Henry Mayhew

Twayne's English Authors Series

Herbert Sussman, Editor
Northeastern University

TEAS 396

HENRY MAYHEW
(1812–1887)
Engraving from *London Labour
and the London Poor,* volume 1 (1851)
Photograph courtesy of Columbia University Libraries

Henry Mayhew

By Anne Humpherys

Herbert H. Lehman College
City University of New York

Twayne Publishers • Boston

Henry Mayhew

Anne Humpherys

Copyright © 1984 by G. K. Hall & Company
All Rights Reserved
Published by Twayne Publishers
A Division of G. K. Hall & Company
70 Lincoln Street
Boston, Massachusetts 02111

Book Production by Marne B. Sultz

Book Design by Barbara Anderson

Printed on permanent/durable acid-free
paper and bound in the United States of
America.

Library of Congress Cataloging in Publication Data

Humpherys, Anne.
  Henry Mayhew.

  (Twayne's English authors series ; TEAS 396)
  Bibliography: p. 179
  Includes index.
  1. Mayhew, Henry, 1812–1887.
2. Authors, English—19th century—Biography.
3. Sociologists—England—Biography.
4. Labor and laboring classes—England—London—History.
5. London (England)—Poor—History.
I. Title. II. Series.
PR4989.M48Z687   1984   808'.0092'4 [B]   83-22729
ISBN 0-8057-6882-3

For my mother and father

Contents

About the Author

Anne Humpherys received her degrees from Stanford University and Columbia University. She is a professor in the Department of English at Herbert H. Lehman College of the City University of New York. She was editor of the *Cass Library of Victorian Times,* in which series several volumes by Henry Mayhew and his associates were reprinted. She edited *Voices of the Poor* for the same series in 1971, a collection of Mayhew's contributions to "Labour and the Poor." She is the author of *Travels into the Poor Man's Country: The Work of Henry Mayhew* (1977) as well as of articles on Dickens, G. W. M. Reynolds, and other Victorian writers. She is a member of the Modern Language Association, on the board of directors of the Research Society for Victorian Periodicals, and serves as Publications Coordinator for the Northeast Victorian Studies Association.

Preface

In the winter of 1849–1850 Henry Mayhew reached the pinnacle of his career and his reputation. Within a year he was finished as the "Metropolitan Correspondent" for the series "Labour and the Poor" in the *Morning Chronicle*. In retrospect we can see that at that point his reputation began to decline, though he continued to write his social surveys, including all of *London Labour and the London Poor* during the next decade. He nevertheless slowly slid into obscurity, where he finally landed totally in the late 1860s and where he remained for the duration of his life. His work on London's poor also disappeared from view after the 1860s.

For a hundred years this condition of neglect remained, though there were intermittent readers who tried to revive his reputation and restore his work to the center of Victorian studies. This effort was not successful, however, until Peter Quennell's three volumes of selections from *London Labour and the London Poor* were published in the 1950s. These volumes laid the groundwork for the rediscovery of Mayhew. In the 1960s his reputation began to grow again, his work on London's poor was once more in print, and Mayhew enthusiasts grew in number among both specialists and general readers.

The reputation of *London Labour and the London Poor* continued to grow to such an extent that the inevitable counter-reaction set in and the 1970s brought a number of negative evaluations. Despite these nay-sayers, however, Mayhew's social investigations remain a major source for Victorian studies as well as popular books with the nonspecialists who come in contact with them. They have also become in many colleges standard reading for undergraduate students of the Victorian period.

In the midst of this "Mayhew revival" I began my efforts to track down the details of his life, to determine the shape of his surveys, and to move toward an evaluation of his contribution to the literature of the period. This turned out to be a difficult task. Little information about his life has survived, and the development of his work has proved confusing and often misleading. Further, placement of his achievement and evaluation of his importance has been a perplexing enterprise. The result of my initial effort was *Travels in the Poor Man's Country* in 1977, the first book-length study of Mayhew and his major work.

Since the appearance of that book some additional information about Mayhew's life has emerged, but, more important, the issues raised by his subject and his methods of working, as well as we can determine them, have been sharpened and hence clarified. In this new work on Mayhew I have been able to address the questions of his sources, his format, and his techniques more directly; also as a result of this reading of *London Labour and the London Poor,* I have emphasized some different aspects of his social surveys in the process of describing and analyzing them. Though my position about the ultimate strengths and weaknesses of his achievement has not significantly changed, it has been enlarged and in some cases modified. Finally, my first book on Mayhew, in addition to analyzing his social surveys, developed at length questions about his style and relationship to other major literary figures of the period; these issues are not part of the present volume. However, other considerations do appear here for the first time ever. Half of the following book traces the development of Mayhew's career outside the handful of years he spent on his social surveys. There is a full consideration of all his "other" work—his plays, journalism, novels, educational and travel books—to which he devoted the majority of his working life. As a result, his work on the London poor can be evaluated in a much larger context. As a second advantage of this new material, the reader can get some insight into the multi-faceted aspects of Victorian popular writing. This book, then, though in some ways based on my earlier investigations of Mayhew's social surveys, presents a different and broadened perspective on them at the same time that it illuminates the career of a representative Victorian journalist for the popular press.

I am grateful to Herbert Sussman and Twayne for giving me the opportunity to gain this new perspective on a writer to whom I have given a good deal of my professional life. I also want to thank several others who have contributed in different ways to the present work. I want to thank my old friend Graham Parry of York University in England, whose encyclopedic knowledge has frequently given me just the reference I was looking for, and also Janet Careswell, who read the manuscript and made many helpful suggestions. I appreciate the grant from the George Shuster Fund, administered by Herbert H. Lehman College of the City University of New York, which again

Preface

aided me in the preparation of the manuscript. Finally, I want once more to thank John Mineka. This time his aid was quite practical— the shouldering of what turned out to be more than his share of child care.

Anne Humpherys

Herbert H. Lehman College
City University of New York

Chronology

Sandboys with George Cruikshank; edits the *Comic Almanac;* writes articles on Great Exhibition for *Edinburgh News; Low Wages.*

1852 Suit in Chancery stops publication of *London Labour and the London Poor* 21 February.

1853 Speaks in favor of opening the Crystal Palace on Sunday.

1854 In Germany; *The Story of the Peasant-Boy Philosopher.*

1855 *The Wonders of Science, or Young Humphry Davy;* returns from Germany.

1856 Interviews Dr. Alfred Taylor and surveys insurance firms for the *Illustrated Times; The Rhine and Its Picturesque Scenery;* "The Great World of London" (March-December); "On Capital Punishments." Volume 3 of *London Labour and the London Poor* written but not published.

1857 Begins *Paved with Gold* with brother Augustus in April but leaves project after fifth number; "Punch on the Platform."

1858 Father dies, leaves Mayhew a pound a week in his will; *The Upper Rhine and Its Picturesque Scenery.*

1859 Edits *Morning News* for month of January.

1861 *Young Benjamin Franklin; London Labour and the London Poor,* 3 vols. in book form; goes to Germany.

1862 Volume 4 of *London Labour and the London Poor; The Criminal Prisons of London.*

1863 *The Boyhood of Martin Luther;* returns from Germany.

1864 *German Life and Manners as Seen in Saxony at the Present Day.*

1865 Edits *The Shops and Companies of London;* second printing of *London Labour and the London Poor* in four volumes.

1870 Edits *Only Once a Year;* with son Athol correspondent in Metz.

1871 Report on Working Men's Clubs for the Licensed Victuallers.

1874   Some early material reprinted in *London Characters* and his name appears on title page; play *Mont Blanc,* with son, fails.

1880   Wife dies 26 February.

1887   Henry Mayhew dies 25 July of bronchitis.

Chapter One
Life

The information about Henry Mayhew's life is uneven, inadequate, and in some cases unreliable. Long periods, particularly before 1830 and after 1864, are blank. Even his creative middle years are known to us primarily through anecdotes handed down by his contemporaries long after the events. There is some internal evidence in his works themselves, not just the monumental *London Labour and the London Poor* and its predecessor, the articles on "Labour and the Poor" in the *Morning Chronicle,* but also his little-known light novels, miscellaneous journalism, his books for children, and his travel books. Still, the picture of his life and puzzling personality is vague and uncertain. Not the least of the puzzles is why, during the long, silent last twenty years of his life, he never wrote a "Memoir of My Time," as did nearly every one of his contemporaries who survived middle age.

Early Life

We can construct some outline of a biography for him, however.[1] He was one of seventeen children and the fourth of seven sons of a successful London solicitor. He was born on 25 November 1812, the same year which saw the birth of Charles Dickens, many of whose works and a part of whose career parallel those of Mayhew. Mayhew's father, Joshua Dorset Joseph Mayhew, seems to have been something of a family tyrant. He was obsessive about respectability, about saving pennies (he bought umbrellas by the gross to get a better price), and had a terrible temper. He is supposed to have made up to his wife after each outburst by giving her a piece of jewelry. In the late 1840s Henry and his youngest brother Augustus satirized their father in a bitter comic poem, "A Respectable Man," in which they ran down the list of his faults: his hypocrisy, his penuriousness, his temper, his capriciousness.[2]

Joshua Mayhew certainly had a clear idea of what he wanted from his sons, namely, that they were to be solicitors like himself, and as each son reached his majority he was duly apprenticed to his father and the cost of his apprenticeship deducted from his future portion of his father's estate. But despite his "good" intentions, only his third son Alfred became a solicitor. As a reward, when his father died in 1858, Alfred was given the bulk of the £50,000-odd estate. Three of the sons—Henry, his next brother Horace, and the youngest, Augustus to whom Henry was closest—after trying one thing and another settled down to erratic existences as journalists. The next-to-youngest, Julius, never settled to anything, though he tried many things—art, photography, writing—but because he kept his father's goodwill by keeping his father's rules (for example, never staying out past 11 at night), he was left independently wealthy at his father's death, reportedly married his cook, and retired into what we hope was a happy obscurity. After trying out drama criticism, the second brother Edward became at around age thirty-five a writer on veterinary medicine. The eldest brother Thomas had a tragic end, for after a vigorous number of years devoted to radical journals like the *Poor Man's Guardian* (remarkable for an upper-middle-class son of such a staunchly conservative father), Thomas committed suicide at age twenty-seven, apparently to avoid the disgrace of personal bankruptcy, which for him would have meant prison. Mayhew senior's influence on the direction of his sons' lives had been mixed indeed.

Henry Mayhew followed somewhat erratically in his oldest brother's footsteps by taking up liberal causes in journalism, and in his major surveys of London's lower classes moving close to a radical political position. He also, unhappily, followed Thomas's path by going bankrupt.

Henry Mayhew apparently had a traditional early childhood. His family recognized his intellectual potential; Mayhew later recalled that his father expected Henry with his talents could become Lord Chancellor of England. His father did the best he could think of for his brilliant son; he sent him to one of the top secondary schools in the country, Westminster. But the educational regime at that school was uncongenial to Mayhew's interests and temperament; after a number of years there, he ran away at the age of fifteen.

We can imagine the ensuing scene. Father: What *do* you want to do, then? Apparently the boy answered that he wanted to be a research chemist, a surprising desire in the 1820s when such an occupation was not respectable and certainly nothing one could be trained for. (One thinks of Daniel Doyce in Dickens' novel *Little Dorrit* [1857], an "inventor" or scientist of genius but eccentric and scruffy, who has to leave England for his talents to be recognized and nurtured.) Where Mayhew got the idea is unknown; a family tradition says that the great Victorian scientist Michael Faraday was a friend, and Mayhew wanted to model himself on the older man. The family certainly had good connections; the well-known composer John Barnett was Mayhew's early music teacher and friend. Perhaps these connections were made through Mayhew senior's extensive law practice.

Wherever the idea came from, there was little formal training that could be given. The only "training" in chemistry that existed in Britain at that time was at a Scottish university; otherwise one could study medicine or take an apprenticeship to an apothecary or druggist. The same family tradition says that his father offered Mayhew the last, but not surprisingly, in view of the loss of class status that would be involved, Mayhew did not take him up on the offer. Instead he went as a midshipman to India, where his steady older brother Alfred was working with the East India Company. Henry's stay there was not long either, for in the late 1820s, when he was in his late teens, he was back in London where he worked in his father's office and embarked on a system of self-education in natural science with his £1-a-week allowance. With his old school friend Gilbert à Beckett, he also entered the bohemian world of journalism and drama, where eventually he was to discover his true vocation.

During the 1830s Mayhew set up a laboratory in the house of his long-suffering brother Alfred (now returned from India) and later in his own quarters in various parts of London. In our age, when we take a formal course for almost everything, it is easy to dismiss such self-training. But Mayhew's later works show that he learned a great deal on his own, that he read voraciously, and that he mastered the fundamentals of natural science. He later claimed to have discovered a dye similar to our aniline dyes. Altogether, his scientific education was a significant achievement, and it led Mayhew to have a high—perhaps too high—estimation of the value of "self-help" in education.

The self-training in chemistry also had an important effect on Mayhew's conception of scientific method, which he later tried to introduce into his social surveys. The other half of his life during this period, however, was equally important in preparing him for these major works.

Following a debacle while working at his father's office around this time (Henry forgot to file some important papers and nearly caused his father to be arrested at his own dinner table), Henry escaped to

Paris, where he met the already well-known writer Douglas Jerrold, himself avoiding creditors, and the young W. M. Thackeray, also trying to live cheaply. Out of this association, when all three apparently settled their affairs and returned to London, grew a close-knit, creatively supportive, and happy-go-lucky circle of friends and acquaintances in the world of London journalism and light drama. The young men, whose group included Charles Dickens, soon to rocket into fame with *Pickwick Papers* (1837), formed social and professional clubs at the drop of a hat, and at the drop of a £5 pound note they brought out a new comic magazine or journal. Earlier Mayhew and à Beckett founded a popular and successful weekly journal which lasted for most of the decade of the 1830s, *Figaro in London,* modeled on the well-known French satirical newspaper *Figaro.* Mayhew edited this journal in its last years, from 1835 through 1838.

The young men also joined together in writing farces and burlettas for the popular stage; Mayhew himself wrote the successful *The Wandering Minstrel* (1834) and with Henry Baylis *"But however—"* (1838). He collaborated in works with Mark Lemon and others. Also he is said to have produced various ephemeral pieces under the pseudonym Ralph Rigamarole to prevent his father's knowing what he was doing with his time.

At this time in his life and indeed throughout it, Mayhew was a man of sanguine temperament, an apparently inexhaustible supply of ideas, and a totally "indolent" nature, as M. H. Spielmann has said.[3] He was a gay but irresponsible companion, unable to follow through on many promises and plans. This combination of talent and temperament plagued him all his life and contributed to many of the frustrations and uncompleted projects that define his life and work.

Of the many journalistic endeavors of Mayhew and his group during this period, one, *Punch,* became spectacularly successful. The brain-child apparently of Mayhew, the magazine began in 1841 under the joint leadership of Mayhew, Mark Lemon, and Stirling Coyne, but most of their talented friends—Jerrold, Thackeray, and à Beckett—wrote for it. (Dickens had, with *Pickwick* and *Oliver Twist* in 1838, gone on to bigger things.) Mayhew edited the magazine for a short time after its beginning, but new publishers in 1842 felt that he was not completely dependable in such a position and from 1842 on Mark Lemon was the sole editor. Mayhew continued his association with *Punch* until March 1846, but he was gradually moving away from his old friends of the 1830s and early 1840s. He joined with many of them in Dickens's celebrated amateur theatrical of Ben Jonson's *Every Man in His Humour* in 1845 (Mayhew played Knowell), but his diminishing connection with *Punch,* his bankruptcy, and other problems seem to have loosened the ties to his old circle. After 1845 he appears to have joined with different associates and collaborators: his brother Augustus, Henry Wood (who helped him on the *Morning Chronicle* series and *London Labour and the London Poor*), and Henry Vizetelly with whom he worked closely in the mid-1850s.

Shortly after his ouster from the editorship of *Punch,* Mayhew, undoubtedly needing money and also looking for an outlet for his more "philosophical" ideas, began on his own a two-pronged publishing venture about education. Using the popular serial-part format, in 1842 Mayhew brought out one monthly number of a theoretical work *What to Teach and How to Teach It* and in 1844 followed it with one number of the practical example *The Prince of Wales's Primer.* Neither serial was completed.

Mayhew was married in 1844 at the age of thirty-two to Jane, the oldest daughter of his friend Douglas Jerrold, and nineteen at the time of her marriage. They subsequently had two children, a son Athol and a daughter Amy. Throughout his twenties, Mayhew had lived on the pound-a-week allowed him by his father and whatever he could make with his journalistic and dramatic writings. He never held onto money for long though some of his works brought him good returns. Throughout his life, except for the handful of years when he was doing his major social surveys, he was always on the brink of financial disaster. Such a life had to be a difficult one for his family, and there were a number of separations between Mayhew and his wife, one only three years after their marriage, but none permanent until later in the 1860s. Jane took good care of her undependable husband, doing his correspondence, dealing with his creditors, being the amanuensis for his books. It could not have been an easy life for her, however, and the difficulties and problems she faced were probably the reason for the break in relations after 1850 that occurred between her father, Douglas Jerrold, and her husband, his old friend Henry Mayhew.

Mayhew's marriage was the highlight of his personal life during the 1840s, even as his designation as Metropolitan Correspondent at the end of 1849 marked the beginning of his most significant work. In between these two events, however, was an unmitigated disaster: a bankruptcy in 1846. This event probably drove his wife back to her

father for a while and finished Mayhew's standing with his own father, who effectively cut him out of his will as a result.
    The fiasco was characteristic of Mayhew's happy-go-lucky attitude
toward life. Upon marrying Jane Jerrold, with his usual buoyancy of
spirit and carelessness about details, he bought and furnished a beautiful home for his bride at a cost way beyond his means. He was encouraged to do so, apparently, because he expected to make a pile of
money on a new publishing scheme he was entering into with an unreliable publisher, Thomas Lyttleton Holt. The two planned to take
advantage of a mania for railroads which developed in England in the
mid-1840s and which contributed both to the enormous expansion of
the railroad lines imaginatively chronicled by Dickens in *Dombey and
Son* and to the panic of 1847.
    Mayhew and Holt were speculating with their proposed publica-
tion the *Iron Times,* a daily journal to be made up exclusively of railroad news. The newspaper failed, however, in 1846, and Holt went
bankrupt, followed very closely by Mayhew himself, who escaped
going to jail only because there had been a recent change in the law.
    After the bankruptcy Mayhew joined with Augustus for three years
in writing a series of six novels. "The Brothers Mayhew," as they
were listed on the title page, wrote these novels in a spirit of conventional light satire, and they managed to get some of the best illustrators—such as H. K. Browne or Phiz, Kenny Meadows, and George
Cruikshank—to provide the plates. The novels include *The Greatest
Plague of Life* (1847), *The Good Genius that Turned Everything into Gold*
(1847), *Whom to Marry and How to Get Married!* (1848), *The Image of
His Father* (1848), *The Magic of Kindness* (1849), and *The Fear of the
World* (1850). The Brothers Mayhew also published in 1850 a Christmas book of *Acting Charades* for family parties.

"The Metropolitan Correspondent"

    Also at this time Mayhew began his major work. In late August or
September 1849, in his role as journalist, Mayhew made a visit for
one of the two major daily London newspapers to Jacob's Island, a
slum south of the river. He went there because the recent murderous
outbreak of cholera in London (14,000 people had died of the disease
in the preceding year in London alone) had been particularly bad in
this neighborhood, which housed a large number of tanning operations and which had, a decade before, been made infamous by Dick-

ens in *Oliver Twist*. In 1849, though no one knew how cholera spread (by water), there was a sense that, since the worst outbreaks seemed to be in the slums, it must have something to do with dirt, bad sanitary conditions, even overcrowding. Mayhew's job as reporter apparently was to look around and see what he could turn up about the conditions amid which the area's inhabitants lived. (Because there was no cheap transportation before the 1860s, workers had to live within walking distance of their places of employment, and the petty tradesmen that served the workers as well as the cadgers and con men who lived off the poor all were crowded together in old dilapidated housing scattered throughout London's commercial and industrial areas.)

What Mayhew found in that visit to Jacob's Island shocked him profoundly, and the subsequent report he wrote for the *Morning Chronicle* was not only the genesis of his famous articles on "Labour and the Poor" and his work as a social historian, but was a powerful piece of writing in and of itself.

Almost immediately after Mayhew's description of Jacob's Island was published, the newspaper announced a forthcoming major series called "Labour and the Poor," which was going to survey the condition of the lower classes all over England. They sent special reporters to manufacturing towns like Manchester and Leeds and others to rural agricultural counties like Dorset and Cambridgeshire. Henry Mayhew was appointed "Metropolitan Correspondent," to report from London.

In the course of the following year, from October 1849 through December 1850, the *Morning Chronicle* published eighty-two articles (or "letters" as they were called) by the Metropolitan Correspondent. In the beginning they appeared three times a week, alternating with the letters from the manufacturing and rural districts. After January, however, the *Morning Chronicle* was committed to using a great deal of its space for publishing verbatim accounts of the debates in Parliament, and Mayhew's articles eventually appeared only once a week. But his articles had grown in length in the previous months because he included longer and longer interviews with the various workpeople he met during his investigations. At the height of his production for the *Morning Chronicle* a letter could run as much as eight full-length columns.

The readers of these articles were very enthusiastic about them. People wrote laudatory letters and sent in donations to a special "Labour and the Poor Fund" which at one time contained £869; there did not seem to be a single newspaper in the country that did not comment on the series, nearly all favorably and many enthusiastically. Mayhew himself became an instant expert in demand as a speaker by both middle-class philanthropic groups and working men's pressure groups alike. Two famous philanthropists, Sidney Herbert and Lord Ashley (later Lord Shaftesbury), started a Female Emigration Society to help the "distressed seamstresses" described by Mayhew to emigrate.

This heady response did not last. Mayhew and the editors of the *Morning Chronicle* had differences over editorial practices which grew ever more exacerbated, and Mayhew finally quit as Metropolitan Correspondent almost exactly one year after his first articles had appeared. The quarrel apparently was over economic theory. The *Chronicle* editorially was a strong supporter of the benefits of free trade to all classes of society. A number of the working people Mayhew interviewed expressed opinions contrary to this position. For example, some shoemakers thought cheap shoes imported duty free from France resulted in a lowering of the English workman's wages. The *Morning Chronicle* cut these comments out of Mayhew's reports, later justifying the practice as simple elimination of a "hacknied common-place."[4]

Mayhew was understandably irritated by these editorial depredations in his work, particularly since his purpose in his investigations, he said, was to "scientifically" determine the truth about the condition of the lower classes through an impartial examination of all the evidence. Such an examination was impossible if the *Morning Chronicle* editors insisted on editing out all the evidence on one side. Mayhew also was beginning to suspect that free trade, which he had initially believed in as strongly as his editors did, was not a good thing for all workers and also that the level of wages for many was not determined by the simple and supposedly infallible laws of supply and demand. These changing attitudes of his probably made a break with the *Morning Chronicle* inevitable. In addition, the paper had devoted a full year to its survey of "Labour and the Poor." Public interest had dwindled and the paper more than likely wanted to go on to something else.

The *coup de grace* was an argument between Mayhew and the editors over an article published in October 1850 praising one of the big ready-to-wear tailoring firms. Mayhew was angered by this article because this firm, the Nicholl Brothers of Regent Street, was among what he considered the worst employers in regard to the wages and the conditions of their pieceworkers. Mayhew was afraid readers of the laudatory article, which was published anonymously as was all journalism during this period, might think it was by him.

London Labour and the London Poor

Sometime during this final breakup of the *Chronicle* series, Mayhew made the arrangements for his next project, the one by which nearly all twentieth-century readers know him—*London Labour and the London Poor*. In the beginning Mayhew saw this work as a continuation of his *Chronicle* investigations into "Those that Will Work, Those that Cannot Work, and Those that Will Not Work" in London. The format of the new publication was a serial like that of the earlier *What to Teach*. It appeared in installments of about eighteen pages from December 1850 through February 1852, a total of sixty-three issues. The page numbers of each part were consecutive so that the various numbers could be bound together and sold as a single volume.

Despite his desires, Mayhew was not able to complete his *Chronicle* surveys in *London Labour and the London Poor;* indeed he was not even to begin them again. Instead the whole of his efforts for the next year and two months was devoted to an increasingly detailed survey of the "street folk," the men, women, and children who sold different types of food and articles in the streets and also those who collected the various street refuse either to sell again or to cart away. He also tried to formulate some of his evolving ideas on economics on the weekly covers of *London Labour*.

At the same time that Mayhew was working on his major work, he had other projects in hand. He edited the *Comic Almanac* for 1850-1851 and planned a new novel, *The Shabby Fammerly*, with Augustus. He also undertook two simultaneous and quite different assignments in connection with the Great Exhibition of the Industry of All Nations in 1851. On the one hand, in collaboration with the artist George Cruikshank, once a month from January through September he brought out a nine-part comic novel, *1851; or, the Adventures of Mr. and Mrs. Sandboys and Family. . . .* On the other hand, as a straightforward reporter in May-July of 1851, he did a series of nine articles critically commenting on the various exhibits at the Exhibition. Also in November and December of 1851, again as his own publisher, he issued four numbers of a projected nine-part "philosophical" treatise on political economy, *Low Wages*.

This flurry of activity, however, lasted only two years. In February 1852 Mayhew had a falling out with the printer of *London Labour and the London Poor* over financial arrangements. The printer seized all the unsold copies of *London Labour,* including a number not yet distributed; he then got an injunction to prevent Mayhew from selling any more copies of the work. There were various court appearances and some negotiations but nothing came of them, and this was the end of *London Labour and the London Poor* for another four years.

During these four years Mayhew effectively disappears. He was clearly in financial trouble after the failure of *London Labour and the London Poor.* As he had after his bankruptcy the decade before, he embarked on a series of books which he hoped would sell. This time, rather than the novels he had written earlier with Augustus, he produced two children's books, both biographies of scientists whose lives were meant as models for young boys. In 1854 *The Story of the Peasant-Boy Philosopher,* the biography of Owen Ferguson the astronomer, was published and the next year saw *The Wonders of Science, or Young Humphry Davy.*

As another measure in his effort to right his financial situation, Mayhew and his family went to Germany for somewhere around two years (1854-1855) where they could live more cheaply than in England and, in the time-honored tradition, could also avoid his creditors.

Early in 1856, however, Mayhew was back in London. Perhaps his children's books did well enough to justify a return; but Mayhew also had a number of new projects that augured well for him. Not only did he have enough material gleaned from his stay in Germany to produce two travel books, but he had also reached some kind of agreement with David Bogue, an old publisher of his, who not only was going to finance him in a new survey of London but was also going to issue the previously published numbers of *London Labour and the London Poor* (the lawsuit with the old publisher being in the process of settlement) in two volumes and enable Mayhew, with the help of Augustus, to research the street entertainers for a third volume.

The first product of Mayhew and Bogue's new association was the survey "The Great World of London" issued in monthly parts beginning in March 1856. It was to be a broad survey of London life and occupations, but after the first number it became a survey of the various London prisons.

The more Mayhew took on the more he found to do. The year 1856 contrasts sharply with the previous two years. While researching the London prisons for "The Great World of London" he also published his first travel book, *The Rhine and Its Picturesque Scenery.* He was asked to address the committee working to abolish capital punishment and his thoughtful speech on that subject was subsequently published by the committee. He was involved again in free-lance journalism, writing for Henry Vizetelly's cheap daily the *Illustrated Times.* Mayhew delivered a lecture based on *London Labour and the London Poor* at the Royal Polytechnic Institution in June 1856. He joined Jerrold and other journalists and dramatists in "The General Exhibition Company" to develop the "georama," a panorama on a new principle. (Instead of moving across the screen, the images would move toward the spectator and diverge on either side. The project never materialized.)[5] He continued his interests in working-class concerns by supporting various plans for inexpensive and accessible entertainments for the lower classes. He also stage-managed several unusual gatherings of parolees and "swell mobsmen" (con men who dressed as gentlemen) to gather information for his ongoing investigations of prisons and criminal life. There were two such meetings in 1856 and one in 1857 with Lord Carnavon in the chair.

Despite the variety of activity, Mayhew's major hopes were undoubtedly fastened on the two-part project with Bogue. Sadly, Bogue died very suddenly (he was only forty-four) and both "The Great World of London" and the plans for *London Labour and the London Poor* died with him.

Later Years

Mayhew's bad luck drove him back to earlier enterprises but none were long-lasting. In 1857 he and Augustus began to publish serially the novel *Paved with Gold,* but Henry did not stay with the project beyond five numbers. He returned to his earliest activity, the drama, by putting together a comic review where he spoke about his work on *London Labour and the London Poor* and imitated various street people and another friend played the piano and sang comic songs. This review had some success in London, it seems, and in the summer was to make the rounds of the watering spots. But in Brighton, Mayhew was driven off the stage when he saw his father grimly sitting in the

front row. After Joshua chastised him for "compromising the respectability of his family by continuing so 'degrading' a pursuit"[6] Mayhew
abruptly abandoned the project. This may have been one of the last
encounters between Mayhew and his father, for Joshua died the following year.

Mayhew tried a little of everything in the following years. He published another travel book, *The Upper Rhine and Its Picturesque Scenery*,
in 1858 and edited a newspaper the *Morning News* for a short time in
1859. He wrote another children's book, *Young Benjamin Franklin*
(1861) and then, probably as a last resort, went off to Germany
again.

Mayhew later said he went to Germany to research a book on Martin Luther and indeed in 1863 his last children's book, *The Boyhood
of Martin Luther*, was published. It is equally likely, however, that
the trip was a financial necessity as before. His wife and children
went with him and the family lived for two or three years in Eisenach. Either just before he left or while he was away, *London Labour
and the London Poor* finally reached the form Mayhew's modern readers
know him by. In 1861 the first three volumes were published in book
form, while volume four and *The Criminal Prisons of London* ("The
Great World of London") appeared the next year.

The mid-1860s really saw the last of Mayhew's work. In 1864 he
published a final book on Germany, the two-volume *German Life and
Manners*, based on his stay a few years before. A Harper Brothers advertisement of 1864 includes a volume by the Brothers Mayhew,
"Model Men, Women and Children" with illustrations, but I have
never discovered any such book. The next year he made some effort
to return to the subject of labor in London, the one topic which had
been productive for him. For several months he edited a monthly
journal *The Shops and Companies of London*, a survey of various skilled
industries in London.

After this Mayhew begins to disappear again. We see him suggesting various projects in the late 1860s and early 1870s, but none
materialized. He tried to get a contract to ghostwrite a book on
horses and to interest some people in a wholesome journal for boys.[7]
He is reported by one source to have been a correspondent in 1870 at
Metz during the first major engagement of the Franco-Prussian war.
He brought out one issue of *Only Once a Year* in 1870 and investigated workingmen's clubs for the licensed victuallers. Some of his
earlier pieces in the *Chronicle* and in *London Labour and the London Poor*

were reprinted in *London Characters* in 1874. For his final publication he returned to the mode of his first: he and his son Athol wrote a play in 1874, *Mont Blanc*.

How Mayhew managed to live in these later years of his life is not known. Presumably he continued to have the £1-a-week his father left him in his will. Perhaps that was all he had. His wife sometime in the years after 1865 moved in with her daughter and husband, and though Mayhew visited Sundays for dinner the separation was permanent. Mayhew was not with his wife when she died in 1880. Mayhew himself died in near obscurity in 1887, leaving an estate totaling £90-10, by today's standards around $500. His work on labor and the poor in London at mid-century was almost completely forgotten when he died. For many years he was remembered only as a founder of *Punch*. Today the situation is reversed. His current reputation as a social observer is as high now as it was low a hundred years ago. But the uncertainties in his life story remain.

Chapter Two
Popular Literature: Drama, Journalism, Fiction, Education, and Travel

Henry Mayhew made his reputation as a crusading journalist. His value for modern readers lies in the same area of endeavor, his social surveys. But these works took up a very small number of years in his life—really only about four. For the rest of his working life, Mayhew was essentially an ordinary journalist turning his hand to anything that might bring him an income. As John L. Bradley, the first scholar to write seriously about Mayhew's work, said, all these other pieces exploited popular interests.[1] So as a young man in the 1830s, he wrote for the popular stage and began various journalistic schemes to cash in on the expanding audience for cheap, popular magazines and journals. After his bankruptcy, he and Augustus wrote their comic novels to try to break into the market the successful *Punch* and the even more successful Dickens had tapped, and he wrote another novel to exploit the tremendous excitement over the Great Exhibition of 1851. During the 1840s and 1850s he was interested in reform of education and tried different kinds of books to demonstrate his theories. He also tried to make a profit from his intermittent trips to Germany by writing travel books, always a popular genre.

Few of these pieces have lasting importance. Yet Mayhew's "other" career has interest for the modern student of the period. Since he tried writing almost everything, he provides a good example of the way one might survive on the "Grub Street" of Victorian England. In addition, by looking at what Mayhew produced, we get a sense of what a majority of people in Victorian England enjoyed reading.

The following sections take up each of the five areas of Mayhew's "other" writing career—drama, miscellaneous journalism, fiction, children's books, and travel books—in roughly chronological order. Each section discusses the conventions within which Mayhew was working and attempts to evaluate the individual pieces in terms of these conventions as well as how they relate to his career as a whole.

Drama

In the 1830s when Mayhew was in his twenties, he devoted himself to his chemical experiments, journalism, and dramatic writing. His friends, before venturing to visit him in his upstairs "laboratory" at his brother Alfred's house, would call from below demanding to know if he were "literary or scientific today?"[2] He collaborated with these friends in the writing of farces for the minor London theaters and in much convivial good times over punch and cigars.

Mayhew's known works during the decade of the 1830s are few. A number have undoubtedly disappeared in the anonymity of Victorian journalism and dramatic ephemera. We know of only two dramatic pieces that were by him alone; there are three others on which he is known to have collaborated. He also claimed in his 1846 bankruptcy suit that he had helped Mark Lemon with three of his plays. One of Lemon's farces, *The Gentleman in Black* (1840), is almost a verbatim dramatization of Mayhew's comic sketch "Mr. Peter Punctilio, the Gentleman in Black," published in *Bentley's Miscellany* in 1838. A note to the sketch said Mayhew was dramatizing it. Probably he abandoned the effort, Lemon taking it up, but there was no rancor over this particular "collaboration," it seems, for Mayhew called Lemon his "best friend" in 1842. Undoubtedly in their conversations and daily exchanges all the young men gave each other ideas and contributed to each other's work. In a similar way, Mayhew and Augustus collaborated on a kind of "drama," a book of *Acting Charades: Deeds Not Words* in 1850 (reissued in 1852). This book gave examples of how to act out thirty words, like *fireworks, cabbage, carpet, blunderbuss,* and so forth. In their prefatory description of what charades are, the reader familiar with *Vanity Fair* will recognize the game that brought Becky Sharp to the pinnacle of her success at Lord Steyne's party: "the two most celebrated performers of the party choose 'their sides' and, whilst the one group enacts the Charade, the other plays the part of the audience. A word is then fixed upon by the *corps dramatique;* and 'my first, my second, and my whole' is gone through as puzzling as possible in dumb show, each division making a separate and entire act. At the conclusion of the drama, the guessing begins on the part of the audience" (vi).

These charades and Mayhew's farces and burlettas, though basically insignificant works, have interest both in terms of his later career and in providing insight into the dramatic conventions of the age. Mayhew's writing of farce certainly influenced the novels of the Brothers Mayhew in the next decade, and both farces and novels have subtle connections with his social surveys. The dramas that we are concerned with here are the two farces of the 1830s which were successful enough to be printed in acting copies and are thus available outside the archives of the Lord Chamberlain's office. *The Wandering Minstrel* (1834) by Mayhew and *"But however—"* (1838) by Mayhew and Henry Baylis demonstrate the characteristics of farce in the 1830s as well as highlight some of Mayhew's attitudes that inform his later works.

The situation in the theater in the 1830s was very different from what it had been in the days of Shakespeare, the great Restoration dramatists, or what it is today. While a detailed survey of early nineteenth-century theater is beyond the scope of this book, some idea of the forces at play will throw light on Mayhew's farces of the 1830s. During the nineteenth century only two theaters—Drury Lane and Covent Garden—were licensed to perform drama and comedy. They were the "legitimate" theaters and had a monopoly on serious theatrical work. At the same time, all new plays produced at these theaters were subject to the official censor, who for most of the 1830s was as rigid as he was arbitrary in his standards. In addition, for complex reasons, the audience for theater had changed from the basically middle and upper-class audience of the seventeenth and eighteenth centuries to an essentially lower-middle- and lower-class audience in the 1830s.

These different pressures—the monopoly, the censor, the change in audience—had a major effect on the dramatic literature written in the early Victorian period. The two "legitimate" theaters had become vast halls seating 3,000 people; clearly, intimate drama and subtle comedy were very difficult to perform in such circumstances. Acting styles coarsened and drama was simplified, becoming "melodrama," the dominant genre in early Victorian theater. In addition, since the monopoly of the two theaters was really not very workable, there was a large, thriving "illegitimate" drama, which had official sanction for performing "burlettas," originally rhymed works with music but eventually any piece with music incorporated. A great many theaters were built in the 1830s to house this "illegitimate" theater, which was devoted to farce, burlesque, pantomime, and spectacle because of the prohibition on performing serious drama and because the new class of audience preferred these lighter dramatic forms.

The easiest and most lucrative market for the playwright was the "illegitimate" or minor theater, though the authors were woefully underpaid and roundly exploited even after a Select Committee investigation in 1832 and the founding of the Dramatic Authors Society in 1833. Mayhew and his friends were charter members of this organization, whose goal was to try to secure a form of copyright for the authors. The need for such reform was obvious. In 1829 Douglas Jerrold received £50 for writing *Black Ey'd Susan,* perhaps the most popular play of the century, and along with £10 for the copyright, that was all he received, though the play was produced over and over throughout the century. This situation finally changed with a bill passed in Parliament in 1843. By then many of the dramatic writers, including Jerrold and Mayhew, had abandoned the stage for more lucrative forms of writing, mainly popular journalism.

The two popular dramatic forms, melodrama and farce, were usually performed on the same bill. The theater started at 6 P.M. with the melodrama; at eight o'clock tickets were half-price and the farce followed. By far the greater number of these "afterpieces" were written for the occasion and disappeared after their first performance, though some, including *The Wandering Minstrel* and *"But however—,"* stayed in the repertory. In addition there were various entr'acte songs, dances, and other types of short acts interspersed in the lengthier pieces. The theater-goer certainly got his money's worth in variety if not in quality. The true inheritor of this tradition, as Raymond Williams has argued, is today's popular television.[3] The attraction was not the play but the actors, and the playwright "existed to make their performance possible, rather than they to interpret his work to an audience."[4] Mayhew's plays were both written as vehicles for comic actors.

Writing for the theater must have come naturally to him. Not only did all his friends do so, but his older brothers did also. Even the politically active oldest brother Thomas is recorded as having written a "drama" in 1830. Edward, the brother who became an eminently respectable writer on veterinary science, seems to have had a strong spurt of dramatic writing at one point. The same month and year as *The Wandering Minstrel* saw no less than three comic pieces by Edward. These three pieces as well as *The Wandering Minstrel* were

produced at the Royal Fitzroy (also called the Queen's) Theater, built
the previous year and probably a stone's throw from the Mayhew family establishment.

Since these farces were viewed by authors, audiences, and theater
managers as ephemera, collaboration was probably the rule rather
than an exception. The point was to churn out something different
for each night's performance and undoubtedly anybody who was available was enlisted to help, including the actor for whom the piece was
to be a vehicle. Mayhew and Baylis dedicated *"But however—"* to
Benjamin Wrench, "the original suggester of the name and subject"
of the "trifle" and the star. Because of the collaborative nature of
these pieces as well as their slight literary merit, we do not place
much weight on what they tell us about Mayhew's talents. But because they conform to type more or less perfectly, they do provide
good examples of the farces of the 1830s and give a sense of some of
the sources of Mayhew's later work.

The Wandering Minstrel. The farce as a form basically turns
on a series of humorous reversals—mistaken identities and unexpected entrances—as well as coincidental meetings of inappropriate
characters, wordplay (mainly puns), and usually one eccentric character, the comic focus of the play. Unlike French farce, the early Victorian version of this old form usually hangs on a sentimental plot of
thwarted young lovers who are allowed to come together at the end.
Michael Booth, probably the foremost authority on Victorian drama
today, has linked this "sentimental outlook" to the "overwhelming
domesticity" of nineteenth-century drama. The best farce, he says
(and Mayhew's two works are good if not the best) is "the disciplined
expression of moral and domestic anarchy, the plausible and logical
presentation of a completely crazy world that all the characters take
with the greatest seriousness."[5]

The Wandering Minstrel is an example. The success of this play is
indicated by its publication in an acting copy after it had been playing for seventy nights, a very good run indeed and quite a good send-
off for what Mayhew says in the preface is his "infant" effort. Like
most farces of the 1830s, it has a middle- to upper-middle-class setting. It takes forty-five minutes to perform, is divided into five
scenes, and is set in the house of Mr. Crincum, an anti-sentimental
gentleman whom Bradley has claimed looks forward to the more realistic characters of the plays of the 1860s.[6] His flighty and snobbish
wife is dead set against the marriage of their niece Julia to Herbert

Carol, the son of an attorney, because of his lack of proper pedigree. In the first scene the family reads in the newspaper of a certain "well-known musical nobleman" who, for a wager, is traveling through the country incognito earning money by singing. Mrs. Crincum is in an ecstasy at the thought of his coming to their town while Mr. Crincum is less than enthusiastic: "Where's the romance, I should like to know, in a fellow's rendering himself amenable to the vagrant act?"[7]

Scene 2 opens on Jem Bags, the cockney "hero" of the piece, who makes a living by playing the clarinet so badly that householders pay him to go away. When he plays outside the Crincum house, Mrs. Crincum takes him for the noble wandering minstrel, and a characteristic dialogue at cross-purposes ensues, including various verbal misunderstandings such as Mrs. Crincum's exclamation "O, the dear melodious creature!" being heard by Jem Bags as "she says I'm a hodious screecher. I sartinly must ax 'em a shilling!" The scene closes with Mrs. Crincum inviting Jem in for "refreshment" and Mr. Crincum bemoaning his fate in marrying a young wife.

Scene 3 opens with Jem meeting the Crincum's maid Peggy who recognizes him as her former lover and who tells him Mrs. Crincum has mistaken him for the wandering minstrel. Mrs. Crincum discovers the two in close communication and Jem talks his way out of her displeasure at his taking liberties with her maid only to discover that she has arranged a concert for the evening to enable him to show off his talents. Another comic dialogue follows between Jem and the concertmaster Tweedle in which Jem has to parry all Tweedle's musical questions by his wits:

Tweed: . . . What may you think of Paganini?

Jem B: What ninny?

Tweed: Paganini sir, the great violinist, who has lately drawn such large houses with his one string. What may be your opinion of his powers?

Jem B: Why, my opinion is, that his powers must be werry great if he draws a house with one string. (10–11)

The scene closes on Jem and Peggy reminiscing over old times and dancing to Jem's clarinet, in the midst of which they upset the tea tray.

Scene 4 introduces the sentimental love story with an exchange of conventional ballads by Julia and Herbert. Julia suggests Herbert disguise himself as the wandering minstrel to show up Jem as an imposter at the musicale that evening and thus win her aunt's consent to their marriage.

Scene 5 is the grand finale. The concert begins, but Jem's clarinet playing and dancing only result in comic disharmony and much turning over of chairs and music stands. The musicians scatter. At this point Peggy introduces Herbert disguised as the wandering minstrel. He challenges Jem to a singing contest, Herbert turning in a conventional love song. Jem is next in what was the show-stopping number, the comic song "Villikins and his Dinah," which has ten verses plus ten "choriuses" including a "moriale," and "encore," and "another moriale." This song was probably a popular street ballad introduced into Mayhew's farce by the actor who played Jem Bags throughout the century, Frederick Robson. Mrs. Crincum finally stops him, though he protests there are sixteen verses. When threatened with the authorities, he turns to appeal to the audience, an almost mandatory ending for farce of the period, and this leads right into the curtain calls in a semicircle with the principal comic actor in the center.

From this summary we can see that the effect of the piece depends on the skill of the actor playing Jem Bags, though the playwright has contributed his share of puns and witty comebacks for all the players. The piece even in the reading is amusing and because it doesn't claim to be anything more than it is has a certain integrity. The mixture of song, dance, slapstick, verbal play, sentimental love, satire on wives, and cockney humor works in a piece forty-five minutes long; anything longer would be pretentious, which is part of the reason the more traditional comedy was so dismal during the period.

"But however—." *"But however—"* follows almost exactly the same pattern though it contains no music. There is a neat plot of intrigue and mistaken identity which begins with the entrance of the comic "hero" Caleb Chizzler, a petty thief hiding from the bailiff, and which unravels consistently until the final tableau at the end. Motivation for Chizzler's accepting the initial mistaken identity is more realistic than in *The Wandering Minstrel* since Chizzler needs to remain incognito. Also it is not too improbable that he could be mistaken for the "squire" who has been fourteen years among the "heathen" of India. Though the plot of *"But however—"* is more intricate—there are no less than four cases of mistaken identity—the farcical mistakes dovetail in a natural way. All these elements provide

a gratifying illusion of realism to the action and the variety of mistaken identities maintains the comic pace. There is less reliance on comic business, the emphasis being on plot and dialogue, the traditional elements of more substantial comedy.

"*But however*—" was performed at one of the more prestigious minor theaters, the Haymarket (still in use), in 1838 and published in an acting edition the same year, accompanied by an etching by Pierce Egan the Younger from a drawing taken during a performance. The play ran for a good while and stayed in the repertory. It takes its title from the comic hero's distinctive mode of speech; he ends most of his explanations with "but however—" to avoid making any direct statements. For example, his first speech to Prowl, the bailiff, who mistakes him for a town resident, is "(aside) No time to be lost; good day to you, sir—snug little place, this, sir—natives devils to talk, sir—no secrets here, sir—capital place for information, sir—I should say you'd come down on a voyage of discovery, sir—you'll excuse me, sir—no wish to appear inquisitive, sir—but however—."[8] His explanation at the end is similar: "Spare me, my good friends, spare me— I respect you all—shall ever respect you—you see, the fact is—temptation was before me—bailiffs behind me—beauty beside me—my wonted modesty forsook me—and I—but however—" (23). In addition to his characteristic tag ending, Chizzler's jerky, incomplete way of talking is distinctive. It is also very similar to that of one of Dickens's brilliant comic creations, Alfred Jingle in *Pickwick Papers,* which was published in parts throughout the preceding year. In the similarities between the two characters we perhaps have an example of the way this group of literary friends both contributed to and drew on each other's work.

The farce opens in a small country inn. The landlady, Mrs. Juniper, and the lawyer Standwell are discussing the return of the squire, Cashmere, who has been in India for fourteen years and has now inherited the estate. He was engaged to Standwell's daughter Julia before he left. She has remained faithful to him, but Standwell doubts that after all these years they would recognize each other.

The stage is thus set for the entrance of Caleb Chizzler, running from the police. He is mistaken for the squire by Mrs. Juniper. Finding she is a well-to-do widow, Chizzler takes advantage of her error and decides to make love to her.

Next Standwell and his daughter arrive at the inn. Mrs. Juniper, caught in the compromising situation of being alone in a locked room with a strange man, is forced to hide in a closet, a stock device in farce. Still maintaining he is the newly returned squire, Chizzler discovers Julia is an heiress to £20,000 and hurriedly begins to make love to her. Mrs. Juniper in the closet hears with shock his treachery, but, in what would be one of the funniest scenes, Chizzler manages to court both women at the same time by means of asides in the dialogue and probably much humorous stage business.

Inevitably the real Squire Cashmere arrives. Before he reveals himself, however, he decides to try to find out if Julia still loves him. To this end, finding him alone, he questions Chizzler, who, because he thinks the squire is the bailiff, now pretends to be a long-time resident of the area. A humorous dialogue at cross-purposes follows. Chizzler thinks Cashmere is referring to himself and tries to throw him off the trail. Cashmere, in turn, is led to think that Julia has "bolted" and is properly horrified. He retires to another room where he is locked in by Chizzler who still thinks he is the bailiff.

Immediately after this, the real bailiff Prowl appears and Chizzler mistakes *him* for the returning squire. Prowl takes Chizzler for a town resident. Another dialogue at cross-purposes takes place. Chizzler tries to make this mistaken squire jealous by telling him Julia (whom he never names) is "quite taken in another quarter"; Prowl of course thinks this refers to Chizzler.

In the midst of this deep water, Prowl mentions Chizzler by name and the crook is suddenly enlightened to all the correct identities. Thinking fast, he tries to pass off the locked-up true Squire Cashmere as himself. Prowl is convinced and is about to drag Cashmere off to jail when Standwell, Julia, and Mrs. Juniper appear. Cashmere establishes his true identity by producing Julia's letters; the lovers are reunited. Prowl starts to take Chizzler away, but to keep the convention of a happy ending for all, Standwell volunteers for no reason other than dramatic convention to pay Chizzler's debts and to rehabilitate him. Chizzler has the last word, however, and the curtain falls on the standard semicircle of actors.

We can assume that Mayhew's other farces and burlettas were in the same mode. These other works include his own burletta *The Young Sculptor* (1839), a sentimental melodrama set in renaissance Italy; another collaboration with Baylis, *A Troublesome Lodger* (1839), and one with G. Smith (who also collaborated with Mayhew's brother Edward) *The Barbers at Court* (1835), a farcical piece with a Restoration setting. Mayhew did not write any more plays except for *Mont*

Blanc, which he and his son adapted from a French comedy by Eugene Labiche, *Le Voyage de M. Perrichon,* in 1874. It was not a success and has survived in the British Library in a privately printed copy.[9] We see the farcical conventions continued in Mayhew's fiction. Also certain elements in his social surveys reflect aspects of his drama: his sympathetic identification with lower-class characters and the verbal byplay parallel Mayhew's response to his later informants. Robson's realistic portrayal of the disreputable street musician Jem Bags was apparently a real innovation in 1834. Mayhew had a good ear for lower-class speech though in his social surveys he did not reproduce the humorous cockney dialect he used so well in his plays. He was to find little comic in the stories he was told in "Labour and the Poor" and *London Labour and the London Poor.*

Miscellaneous Journalism

At the same time that Henry Mayhew was writing his farces, he was also a working journalist and editor. In fact, we could say that everything he wrote was journalism of some sort, a designation that shows both the wide variety of such writing in the Victorian period and the high level some of it could achieve. Though drama would seem outside the journalism label, in the early Victorian period it was not so obviously separate. Minor comedy was closely connected to popular journalism of the period in subject, treatment, and in authorship. Many of the members of the Dramatic Authors Society also wrote for the press. Mark Lemon's ability to turn Mayhew's comic piece "Mr. Peter Punctilio" into a drama with a minimum of change exemplifies the interconnection.

Mayhew's many other kinds of writing are also connected with journalism. The novels by the Brothers Mayhew are expansions of themes and treatments common to comic journalism; they were also published serially, as was much fiction of the period, and read like a periodical. In *1851* large pieces of Mayhew's regular news coverage of the Great Exhibition were incorporated, albeit rather uncomfortably, but in *Paved with Gold,* which began as a joint effort of the Brothers Mayhew, sections of *London Labour and the London Poor* fit easily into the novel's text. Mayhew's more "philosophical" pieces on education and psychology were also issued in periodical parts and written for the same audience as that of popular journalism; his children's books and travel books are again treatments of popular topics in the periodical press. His great social surveys are journalism, too—great journalism. Only our ignorance of the publishing history of *London Labour and the London Poor* has obscured its journalistic base.

Mayhew was not unusual in his many-faceted journalistic career. Dickens and Thackeray both began as journalists and continued their work as reporters and editors even after their reputations as novelists were achieved. Even George Eliot began as a journalist, though of a very different sort from Mayhew and his friends. She was part of the intellectual elite of the quarterly reviews, while Mayhew, Thackeray, and Dickens were associated nearly all their lives with the daily and weekly press, comic journals, and family miscellanies.

As we have seen, in his youth Mayhew wanted to be a chemist, and his more "philosophical" concerns remained a part of his work to the end, differentiating it from all other journalistic work of the period. But by mid-century and the mid-point of his life, Mayhew considered himself a professional journalist, a designation that by then had lost a good deal of its disreputable connotation, undoubtedly partly due to the number of working journalists who were men of good families, such as the Mayhew brothers, Thackeray, and others.

In his memoir of his father Athol says Henry's career in journalism began at the age of sixteen. He edited his first successful journal at age twenty-three. At an early age, then, he had committed himself to the world that was to remain his for forty years. How he, brilliant son of a rich solicitor, chose journalism is not really known. He had the models of his older brothers and some of his friends. One of his contemporaries at Westminster School, Gilbert à Beckett, joined him in his abandonment of the straight and narrow parental path for the world of London journalism and drama. Perhaps no more was needed than the attractions of the life. One modern scholar asserts that for Mayhew and his friends journalism offered "a retreat from the conventionalities of a career in the Church, the law, or the military."[10] There was a free and easy camaraderie loosened from the stiff conventions of middle-class life where, for example, Mayhew senior required his sons to remain standing while he was in the room. Opposed to this were long talks over good food, wine, cigars; collaborative efforts at drama and comic pieces; late nights at theaters and taverns; days free of responsibilities. "Its denizens were young, gifted, reckless . . . working in fits and starts and never except under pressure" according to a contemporary.[11]

Along with this middle-class bohemianism, a strong sympathy for the sufferings of the poor informed their political writings and even their comic pieces. Dickens, Jerrold, and Mayhew also carried it forward into their major work. But their liberalism remained on the safe side; Mayhew, writing for *Figaro in London,* opposed both universal suffrage and payment of members of Parliament as espoused by the Chartists. Their political positions were soft, frequently sentimental, often naive, but always strongly stated.

It was a tremendously exciting period of English history. Richard Altick gives considerable credit to the agitation over the Reform Bill of 1832 for creating a mass reading public devoted to newspaper and periodical writing.[12] Perhaps it was the strong support of that measure, which ended the aristocratic control over Parliament by giving the vote to anyone with £10 of holdings, that led Mayhew's oldest brother from the drama to the radical, illegal, unstamped press. Certainly there was a sense abroad of changing times, of new possibilities, of grand changes. It seemed a revolutionary time without the unpleasantness of a real revolution—chaos, violence, and bloodletting.

Coupled with the heightened sense of new times and new possibilities in the early 1830s were also some dramatic developments in the press. Journalism as we know it is fundamentally a creation of the eighteenth and nineteenth centuries; its rise parallels the development of the novel, and the two forms have always been linked in terms of audience and intention. The newspaper began in the need of farmers, businessmen, and others to get reliable business information quickly; gradually other information was added, and at the end of the eighteenth century the *Times* and the *Morning Chronicle* had taken the shape they were to keep more or less to the end of the nineteenth century. In addition, the desire for other sorts of current opinion—about the arts, the theater, fashion, literature, and gossip—resulted in the periodical journals the *Tatler* and the *Spectator* in the early eighteenth century. Other journals dealt with politics, either rabble-rousing or satirical or both. In addition, there was the older tradition of the broadsheet and street literature that fed the taste for the sensational, the salacious, the curious, and the horrific.

All these threads mixed and merged together in various ways throughout the last decades of the eighteenth and the first two decades of the nineteenth centuries, as the publishers and printers tried various formulas to meet the demands of an enlarging audience. In the 1830s there was a positive explosion of journalistic enterprises. Nearly six hundred separate unstamped periodicals appeared between 1830 and 1836.[13] Journalism became the most characteristic form of the age. Thomas Carlyle, perhaps following Macaulay's usage of the same phrase, called the press "the fourth estate," sensing the power of the press equal to that of Church, Aristocracy, and Merchant. As the editors of the *Waterloo Directory of Victorian Periodicals* state, the growth of newspapers and periodicals during the century "was a direct response to demands for information, for discourse, for instruction, for propaganda, for entertainment, for platforms, each demand corresponding to a new facet of national life."[14] The dominance of the press in every aspect of life continued throughout the entire period, abating only with the emergence of radio and television in our own time.

Though it is impossible to make hard distinctions among the many different types of press that evolved in the early decades of the nineteenth century, we can see some broad demarcations. First, there was the daily press, dominated by the *Times* and subject to various taxes in an effort to control what the ruling powers considered seditious and dangerous sentiments. Then there were the lordly, highbrow quarterlies like the *Edinburgh* and *Quarterly Reviews*. On the bottom were many different "popular" publications—gossip, political, sporting or entertainment, or all of these together. Between the heights of the *Edinburgh Review* and the lower depths of Pierce Egan's *Life in London* (1821), Henry Mayhew and his friends and associates moved in the 1830s and 1840s to provide a new press for the middle classes—a press of liberal sentiment, light literature, good humor, intelligent criticism, and occasionally useful instruction. Not many of these early efforts lasted, though Dickens's ventures *(Bentley's Miscellany, The Daily News, Household Words)* were successful. But the two journals that have pride of place in this development were both associated with Mayhew, *Figaro in London,* begun in the early 1830s, and *Punch,* in the early 1840s and still going strong today.

In the 1830s being a journalist did not mean writing for one newspaper or magazine primarily, though some early journalists were able to find such positions that paid. More often than not it meant founding one's own magazine, usually a weekly selling for a penny. The economics of beginning these journals were simple; with a sympathetic printer, one could begin with as little as £5 or £10; the proceeds of one issue financed the next and so on. If there were no proceeds, the journal disappeared—the fate of most of them, some not even issuing a second number.

Though many different kinds of journals and magazines were started at this time, the branch that concerns us here is what is loosely referred to as "the comic press"—a combination of political satire and commentary, jokes, parodies, burlesques, and—mirroring the interests and occupations of its writers—dramatic and sometimes literary criticism. Most were illustrated with black and white wood-cuts. These journals were read "by people who had been convention-ally educated . . . who read a newspaper daily . . . who were comfortable within one or another of the established political par-ties," for these comic periodicals are "popular journals which ride with strongly established opinions and tastes rather than trying to create them."[15]

Early career through *Figaro in London*.   In this genre of early Victorian journalism Mayhew began his career. Later in the 1840s he was also involved in more conventional reporting, as we understand it. It is not possible at this time, however, to chart his career as a journalist precisely. There are only a handful of references in various reminiscences of the period to journals he was associated with and even fewer pieces that bear his name. Partly this is due to the ephem-eral nature of journalism itself not to mention of some of the actual copies of the journals. The short-lived nature of his journalism is also exacerbated by the tradition of anonymity in Victorian publications. Nearly all material published in the vast array of Victorian journalism was published anonymously. The reasons for this are various; partly it was a convention going back to the earliest days of journalism when a fictitious Mr. Spectator, for example, was projected as author of the pieces. Partly it was protective; the press at this time, even the most prestigious, could be vitriolic, personally abusive, and scurri-lous; anonymity thus protected the writers from libel. The tradition of anonymity died hard. *Punch* maintained it well into the twentieth century, and newspapers have not yet given it up completely. Thus, though a few pieces by Mayhew carried his name, most did not and we only know of his authorship from other sources. All the letters on "Labour and the Poor" for the *Morning Chronicle,* for example, were never published under their authors' names, which has given rise to a good deal of confusion about parts of that series which Mayhew did not write but which twentieth-century librarians have credited to him since he is widely known to be associated with the series.[16] As the

field of Victorian periodicals is mined and rationalized, we will discover more stray pieces here and there that Mayhew wrote in these
years. For now we can only construct a partial outline.[17]

We begin, then, when Mayhew was in his late teens. He had left
Westminster School, tried life as a midshipman, and now under a
begrudging parental allowance, was studying chemistry. With his
school friend Gilbert à Beckett, he tried to launch a series of weekly
comic journals. Perhaps the first was *The Censor: An Entirely Original
Work,* which lasted for sixteen issues in 1829. Certainly they tried
Cerberus, which was "to contain a reliable list of the latest arrivals in
Hades," according to Mayhew's son. The printer, Henry Hethering-
ton, set the first issue in type, payment for which was to be made by
the sales of the first issue. Mayhew and à Beckett needed £5 for advertisements. But, according to the story told by Athol, they did not
have it so they found a man down on his luck, willing for less than
£5 to parade around London dressed as a devil with a sandwich board.
The street urchins, however, tormented the man unmercifully and in
the fracas the poor "devil" was carried off to the police station. With
their last pence the editors paid his fine. *Cerberus* did not have a second issue.[18]

After this, Athol says Mayhew and à Beckett started or were involved with *The Literary Beacon,* a weekly guide to books, the drama,
and the fine arts, which lasted four months in 1831. It featured independent critical book reviews, some of which contained thinly disguised radical political comments. Finally, the first great success not
only for Mayhew and à Beckett but for satirical journalism itself was
launched: *Figaro in London,* whose first issue was on 10 December
1831. Before discussing that important journal and Mayhew's connection with it, however, we should mention one other weekly journal Mayhew and à Beckett founded at this time, *The Thief,* which ran
for twenty numbers between 21 April and 1 September 1832, and
was published by William Strange, who also published *Figaro in London.* As the title honestly acknowledges, this was a scissors-and-paste
job, a miscellany of excerpted tales, poetry, essays, and anecdotes that
were aimed at the working class. The editors gave in their editorial
policy this justification for the melange of light literature: "we considered that the great body of literature which fell into the hands of
artisans and operative mechanics, as either of a nature to take them
from the hard labour of the body to the more severe exertion of the
mind; or as tending to corrupt and debase them by constantly bring-

ing before their eyes the productions of inflamatory politicians, or the prurient fancy of vitiated imaginations" and so they wanted to provide more wholesome entertainments. There are occasional comic pieces written by the editors, one of which is a street scene in front of an oyster stall.[19]

Figaro in London, however, was the most significant journalistic achievement of the 1830s for Mayhew. Athol says his father and à Beckett started *Figaro in London* together, but à Beckett was the editor, by all accounts, from its beginning in December 1831 until the end of 1834 when he quarreled with the illustrator Robert Seymour over a cartoon and quit. In January 1835 Mayhew took over the editorship, though it is possible that he had written some pieces for it during the previous two years. Mayhew edited the journal from 1835 through the end of 1838, when it began to have serious problems. There was a new publisher starting January 1838 and in August he apologized in print for the low quality of the material. But "the Editor being out of town, and having furnished a much smaller portion of copy than requisite, no other source was left but that resorted to" (4 August 1838). (Was this one of Mayhew's periodic disappearances to avoid his creditors?) Worried that his reputation would be endangered by this, the Editor "will for the future avoid the chances of such accidents," but it did not happen. Two months later the paper announced a new format and by November the journal was slipping quickly into a vulgarized, poorly written collection of jokes, dramatic notices, and answers to correspondents. Probably Mayhew had left by this time; in the first issue of the new format there is a negative review of his play *"But however—"* ("we cannot compliment the author on any stretch of ingenuity, either as regards plot, dialogue, or jokes" [5 November 1838]). Athol says à Beckett returned to the editorship and saw the journal end on 17 August 1839.

While it lasted, though, *Figaro in London* was a tremendous success, and its longevity was unequaled at the time. Within a few months a raft of imitations attested to its popularity: Douglas Jerrold's *Punch in London* (Jerrold and Mayhew had not met at this time), *Punchinello!, The English Figaro, Giovanni in London, The Illustrious Stranger, The New Figaro,* and separate *Figaros* in Birmingham, Chesterfield, Liverpool, Sheffield, and Wales. All but the last two disappeared after a few issues.

The journal was a four-page quarto; it cost a penny and came out every Saturday. It featured a standard logo on the front page of the barber Figaro (the name, however, came from the French satirical journal) with the caption "Whigs dressed here." There were also two quotations, one from Lady Montague: "Satire should like a polish'd razor keen, / Wound with a touch that's scarcely felt or seen." On the first page a satirical illustration furnished the text for the leading article. After a while there were additional smaller cuts inside. The well-known illustrator Robert Seymour provided the illustrations until his death in April 1836, after which Robert Cruikshank became the illustrator.

The letter press contained political satire, squibs, puns, jokes, and ironical attacks on social abuses plus a column of good dramatic criticism. It is probably true to say that *Figaro in London* was the first of these comic magazines. Its roots were in the satiric works of the great eighteenth-century illustrators Hogarth, Gillray, and Rowlandson. During the early nineteenth century the comic political commentary could be in very bad taste, frequently obscene and abusive. *Figaro in London* established a new level of responsibility even though it too was sarcastic about institutions and frequently crude in its attacks on politicians and others. When Mayhew became editor, the journal became broader in its political position and Mayhew boasted in January 1836 that "our columns have been free from that reckless severity which used to be laid as a charge against this periodical." This broad satirical thrust, the softer, less personal tone, and the uncompromisingly liberal if not truly radical sentiment Mayhew carried with him from *Figaro in London* to *Punch,* the natural child of the *Figaro in London* endeavor.

Two related projects took shape during the *Figaro in London* years. *The Comic Magazine* (1832-1834), a monthly edited by à Beckett, reprinted illustrations from *Figaro in London,* substituting an innocuous caption for the original political one. Some contemporaries said Mayhew was also associated with this magazine. Robert Seymour wanted to do a series of plates illustrating the misadventures of a "Nimrod" club of cockney sportsmen. He tried to get Henry Mayhew to write the text for him, but finally, through the publishers Chapman and Hall, he got another young, relatively unknown journalist, Charles Dickens, to do the captions. The outcome, though Seymour committed suicide in the midst of the project, was fortuitous: *The Pickwick Papers.*

Punch and after.   From the severing of his connection with *Figaro in London* in late 1838 to the founding of *Punch* in July of 1841, Mayhew must have been involved in various activities but nothing so far has turned up to indicate what. Perhaps he had to leave London for a time to avoid creditors; his son recounts that he went to Wales for such a reason, and in *German Life and Manners* Mayhew reminisces about living on the banks of the Wye when a young man. He was in any case full of ideas, involved in the planning of a comic weekly *Cupid* (based on the satirical nickname given the late Lord Palmerston) to replace the defunct *Figaro in London.* In addition, Joseph Last, the printer of *Figaro in London* at its demise, and the engraver Ebenezer Landells had plans for a miscellany called *The Cosmorama,* in which they tried to interest Henry Mayhew. He in turn tried to get them to help in forming *Cupid.* Both of these projects eventually fed into *Punch,* launched in July 1841.

Even though Mayhew's connection with this august institution was comparatively slight after its first months, it is a high watermark in his early career, for he was a crucial figure in its conception, gestation, and birth. Furthermore, Mayhew's effort to establish a less biting, more generous tone to the political satire tells us something about the attitudes informing his sense of social questions in the decade before his social surveys.

The details of the negotiations leading up to the foundation of *Punch* and the various machinations, personal rivalries, adjustments, and betrayals of its first precarious year of existence have been the source of much acrimonious debate and are even yet shrouded in uncertainty. Mayhew's son was moved to write his memoir of his father, he said, because the obituary of Henry Mayhew in *Punch* denied his formative connection with the journal. Athol's book with its claims for his father, in turn, greatly angered the families of Douglas Jerrold and Ebenezer Landells. R. G. G. Price, a modern historian of *Punch,* tried to sort out the details of the story, which he published as an appendix to his *A History of Punch* in 1957. The following summary is based on Price's account.

In the year or so preceding 1841 Mayhew was trying to get funding for *Cupid.* In conversation among at least some of the following people—Mayhew, Last, Landells, and à Beckett—the idea for a comic weekly began to take shape. At the same time, at a tavern Mark Lemon ran for his mother, the Shakespeare's Head, Lemon and his friends were formulating a plan for a journal called *Pen and Palette.* "In some way that is not clear," Price says, Mayhew brought the two enterprises together.[20]

Several meetings occurred and out of them came the name *Punch, or the London Charivari,* probably suggested by Mayhew though he was hesitant since he felt Jerrold, who was out of the country at the time, might feel he had a claim to the name, having used it in 1832 for *Punch in London.* The meeting also produced an agreement that the ownership of the journal was to be split three ways: Landells the engraver, one-third; Last the printer, one-third, and the three editors—Mayhew, Lemon, and Stirling Coyne—one-third share. There was also a Prospectus, written in Lemon's hand but generally agreed to be dictated to Lemon by Mayhew.

The first year the magazine lost money consistently. In 1842 Mayhew conceived the idea of the *Almanac,* with humorous cuts and a joke for every day of the year. According to Athol, though doubted by others, Mayhew and H. P. Grattan wrote the whole thing in a week in the Fleet prison where Grattan was incarcerated for debt. The *Almanac* when published had a tremendous sale—around 100,000 versus the less than 10,000 a week *Punch* itself was selling. Numerous writers, including the early historian of *Punch,* M. H. Spielmann, credit Mayhew's *Almanac* with saving *Punch.* Now Bradbury and Evans became the printers, and in a set of negotiations that are not clear and were subject to much bitterness in later accounts, they bought all the shares of the editors and the engraver, and by Christmas 1842 were sole proprietors of *Punch.*

Considerable hard feelings resulted from the readjustments involved in this transfer of ownership. Lemon became sole editor, Mayhew having no official capacity, though his connection with the magazine continued for three more years. He was understandably "nettled," as Athol says, by all of this. A coolness developed between himself and Mark Lemon, though Mayhew dedicated his educational work *What to Teach* to Lemon as his "best friend" in 1842. Mayhew's sanguine temperament seems to have extended even to what seems on the surface and from his point of view rather shabby treatment. Athol, writing long after the event, quotes his father as saying, "To me *Punch* was always a labour of love, and certainly never proved a source of profit; for, after planning and arranging the entire work, selecting the whole of the *old* staff of contributors, and having edited it for the first six months of its career without having received a single farthing for my pains, it so happened when those who started it were obliged to sell their bantling to Bradbury and Evans, that on the payment of all the debts connected with the production of the work, there remained a clear surplus of seven and sixpence to be divided among the three original proprietors, of which *the munificent sum of half-a-crown* fell to my share."[21]

One contribution Mayhew does not claim for himself but with which both Spielmann and Price credit him is the early tone and direction of *Punch*. The prospectus for the new journal laid down certain vague, conventional guidelines. Mayhew apparently insisted that it should be clean and nonsectarian: again, Mayhew, as quoted by his son: "At that time the only journals of 'a light character' were about as coarse, and indulged in the same foul aspersions as is the wont of your 'light' characters in general. Their satire was simply slander, their wit obscenity, their humour vulgarity, their ridicule abuse, and their means of existence 'black-mail.' " For this Mayhew wanted to substitute a healthy comic journalism "which should be as pure and joyous as a baby's laughter, and the satire as refined and yet as pungent, as aromatic vinegar."[22]

Most accounts agree that he achieved this, and *Punch* "became or aimed at becoming, a budget of wit, fun, and kindly humour, and of honest opposition based upon fairness and justice."[23] Soon Douglas Jerrold's harsher political satire came to dominate; Price says Mayhew disagreed strongly with this direction and sometime after his ouster wanted to start a rival to *Punch*.[24] But despite Jerrold's influence, nineteenth-century comic journalism, as Donald Gray has said, had moved "toward a genteel amusement combed of those relics of rude manners and satirist's license which still seemed to be a part of the popular humorist's trade in the early decades of the century."[25] Mayhew's influence on the second half of *Figaro in London*'s life as well as on the early days of *Punch* must be credited with a crucial role in this shift.

While at *Punch* in the early 1840s, Mayhew must have enjoyed himself. It was the end of his youth really; he was still a footloose bachelor, with few cares. All that was to change in a few years. The magazine was usually the result of a communal effort by a small number of men, all good friends, who planned the issues over convivial dinners every Wednesday at various taverns, particularly the Crown Inn in Vinegar Yard. A personal memoir by one who served as a copyboy in those early days recounts the lad's efforts to get corrected proof from Mayhew, whom he found with others at Mayhew's apartments in Clement's Inn in the Strand "with a very long pipe with a very large bowl, a copper kettle singing merrily on the hob, and they were enjoying themselves immensely."[26]

The ostensible reason for the *Punch* dinners was to establish the subject of the "big cut" which became a hallmark of the journal. Undoubtedly many other suggestions and ideas evolved over the brandy. In the absence of a complete index of authorship of the articles, we have only sketchy information about who suggested and who wrote what. Some information does exist on the years Mayhew was connected with *Punch* (he left permanently in March 1846 about the time of his bankruptcy). He suggested nineteen of the topics for the "big cut" during these years,[27] wrote a couple of "scholarly" pieces, including an etymology of the word *humbug,* and several good satirical pieces. One is "A Synopsis of Voting, arranged According to the Categories of Cant," a clever breakdown of why people vote, as applicable today as in 1841 when it first appeared. In the *Almanac* for 1845 Mayhew was also responsible for what was reputedly *Punch*'s most famous joke: "Worthy of Attention! Advice to persons about to marry,—DON'T"—a parody of a well-known advertisement for a furniture company. In all of this there is little that is extraordinary in terms of literary merit, although in the interest in etymology we see the more "philosophical" bent that distinguishes him from his colleagues. In 1865 he said that while editor of *Punch* he had translated several popular songs into Anglo-Saxon.[28] But his influence on the magazine was more personal, more indirect than in what he actually wrote, which is probably one of the reasons the tone of Jerrold's written contributions came to dominate *Punch.*

The early reforming spirit of *Punch* is important though, for it underlines the general sympathy with the poor and oppressed that propelled Mayhew into his major work at the end of the decade. But between *Punch* and "Labour and the Poor" lay Mayhew's marriage and his almost immediately following bankruptcy with the personal trouble that that failure brought him with his father and his father-in-law.

Mayhew's marriage in 1844 could be seen, facetiously, as a product of his journalism, for he met his wife through his friendship with her father's circle of journalists. Certainly his bankruptcy was a direct result of a journalistic endeavor. After he married Jane Jerrold and several months before he severed all connection with *Punch,* he joined with a well-known but fairly disreputable journalist, Thomas Lyttleton ("Raggedy") Holt in launching a daily newspaper called the *Iron Times*, in a format like the *London Times* but designed to exploit the tremendous enthusiasm over railway expansion in England in the mid-1840s. (Over nine thousand miles of new railways were authorized between 1844 and 1847.) The paper at its inception in July 1845 limited itself to railroad news and was aimed at an audience who speculated in railway stocks. Unfortunately—and disastrously for both Holt and Mayhew—there was a crash in 1847 in railway speculation; the paper had sunk the year before, being too late to exploit the market. Both Holt and Mayhew went bankrupt.

This episode has more to do with biography than journalism, for there is no significant writing in the *Iron Times*. The failure of the newspaper propelled Mayhew into a spurt of literary and journalistic activity in order to recoup his losses. He wrote a series of novels with Augustus which are discussed in the next section. He also may have been associated with a satirical weekly *Gulliver* (now lost), which, along with narratives and criticism, apparently had "some satire . . . in the worst taste."[29] During this period he also worked in some capacity for *Era,* the leading trade journal for the stage. In December 1847 he contributed a long "philosophical" piece called "What is the Cause of Surprise? and what connection has it with the Laws of Suggestion?" to *Douglas Jerrold's Shilling Magazine.* In this piece he tries to analyze the emotion surprise "scientifically" and in doing so he uses various methods of categorization familiar to the readers of his social surveys. He concludes by drawing attention to the analogy "between the cause of Surprise and the phenomenon necessary for the production of the electric shock, as well as between their effects upon the animal economy" (566). The emotions wonder and surprise are fundamental to Mayhew's educational theories. His discussion of them in this article shows again how he tended to bring a "scientific" orientation to his work.

Morning Chronicle, Comic Almanac, and *Edinburgh News.* In 1848 Mayhew is reported to be working for the popular *Illustrated London News* under the editorship of Charles Mackay, who was later to be the correspondent from Liverpool and Birmingham for the "Labour and the Poor" series. Finally in October 1849 he began his work as Metropolitan Correspondent for the *Morning Chronicle.* In this context, we can see that Mayhew's social surveys were a natural outgrowth of his previous twenty years as a journalist and that however high his sympathetic identification with the poor and his scientific leanings raised these newspaper articles, they were the products of a working journalist.

While surveying London's lower classes, he did not abandon the comic journalism that had been his forte since the beginning. In 1850 and 1851 he edited and wrote some pieces for the *Comic Almanac,* a yearly publication started in 1835 by George Cruikshank and illustrated by some of his best work. The issue for 1850 is made up of conventional puns and jokes, many of them about women and marriage, but the 1851 issue is quite different in tone. There are conventional comic pieces, but there are several more sombre satires. In one, on the census, Mayhew attacks the adequacy of the count by imagining all the people who slept no place on the day of the census, such as the clerk who caroused all night and the cabman who slept on the move. He included another satire in this issue on "Female Emigration," a philanthropic endeavour launched in response to his revelations about underpaid and overworked London needlewomen, which turns on the joke that having exported so many poor women, the government is thinking of importing various native women from Africa and the Far East to make up the difference. A bitter poem on "Overpopulation: A Malthusian Lamentation" lists all the classes of which England has a surplus, including lawyers, actors, artists, and policemen, and then, turning abruptly serious, the "underpaid." A final piece clearly by Mayhew is a semi-serious report on "Our Pet Thief." It tells the story of the misadventures that resulted when a husband tried to reform a pickpocket he had met at a low lodging house by introducing him into his own household.

In all of these pieces the social criticism merges easily with the humor, but the reforming intent is clear. The difference between the conventional 1850 issue of the *Comic Almanac* and the much more socially critical 1851 issue is the clearest evidence we have of the effect Mayhew's years as "Metropolitan Correspondent" had on his social awareness. Nothing in his work before this had had an edge of bitterness like that in the poem on overpopulation nor had he gone to such lengths before to project himself into the lives of a different class as in "Our Pet Thief."

This newly intensified social vision also determined his next work of journalism, the series of nine articles he wrote for the *Edinburgh News and Literary Chronicle* in May through July of 1851 on the Great

Exhibition of the Industry of All Nations. This Exhibition was one of the wonders of the Victorian period. Conceived by Prince Albert and housed in one of the first examples of modernism in architecture, Joseph Paxton's steel and glass "Crystal Palace," it dominated the news and the lives of most Londoners in 1851. Several different countries sent examples of their industry and their arts, but England's industrial achievement was, quite rightly, the lynch pin of the show. Mayhew said in one of his reports that grown men were known to break down in tears at the sight of the "Machine Room" where the technology of modern industrialism was on display (24 May 1851). It was a World's Fair in which both the industrial prowess and the meretricious taste of the age were enshrined.

Mayhew, however, in his reviews was not interested in matters of taste and design. His sense of value of the Great Exhibition was the dignity that it gave to labor in the eyes of the world. Thus Mayhew views the Exhibition from a peculiar stance; based on his experiences of the lives of London working people in the previous year and a half, he sees it as he thinks the working classes must see it, and he also sees it as an upper-middle-class, "philosophically" inclined journalist. The blend of these viewpoints makes his nine articles different from other writing on the Great Exhibition as well as further demonstrating the way his experiences as a social historian shaped his outlook.

He begins with a conventional overview of "The Swarming of the Great Hive," but at the end of the description his special perspective emerges and continues to dominate the rest of his series: the Exhibition "is the first public expression of the dignity and artistic quality of labour that has been made in this country" (3 May 1851).

In his second letter on 10 May a number of Mayhew's current concerns merge. First he compliments the Exhibition on the way it brings to England the best aesthetic productions in Europe, a sentiment like many in these articles he will incorporate in his comic novel *1851,* running concurrently with his reporting. Then he attacks the inadequacy of the system of classification, a charge that he will expand and elaborate in the opening pages of the "extra" volume of *London Labour and the London Poor* two months later. He complains that there is no unity or harmony in the system of division. His next piece is more descriptive, though he expresses his dissatisfaction with the authorized catalogue. Before continuing his description of raw materials in article four, Mayhew takes up the question of the relations of the working classes to the Great Exhibition, something he had touched on in the previous letter and would also introduce into his novel *1851*, though with quite different conclusions.

Initially the Exhibition ticket cost five shillings. Late in May "shilling days" were introduced to enable the working classes to attend, but the Exhibition sponsors were disappointed at first that the attendance seemed to drop on shilling days (actually by the end of its run, shilling tickets had outsold all other priced tickets combined). Why were the working classes staying away? Mayhew said it was because they distrusted the goals of the Exhibition, fearing the employers would use it to find out ways of getting goods produced more cheaply. He disagreed with this supposed working-class perception, but he did feel very strongly—and said so in his fifth article—that the Exhibition only glorified the capitalists and ignored the part the workers played in production. As a result the working man is "filched of his fair fame" (21 June 1851). Because of this, in this same article Mayhew modified his belief that the Exhibition was beneficial in stimulating artisan skill. "The goods exhibited are not the productions of industry but the purchases of mere money." However in the continuation of this argument in the next article he reverses himself and asserts the "great glory and benefit" that the Exhibition will bring to the workpeople. Clearly Mayhew was having a hard time deciding between the two points of view, representing as they do the two different vantage points from which he was reviewing the Exhibition and, indeed, the total social reality at the time. He never resolved the uncertainty of opinion here. The conflict simply disappears in the abrupt end of his contributions. His next-to-last piece includes a glance at the various types of people attending the Exhibition, many paragraphs of which he transposed into *1851*, and a closing expression of hope in the ameliorative effect of the Exhibition on the "elevation of the people." His final article touches on the educative value of the Exhibition in its practicality and example, and a further discussion of the raw materials and the machinery for processing them on display.

Mayhew's articles ceased because he was ill and "had to leave London for a season." His novel *1851* was also hurriedly completed. There was no interruption in *London Labour and the London Poor*, though the "Answers to Correspondents" column had been omitted for two weeks in May because of Mayhew's illness.

Illustrated Times and *Morning News.* *London Labour and the London Poor* continued for another year and seems to have been Mayhew's sole occupation. At its collapse in February 1852 he disappears, going to Germany at some point after 1853, returning in the late months of 1855, in which year the repeal of the Stamp Tax had made possible, finally, cheap newspapers. His friend and fellow journalist Henry Vizetelly almost immediately launched the *Illustrated Times,* a daily which began with a circulation of 200,000 and which lasted until 1872.

While writing "The Great World of London" in 1856, Mayhew was also connected in some way with both the *Illustrated Times* and another new cheap daily the *Morning News,* an offshoot of the *Morning Chronicle.* Both journals report his doings, his lectures, his meetings with London low life, his problems, and review his books. How much he himself wrote for them is not known; we have evidence of only three specific contributions. For the *Illustrated Times* in early 1856 he interviewed Dr. Alfred Taylor, professor of medical jurisprudence, in connection with the notorious William Palmer murder case. He also investigated insurance claims for the same journal, and then edited the *Morning News* for the month of January 1859, after which the newspaper abruptly folded. (The way Mayhew's various endeavors kept failing gives particular pathos to his remark about *Figaro in London,* as reported by his son: in 1838 all his enterprises with "Gil" à Beckett had failed except for *Figaro in London* "possibly, as my father used to laughingly remark, 'because he had long since resigned the co-editorship of it.' "[30])

The William Palmer murder case was one of several well-publicized murders during the Victorian period. Palmer had coolly poisoned three if not more people, receiving £13,000 in insurance money from his wife's death. The *Illustrated Times* followed the story of his trial and execution closely, issuing a special number on 16 February 1856 entirely devoted to various aspects of the case. This number included an anonymous interview with Dr. Alfred Taylor, who had analyzed one of the victims' remains, and who was the chief witness for the prosecution. There was also an investigative piece signed by Mayhew: "An Inquiry into the Number of Suspicious Deaths Occurring in Connection with Life Insurance Offices." This inquiry was conducted and written much like Mayhew's social surveys; he visited a number of insurance companies of all different sorts to determine how prevalent suspicious death was in connection with insurance claims. He reports what he was told at each insurance company in the same way that he reported his interviews with London workers, without, however, any personal interest in the speaker and hence with little interest for the modern reader. He concludes that "tampering with life with a view to become possessed of the insurance money is more general than the public believe." Further interviews with insurance company spokesmen to the same end appear on 23 February and the first and eighth of March.

The interview with Dr. Taylor is also of limited interest, except that it later created a small fracus similar to that following Mayhew's criticism of the Ragged Schools in 1850 which reveals some details about Mayhew's working methods. He carried a letter of introduction to Dr. Taylor from Michael Faraday, the well-known scientist, whose connection with Mayhew went back a number of years. Mayhew's interview with Dr. Taylor was a kind of scoop for the *Illustrated Times.* The doctor is reported as saying that poisoning is on the increase but medical technology has developed to the degree that it is impossible that it go undetected. Later on, during Palmer's trial, Taylor denied that he had given Mayhew permission to publish these sentiments. He was under attack by the defense because he had not been able to find strychnine in the victim's remains but still insisted on poisoning as the cause of death based on circumstantial evidence. The defense wanted to discredit him as a witness and used Mayhew's interview as part of their effort. Mayhew was forced to vindicate himself by writing letters to the daily press demonstrating that Taylor knew full well he was being interviewed for the press and had even corrected the proof before the article was printed. Perhaps because of this altercation, Mayhew's series on the insurance offices stopped rather abruptly.

What Mayhew's connection was with the other cheap daily, the *Morning News,* during the years 1856–1858 is not clear. In a leader (editorial) at the time of his trouble with Dr. Taylor, the *Morning News* supported Mayhew, and his position is fully articulated in the pages of the newspaper. The paper also favored more liberal opening hours on Sunday, as did Mayhew. In a debate over capital punishment the paper published a long excerpt from Mayhew's pamphlet advocating its abolition, but the leaders arguing that the ticket-of-leave system paroling convicts will not work take a position different from Mayhew's.

Both the *Illustrated Times* and the *Morning News* report on Mayhew's meetings of swell mobsmen (con artists) and ticket-of-leave men as well as on the threats against him by one disgruntled exconvict. (The *Illustrated Times* has a picture of one of these meetings with Mayhew taking notes.) In 1857 there is very little in either paper about Mayhew, which suggests that he had separated himself from both journals after the collapse of "The Great World of London." In January 1858 the *Morning News* has a new publisher, and still another in October 1858, at which point it ceased to have any connection with the *Morning Chronicle,* which itself was undergoing difficulties. On 5 January 1859 the masthead announced that the paper is now edited by Henry Mayhew, author of *London Labour and the London Poor.*

In the leaders he wrote during the month the newspaper lasted, two current topics dominate, one the debate over a new reform bill (which was actually passed in 1867) and the other education reform. On both of these issues Mayhew takes a conventional stand. He is against universal suffrage because it will give too much control of government to one class, namely, the lower class. He wants a balance of interests in control, believing that artisans should receive the vote but not farm laborers or unskilled workers. In the matter of education, one of his longtime interests, he is against compulsory schooling or total government financing of education. Children should not be kept off the labor market if they want to enter it, and later they can continue their education while working. Government support of education should be limited to "rendering assistance to the voluntary efforts of all recognized religious denominations." His justification for this is a familiar appeal to the value of self-help: were the government to take over education, the people would be induced "to lay aside one of the greatest of their national virtues—their self-reliance" (25 January 1859). These sentiments are part of his lifelong educational theory.

The *Shops and Companies of London*.   This conservative position, though not completely new to Mayhew (he had argued against universal suffrage twenty years before in *Figaro in London*), parallels the more depressing jingoism of his travel books, written during the same period, and the complacency of his view of British industry in his next and seemingly final journalistic endeavor, the *Shops and Companies of London.* The tone and direction of his thought after "The Great World of London" is rightward. Without the subject of London's lower classes, which released his talents and his energies, he slipped into meretricious and undistinguished work. His career was over.

After more years in Germany, a couple of children's books, and the publication of *London Labour and the London Poor* in four volumes, there remained only this one project, the *Shops and Companies,* before Mayhew disappeared into a twenty-year oblivion.

Joseph Last, earlier connected with the initiation of *Punch,* brought out a monthly periodical in 1865 called the *Shops and Companies of London, and the Grades and Manufactories of Great Britain* modeled on the French *Les Grandes Usines,* and whose purpose turns out to be to glorify various London manufacturers. In some sense it is a high-class advertising special. Last got Henry Mayhew, back from Germany, to edit the journal for him. It continued for a year. In the course of that time Mayhew and probably some other contributors, perhaps Arthur à Beckett, a son of his old friend, now dead, visited a wide variety of London manufacturers: biscuit makers, beer distilleries, jewelers, toolmakers, musical instrument makers, cloth mills, perfume makers, carriage makers, makers of billiard tables, and so forth. In the report of each place the process involved in making the goods is described, followed by a personal account of the trip to the firm and a tour of the plant, a rhetorical device Mayhew had developed while writing about the London prisons. The piece usually closed with an account of a talk between the reporter and the owner of the firm. There are no interviews with workers and no apparent concern over their conditions; Mayhew worries about mercury poisoning in a mirror-making establishment, but he is quick to assure the readers of management's effort to eliminate the danger.

The series is lightened by a number of personal references and revelations made in passing; the voice of Mayhew as a person is more evident here as it is in the travel book he wrote about the same time. There are some evocative descriptions of the streets of shops and of the shoppers but none rise to the level of his descriptions in *London Labour and the London Poor.* Mayhew editorializes occasionally, taking a harder line on crime and punishment than he had ten years before during his survey of prisons. These pieces, despite the tantalizing glimpses of Mayhew's personal life, have practically no interest for the modern reader. They are journalism of the most ordinary sort, expressing conventional, even sycophantic opinions about the glory of British industry and the impressiveness of its capitalists. Mayhew had come a long way from his arguments about the inadequacy of the English economic arrangements in 1851.

This was really the end of Mayhew's journalistic work though not of his life. In 1870 he edited an annual of low-level poetry and fiction, *Only Once a Year*. He and his son Athol are reported to have been war correspondents in the Franco-Prussian war in the same year, perhaps for the *Illustrated Times*. There were schemes for various other journalistic projects, and finally in 1871 a survey of working men's clubs for the licensed victuallers who were worried about the competition these clubs presented. (The 1874 *London Characters*, though bearing his name on the title page, contains only some reprints of the much earlier *Morning Chronicle* and *London Labour and the London Poor* material.) Then silence for thirteen years until his death.

Comic Novels

The Brothers Mayhew.   In 1846, at the time of Mayhew's bankruptcy, Henry was thirty-four and his brother Augustus was twenty years old. All the Mayhew brothers except the steady Alfred and hopeless Julius had dabbled in popular journalism, and when it came time for "Gus" to cut loose from his father's establishment, he moved right into the world of his older bohemian brothers. Family tradition says that "Gus" and "Harry" (as Henry Mayhew was familiarly known) were the closest of all the brothers, and their collaboration as the Brothers Mayhew supports this view. Together they wrote six novels during the years 1847–1850. The dates suggest that the collaboration was an effort by Mayhew to make money after the fiasco of his bankruptcy. The first novel by the Brothers Mayhew appears within months of Mayhew's bankruptcy and the last one shortly before *London Labour and the London Poor* begins. In 1857 they began a seventh novel, though Henry dropped out of the project, and when it was published in volume form it bore Augustus's name only. This final effort at collaboration starts just after "The Great World of London" project collapses. So for Henry at least these fictional efforts reflect his need for money and something to do. Augustus himself wrote five novels in the 1850s and 1860s as well as six farces in collaboration with H. Sutherland Edwards. Augustus also helped his brother with *London Labour and the London Poor*. They had several other projects that did not materialize.

As in any collaboration, how much is due to one or the other of the partners is hard to determine. For what it is worth, one contemporary said later that the ideas for the books by the Brothers Mayhew came from Henry but Augustus did the writing.[31] From what we know about Mayhew's indolence in any matter except his surveys of poverty this is not an unreasonable hypothesis. In *1851,* which appears to be the only novel he wrote by himself, his collaborator providing the illustrations, there is much more social philosophy, but whether that was due to Mayhew writing the piece or to the work appearing after the education given him by his social surveys we cannot know. In any case, there is nothing in the novels by the Brothers Mayhew that is counter to Henry Mayhew's concerns and ideas, and we may discuss them if somewhat cautiously as products of his literary imagination.

The first three novels are related to Mayhew's farces both in treatment and in conception. They are also related in the same way to the nonpolitical comic journalism of *Punch.* Mayhew's fictional piece "Mr. Peter Punctilio," a conventional farce of mistaken identities and puns, was dramatized with very few changes. *The Image of His Father,* a novel by the Brothers Mayhew, on the other hand, turns on a similar farcical plot of mistaken identity. In the same way, the early numbers of *Punch* are full of satire of middle-class pretensions, particularly those of women, the central focus for *The Greatest Plague of Life* and *Whom to Marry,* both told by women narrators who are the primary butt of the satire. Yet the novels also incorporate the individual experiences of their authors: in 1848 *Whom to Marry* and *The Image of His Father,* like their comic poem "A Respectable Man" (published in the *Comic Almanac* by their brother Horace), contain several satiric portraits of their father. (It must have been a bad year in the Mayhew household—the result of Henry's bankruptcy perhaps?) *Whom to Marry* and *The Fear of the World* have strong descriptions of what it is like to go bankrupt and be sold up. An interest in the Condition-of-England is briefly visible in *Whom to Marry,* and this concern shapes nearly all the authorial comment in *1851.* The strange and uneven fairy tales, *The Good Genius* and *The Magic of Kindness,* are imbued with Mayhew's ideas about the education of the moral sensibilities and provide a bridge to his children's books of the 1850s and 1860s. Thus, a survey of the novels by the Brothers Mayhew plus *1851* serves a twofold purpose: on the one hand, it can demonstrate common liberal sentiments about domestic arrangements and human behavior in the 1840s, and, on the other, it can give the reader of

Mayhew's social surveys a glimpse of his attitudes and concerns just prior to the launching of his social surveys.

The Greatest Plague of Life.   We begin then with *The Greatest Plague of Life; or, the Adventures of a Lady in Search of a Good Servant* (1847) with illustrations by George Cruikshank. The narrator is Caroline, a snobbish, selfish, and grasping woman obsessed with food. Counterpoised to her is her attorney husband Edward, the soul of patience and wisdom, who delivers the moral: be kind and loving to your servants, BUT FIRM, and they will respond with obedience. In addition he enjoys the idiosyncrasies of the various servants his wife hires. He is quite sanguine and humorous about the Irish maid's temper and even his deceased first wife's hypochondria. He likes to joke with the nursemaid, much to his wife's disgust, and he loves to listen to the stories of Dick Farden, a cockney seller of "smuggled" tobacco and brandy, who comes to clean the boots. Farden is a character straight out of Mayhew's farces of the 1830s. The husband's is clearly the voice of the authors, and in his even temper, his pleasure in the oddities of London low life, and his conventional sentiments we see the shadow of Henry Mayhew's personality before he became "The Metropolitan Correspondent."

In the course of her story Caroline recounts the "plagues" visited on her by a drunken cook, a charwoman who steals, a hot-tempered Irish maid, and a much-too-pretty Rosetta, whom Caroline, à la Dombey, insists on calling Susan. The maid is addicted to popular romance of the period—silver fork, gothic, Newgate. She buys all the "dying speeches" from the street sellers. A boy "Wittals," a lovable villain like the Artful Dodger, comes from the workhouse. The novel is in fact a catalog of all the servant complaints that have existed from time immemorial. There is no plot to speak of but a succession of misadventures that are stopped only when the husband decides to educate his wife to be a good mistress.

But even though the husband has the last word, the pleasure in the novel lies in the wife's unconscious self-revelation. She unmasks her obsession with food, for example, by parenthetically remarking: "I do think sage and onions *so* delicious when one is not going to see company, and one can only get one's husband just to take a mouthful or so of it; and then 'pon my word, I verily believe, I could devour my own dear mother, if she was only stuffed with plenty of it, and nicely browned."[32] It is a passage we would not be surprised to find in a novel by Dickens.

As the *Literary Gazette* of 1847 said, "there are genuine observations of life, good drawings of character, a whimsical appliance of ridicule to folly, and useful household and family lessons" (13 November 1847). The elements of satire on women and the lower classes plus the liberal sentiments of the husband were a sure-fire popular mix, and one source says *The Greatest Plague of Life* sold more copies than any novel published serially since *Pickwick Papers*.[33]

Whom to Marry. The success must have prompted the Brothers Mayhew to repeat the formula, for *Whom to Marry and How to Get Married! or, the Adventures of a Lady in Search of a Good Husband* (1848) followed more or less the same pattern, though there is a shift in tone in some places that makes the piece more uneven. (In 1851 Henry and Gus planned an actual sequel to *The Greatest Plague,* the same story told from the servant's point of view, *The Shabby Fammerly.* It was advertised but apparently not published.) The *Literary Gazette* did not like *Whom to Marry* as much as *The Greatest Plague,* finding its characterization and moral too forced. Yet, from this distance, it seems the more interesting of the two if not as artistically coherent as *The Greatest Plague.* There is a stronger satiric edge in this novel, and at times the comic element disappears altogether. The difference is seen in the dedication to Joshua Mayhew, surely an ironic one, for in the novel itself several of Mayhew senior's more notorious eccentricities are given to Sir Luke Sharpe, a very unpleasant old miser very much like Sir Pitt Crawley in *Vanity Fair.*

The story is told by Charlotte de Roos, a silly, money-grubbing woman. She continually falls for the wrong men. Her father, a doctor, takes the position here that Edward the husband did in *The Greatest Plague* in delivering the appropriate sentiments. His moral, and that of the book, is that "something *more than love* was required to constitute a happy union, still I never gave her to understand that something *less than love* could, by the remotest possibility, do so."[34] The father's attitude toward marriage and women is conventional: children, kitchen, and church.

Charlotte and her equally ridiculous mother make several botched efforts at securing a good match. Interspersed with their farcical mixups are two scenes in which the tone shifts sharply. In one Charlotte visits a distressed needlewoman, in a scene that looks forward to the "Labour and the Poor" series but which is marred by a sentimentality Mayhew will shed under the experiences of his social survey. And Mr. Gee, a nobleman's brother who pays to drive a coach and keeps all his tips, is quite biting about Charlotte and her mother's machinations when he shears off.

Other potential suitors include various stock types: an Irishman with a gift of gab and a soldier who imitates a costermonger. The knowledge of the cockney accent and costermonger life again looks forward to Mayhew's *London Labour and the London Poor.* Finally Charlotte marries a sporting gentleman, who turns her into a sporting type as well. But after "six weeks of bliss" he is killed in a steeplechase, leaving Charlotte penniless. However, the story is not over yet. As a widow, Charlotte provides the authors with a chance to satirize pretensions of the middle classes that lead them to live beyond their incomes and the snobbery associated with funerals. Again a quick shift in tone provides a moving account of what it feels like to be sold up. Finally, Charlotte, like Becky Sharp, goes as a governess to Sir Luke Sharpe, who lives in a grand and unkempt old house in an uncouth, miserly, and vain way. Again like Becky, Charlotte makes herself indispensable and then threatens to leave, forcing the old baronet to propose marriage. He does; she accepts. But he has the last word, leading her a miserable life of penny-pinching and jealousy.

As this summary shows, *Whom to Marry* is a more complicated novel than *The Greatest Plague* and sharper in its indictment of middle-class hypocrisy and pretension. Yet though the novel mirrors a combination of seriousness and facetiousness common in *Figaro in London* and *Punch,* its shifts in tone are not very successful. In a comic journal the dual direction is absorbed more easily because journals are made up of different short pieces and the variation in tone is an advantage. Coming out of the same tradition, Dickens and Thackeray have the same mixture of serious and comic parts in their novels, and one mark of Dickens's maturity is the way he learns to integrate the two through plot and symbol. His earlier novels are more uneven.

The Image of His Father. The Brothers Mayhew did not write any novels with the scope or depth of those of Dickens and Thackeray. But in *The Image of His Father* (1848) the topics of satire are similar to some in Dickens's early novels. The Brothers Mayhew are softer in their approach, and reconciliation is achieved with much less cost than in *Oliver Twist* or *Nicholas Nickleby. The Image of His Father* is a more promising but less successful novel than either *The Greatest Plague* or *Whom to Marry.* It moves away from the easy, traditional satire of female pretensions and hypocrisy as they are reflected in the middle class to the more socially significant satiric topics of schools that don't teach and lawyers who steal their clients' money. Yet these Dickensian subjects are foisted onto the plot of a standard farce: mistaken identities, dialogue at cross-purposes, sentimental lovers separated by duped and ignorantly authoritative parents. The two elements—the more serious social comment and the traditional comic plot—never mesh. The satire on Impey, the lawyer whose machinations are responsible for all the misunderstandings, and Vyse, his brother-in-law schoolmaster who acts as his dupe, is tame. But the comic scenes, particularly those involving the streetwise cockney lad, Dando, to whom the subtitle of the novel refers *(one boy is more trouble than a dozen girls, being a Tale of a "Young Monkey")* but who is not in any way a central character in the plot, are very entertaining. We wish there were more scenes such as the one where Dando takes the hero Walter Farquhar on a wild goose chase through the byways of the East End of London.

The plot of this novel is complicated; it is a farce drawn out to nearly three hundred pages. It involves the impersonation of Walter Farquhar, who ran away from Vyse's school eight years before, by his friend and fellow school chum, Hugh Burgoyne. Farquhar's parents, who have not seen him for sixteen years, accept Hugh as Walter, but when Hugh's father and sister Nelly also return unexpectedly from India after a similar length of time, the lawyer Impey, who has been pocketing the Farquhar's remittances for Walter ever since he disappeared, gets Dando, an errand-boy in his office, to impersonate Hugh. In the meantime Nelly Burgoyne has met and fallen in love with the real Walter Farquhar, who has been at sea. The ins and outs of the various confrontations and near-revelations that follow this situation, and the operations of Impey and Vyse, who must keep up the pretense to avoid jail as thieves and cheats, take up over two-thirds of the novel. The social satire is limited to the opening pages, where, in the very first scene, Impey is seen in an altercation with a cab driver exactly like those for which Joshua Mayhew was known.

Finally Dando, seeing the game is up, confesses all; Impey escapes to America, where he is reported living in poverty; Vyse gives up his school but because his wife has been thrifty is enabled to be a lodging-house keeper; Dando through Walter's influence goes to sea; and Nelly and Walter get married. Nobody is really hurt, even the sensitive Hugh; nobody is badly punished, even the villain Impey. In this resolution we see the soft center of the Brothers Mayhew's liberalism as compared to that of Dickens, whose early novels contrive happy endings but not for all—not for Nancy in *Oliver Twist* or Smike in *Nicholas Nickleby*. Dickens wanted the fairy tale to be true, but a part of him recognized its impossibility—a split that has its own detrimental effect on the unity of his novels. But the Brothers Mayhew in their works never admitted the qualification, as we shall see more clearly in their fairy tales. As a result their novels do not rise much above the level of good comic journalism.

The Fear of the World.   In their last complete novel together the Brothers Mayhew move farther away from farce toward a more serious social commentary. The subject of *The Fear of the World; or, Living for Appearances* (1850) is the all-consuming middle-class concern about "what the neighbors will say" and the resulting financial overextension of such a total devotion to show. Because it is limited to this topic, however, the novel lacks scope, and because the characters are types out of stock comedy—the spendthrift wife, the honest farmer—the novel lacks depth. Nonetheless, parts of the work are moving, particularly those that, we suspect, come from personal experience. At one point in their downward plunge to the poorhouse, the barrister Wellesley Nicholls and his wife lease and furnish a large showy house (like "The Shrubbery" in Parsons Green that Henry Mayhew bought just before his bankruptcy?). Nicholls is astonished at how easily and quickly they are driven into debt over this house. First there are unexpected attorney fees for the lease and the broker's valuations of the fixtures. The upholsterer, who claims he is "in a large way of business and had never pressed much for his money," convinces the couple it would be better not "to spoil the ship for a ha'porth of tar," especially as it was a thing they didn't do every day; and, besides, what would their friends say, when they came and saw a large handsome room only half filled with furniture?[35]

Perhaps because of the painful personal connections, the satire against Nicholls is uneven. We are as often sympathetic to as critical of him as he alternates self-recrimination with self-delusion. If this were the intended effect of the novel, the Brothers Mayhew might have written an interesting character study, but the intention if not the consistent performance is clearly to ridicule and criticize the Nicholls's "living for appearances."

The story is simple; it is a step-by-step account of financial ruin brought about by living beyond their means. Nicholls buys showy diamonds; they get an opera box, buy a carriage and horses, and fi-

nally a house and furnishings all on credit since they have no money
to pay for them. Then the bills begin to come in, and to escape the
creditors the Nichollses go into the country to live with Mrs. Nicholls's honest brother, Reuben, a farmer. Nicholls forges his
brother-in-law's name on a check; the two return to London where at
a lavish party he is served with several writs. Just in time his father
dies, but to everyone's surprise leaves no estate for his son, having
spent it all himself. Now the writ-processors descend in earnest; Mrs.
Nicholls flees to her brother for help. Wellesley is imprisoned in a
sponging house. Reuben agrees to bail him out if he will go through
the Insolvency Court and then live quietly with him in the country.
Wellesley reluctantly agrees, but the last paragraph assures us he was
a better and happier man with a small country law practice, and even
his wife, though she nostalgically remembers the days of her London
triumph, enjoys making puddings.

Perhaps the more serious bent of *The Fear of the World* was partially
due to the other work Mayhew was doing in 1850, namely "Labour
and the Poor." Certainly when the Brothers Mayhew, seven years
later, begin their last joint project, *Paved with Gold* (1857), the subject of Mayhew's social surveys dominates the first five numbers,
which were all Henry worked on. Scenes of the Asylum for the
Homeless in Cripplegate and the poor street-children buying watercresses at the pre-dawn Covent Garden Market set a somber tone for
what turns out to be a thoroughly clichéd novel. In the latter half it
degenerates into stock melodrama. What keeps *Paved with Gold* from
total banality are the scenes taken from Henry and Augustus's investigations for *London Labour and the London Poor.*

Thus we see that from 1847 to 1857 the Brothers Mayhew gradually shed the light-hearted fun of farce in their fictions and moved
toward a more serious evaluation of their subject. Yet only Gus carried on this movement; after 1857 Henry Mayhew wrote no more
fiction.

1851; or, The Adventures of Mr and Mrs. Sandboys.   There
was one comic novel that Henry Mayhew wrote entirely by himself,
1851, published to exploit the enormous excitement over the Great
Exhibition throughout England. The novel began publication in parts
four months before the Exhibition opened and was scheduled to end
when it closed.

Beginning in January 1851, the first four parts chronicle the Sandboys's trip to London and their efforts to find lodgings in the over-

crowded city before the Great Exhibition opened. Part 5, published in May, recounted the events surrounding the actual opening on May 1. The May and June numbers have interesting connections to Mayhew's reports on the Exhibition for the *Edinburgh News*, written at the same time, and are discussed in detail below. The July number continues the comic account of Curtsy Sandboys's adventures; the August and September numbers are collapsed into one number and the story hurriedly finished with the Sandboys returning home. Mayhew's illness aborted the project. Mayhew collaborated in the work not with another writer but with the artist George Cruikshank, for whom he was editing the *Comic Almanac* who had also illustrated *The Greatest Plague* and *Whom to Marry*. Cruikshank's grand fold-out illustrations to each monthly part are the real attraction of this work. Each of the nine illustrations, with one exception, is a general impression of the Great Exhibition rather than a pictorial account of the events of the novel. All are first-rate. The double views of "London Crammed" and "Manchester Deserted" which adorned the third number show Cruikshank at his best.

The novel recounts the comic misadventures of a couple of country cousins and their two children who "came up to London to 'enjoy themselves,' and to see the Great Exhibition" in the words of the subtitle. They suffer all the classic city dodges: they are robbed, cheated, and diddled in a wide variety of ways, and the hero Curtsy Sandboys is even frustrated in his effort to get inside the Crystal Palace to see the exhibits. A reviewer of the second number in fact cautioned the author "not to exaggerate misfortune, or strive too much after novelty of incident" in the following numbers.[36]

Mayhew seems to have taken the criticisms to heart, for the May and June numbers are much more serious in attitude about the Great Exhibition. Parts 5 and 6 of *1851,* written roughly at the same time as the articles for the *Edinburgh News,* minimized the farce and instead turned to a discussion of the strengths and weaknesses of the Exhibition, and, most important, the attitude of the lower classes toward it. The descriptions of the visitors and the rooms of the Crystal Palace are vivid and lively but not satiric by and large.

In the discussions of Mayhew's articles for the *Edinburgh News* we noted how he believed the value of the Exhibition was the dignity it gave to work and the superior models it gave to English workers. Mayhew repeats these sentiments verbatim in the May number of *1851.* But he makes one very interesting change in the next number when he takes up the question of why the working classes were staying away from the Great Exhibition on shilling days. In the elaboration of the issue, the article in the *Edinburgh News* and the pages in the novel *1851* are almost identical; but the conclusions are quite different. We have seen that in the *Edinburgh News* Mayhew said the workers had no faith in the Exhibition because it was only a celebration of the capitalists: "Glance your eye through the whole catalogue and see if you can find in any place the mention of any one working man's name as having been even *partly* concerned with his employer in the production of the articles exhibited" (21 June 1851). But in the novel Mayhew's explanation is benign: "The reason why the shilling folk absented themselves from the Great Exhibition at first was, because none of their own class had seen it, and they had not yet heard of its wonders, one from the other. But once seen, and once talked about in their workshops, their factories, and—it must be said—their tap-rooms, each gradually became curious to see what had astonished and delighted his fellows."[37] This was probably the right explanation, but its juxtaposition to the more critical *Edinburgh News* articles, written within weeks if not days of parts 5 and 6 of *1851,* show how easily Mayhew could sacrifice the heightened identification with labor which he had achieved through his two years of social surveys. Comparing the two works helps define a mental attitude that will allow Mayhew to slide into conventionality if not outright Podsnappery after 1857.

The Moral Fables

The two moral fables by the Brothers Mayhew further establish the softness that underlay and eventually undermined Mayhew's potentially radical social vision. These two books, *The Good Genius that Turned Everything into Gold* (1847) and *The Magic of Kindness* (1849) are rather hard to classify. *The Good Genius,* the first work by the Brothers Mayhew, is labeled "a Christmas Fairy Tale" on the title page and as such it belongs to the tradition of other Christmas books in which fairy tale and moral comment are combined. The most famous of these works and probably the best is *A Christmas Carol* (1843) by Dickens. These Christmas books were intended as family entertainment and hence tried to have something relevant and interesting for both adults and children, not an easy task in the best of circumstances and not achieved by the Brothers Mayhew.

These two "moral fables" are also related to Henry Mayhew's thirty-year dissatisfaction with the curriculum in formal education and his efforts to reform it. Five years earlier he had published several numbers of *What to Teach and How to Teach It,* discussed in the next section, and in 1848 he wrote his piece on "wonder" for *Douglas Jerrold's Shilling Magazine.* The ideas expressed in these works about what kind of learning is best and how it is achieved remained with Mayhew throughout his working life and shape the two moral fables by the Brothers Mayhew, particularly *The Magic of Kindness.* But these are not successful works either artistically or morally; the sentiments behind them are noble but shallow and the expression of them embarrassing to a modern reader. It is as if all the most simpleminded and sentimental attitudes of Dickens—toward social reform, toward women, toward domestic harmony—were lumped together unleavened by the grim view that reverberates through all of Dickens's work from the interpolated tales and scenes in Fleet Prison in the sunny *Pickwick Papers* to the murder and opium den of *The Mystery of Edwin Drood.*

Yet in their simplemindedness, these moral fables delineate clearly the attitudes Mayhew carried with him into his social surveys and make the more remarkable the powerful social vision he achieved during his investigative work.

The Good Genius.   *The Good Genius that Turned Everything into Gold, or: the Queen Bee and the Magic Dress* is the story of a poor woodsman Silvio, who, given a magic goat's skin dress by a Bee, is enabled to wish himself a beautiful house, a rich kingdom, and a princess for a wife. By the same means—of asking and it being given to him—he restores his kingdom from the terrible agony of democratic rule. He cures his wife's father of a dire illness and ends a drought and famine. The reader is astonished to learn at the end that the Bee is "the Spirit of patient Industry" and that the moral is that patient Industry accomplishes everything. Nothing in the story has been done by industry, patient or otherwise: all has been achieved by a magic goat's skin dress.

The authors in an epilogue justify this disparity, saying that the "magic" only consists "in the shortening of the time ordinarily required for the working out of the results; and so, by removing the intermediate events, and bringing the effects into close connection with their causes, [gives] a fairy character to that which is of everyday occurrence."[38] The theory is a good one, but in *The Good Genius* the practice is a failure since there is no cause for the effect other than a wish that it be so and a magic Bee to wave a wand to make it so. Patient industry involves patience; none is evidenced or even called for in this work.

In addition there are other uncertain opinions. When Silvio is only a woodsman, the Princess scorns his love rather brutally; it is hard to think we are to admire her behavior, especially since the Bee criticizes Silvio for wanting to be a king as a result. The story is similar to the real fairy tale of the fisherman and the magic lamp, and we expect the moral to be that we should be satisfied with what we have. But since it is supposedly industry and not magic that has achieved all the wonders, Silvio is right to want to be a king and the Bee is quite wrong to have criticized him. This uncertainty of attitude is reflected again when Silvio, now a monarch of the rich City of the Diamond Waters thanks to the magic goat's dress, is joyfully accepted as a suitor by the Princess. When he complains that she only loves him for his money since she scorned him when a poor woodsman—a perfectly reasonable complaint—she replies that "to wed unequally is to suffer equally" (44). It appears that the reader is now supposed to applaud as prudence her earlier ugly treatment of the poor Silvio.

The "lessons" this book teaches then are not very clearly thought out. Perhaps this was due to Henry Mayhew's laziness and Augustus's youth. The epilogue suggests they intended to write a series of works like this "designed to exemplify the Magic of different Virtues." In this epilogue a number of Henry Mayhew's key words are present, suggesting his influence on the conception of the whole: "since the feelings of Surprise and Wonder seem to have been given to us only to excite a more than ordinary interest in the objects that elicit them, and so to make us desire to become better acquainted with the nature of that which they have so vividly impressed upon our minds"—this being the whole basis of Henry Mayhew's educational theories—"we have endeavoured to apply these feelings to the inculcation of Industry, and, by pointing out the wonders it can work, to give it a greater charm to the reader, so that it may fasten itself upon his mind, and become a principle in his life" (200).

The Magic of Kindness.   The second and last of these moral fables, published two years later, repeats these principles in the dedication to Henry Mayhew's daughter Amy "in the hope that the principle of kindness may become the guiding principle of her life." But *The Magic of Kindness; or, The Wondrous Story of the Good Huan* suffers a similar kind of confused direction. Its plot is almost identical to that of *The Good Genius,* only here a magic branch is substituted for the goat's dress and, as a way of showing the need for kindness if not its power, the text paraphrases a great deal of material about a plague-stricken city, witch-hunting, war, mistreatment of lunatics, and slavery. (These stories come from Charles Mackay's *Popular Delusions* and other contemporary sources, plus Defoe's *History of the Plague Year.*) With a wave of the branch, the Spirit of Kindness puts out the fires of the witch burnings, stops invading armies, makes the deaf speak, and achieves various other miracles. As Angela Hookum says, "its ingenuous faith in the power of kindness is unacceptable to the most unsophisticated adult mind, yet the realism of its attack on perverted forms of justice, exploitation of cheap labour, and abuse of power, is beyond the comprehension of a child, however precocious."[39]

Yet despite its obvious inadequacy, *The Magic of Kindness* is a very clear example of the nature of much Victorian social criticism from Carlyle to Ruskin: a clear, detailed, and often brilliantly bitter evocation of society's ills and a fuzzy and sometimes saccharine set of solutions for them.

Educational Works

The works by Henry Mayhew discussed in the following two sections represent the major output of his pen during the decade of his forties, 1852-1863. Yet, except in their relationship to journalism, they are quite different from anything else he did. He wrote them like most of his work primarily to make money. But while they show a number of his concerns, none demonstrate his real talents. The most personally revealing of anything he ever wrote, many of these works show a conventionality that is as surprising as it is disappointing to the reader of Mayhew's earlier works. In the case of the travel books he reveals a frame of mind that can be repellent. Because such a reaction is unexpected, these travel books remain the most puzzling of his works.

His treatise on education and his four books written for children are not so much puzzling as tedious, though the intentions behind them are both admirable and correct by modern educational standards. Mayhew was not able to find the right form in which to express his ideas. It is the same problem that the Brothers Mayhew encountered when writing the moral fables discussed above. The frequently maudlin tone of the treatise clashes with the abstract discussion, which in any case is too heavy for the popular weekly part publication in which it was issued. The four children's books have trouble finding a balance between the lessons Mayhew wants to impart and what a child can absorb. This is of course always a problem in writing for children, either textbooks or lighter reading, but in a field that did not really exist when Mayhew entered it—the science book for children—he had to create a new form. He had to do the same thing in writing up his social surveys, and there he was triumphant. But in his children's books he could not find the right medium.

Mayhew had a lifelong concern with education, undoubtedly the outgrowth of his own early experiences. His schooling had been conventional but of the very best offered at the time. Though we know nothing of his primary education, as we have seen he was sent by his father to one of the most prestigious secondary schools in nineteenth-century England—Westminster—one of the nine privileged "public schools." At this time, in the 1820s, and indeed throughout the century, the curriculum at Westminster and the other public schools was limited to the study of the classics in Greek and Latin. Scholars were expected to go on either to Oxford or Cambridge, where they would pursue their "liberal education" (i.e., Greek and Latin) and add theology and a little mathematics by way of Euclid. Neither in the secondary schools nor in the old universities were modern languages and literature or natural science taught. This situation did not change until the last quarter of the nineteenth century. To fill the obvious gap, London University was founded in 1826 and there the curriculum included both modern languages and natural science. There was, however, a social stigma attached to this university and these studies; natural science and engineering were seen as appropriate studies for artisans but not for middle- or upper-class boys. They, on the contrary, went to school to become "gentlemen," which was presumably achieved by the examples provided in Greek and Latin texts and the study of theology. The education turned out civil servants, administrators, and parsons, but no scientists or technicians.[40]

Obviously there was dissatisfaction in various quarters over the limited nature of the education of England's middle and upper classes. John Henry Newman agreed that the function of education was to create "gentlemen," but he argued in *The Idea of a University* (1853) that modern languages and natural science contributed to this end. His is only one of many such voices, including Mayhew's. But the system was very resistant to change, partly because of the state's refusal to intervene in educational matters, partly because of the association of the curriculum to class, and partly because the idea that the purpose of education was to make "good men" tangled education and religion inseparably together and factional strife made it difficult to create a uniform system. Thus three of the most important forces in Victorian England—laissez-faire, class, and religion—all worked to keep the antiquated educational system in place.

Henry Mayhew is an example of the negative results of such a situation. Everyone seemed to recognize that he had a very promising mind. But Henry's interests and talents did not lie in the conventional model; he had an early attraction for natural science or "natural philosophy," as it was called, and an interest in "moral philosophy," or the social sciences, a discipline not yet created. There was very little that could be done formally for such a boy. Without the discipline of a school Mayhew frittered away his time and talents, unable to specialize in one course of self-education, easily diverted by the pleasures of companionship and bohemian good times, and leaving all his major work unfinished. Clearly personality is as important as schooling, but possibly the only way Mayhew's obvious great talents could have been disciplined would have been by a supervised educational program. It is also possible that he would have balked at that every bit as much as he did at the formal "liberal education" curriculum of Greek and Latin. He was from start to finish a strange mixture of rebellion and conformity.

He certainly rebelled against the "liberal education" at Westminster and in the most dramatic way possible: he ran away. He never wrote of the experience at Westminster without bitterness and his sense of its inadequacy informed all his writings on education. Perhaps his most complete indictment came in *The Upper Rhine* (1858): "we ourselves wasted seven of the best years of our life at Westminster School, where we were not even taught our own language, nor even writing nor reckoning, but bored to death simply with the dead tongues, and in proof of the advantages derivable from such a system of education we can safely say, that by the time our whiskers had begun to sprout, and we were sent into the world to get our living out of the elements by which we were surrounded, we were in the same beastly ignorance as any Carib—not only of the physical world about us, but of our own natures and our fellow-creatures, as well as of all that was right, true, beautiful, or indeed noble in life."[41] Allowing for a little hyperbole here, we can still see what Mayhew felt was lacking in his own formal education: natural science, the social sciences, and the "moral" sciences.

What to Teach and How to Teach It.   In his unfinished treatise *What to Teach and How to Teach It: so that the Child may become a Wise and Good Man* (1842) he tried to lay down principles for educational reform. The format of this treatise was not successful; it is an odd mixture of the sarcastic tone of satirical journalism, the deductive mode of scientific writing (a formal principle followed by a narrowing set of classifications and definitions), and the rhetorical flourishes of drama. It should either have been more popularly conceived, or more rigorously thought out and neutrally written. But the ideas it contains are provocative.

Mayhew based his work on a series of lectures by a Dr. Brown on the "Philosophy of the Human Mind." It is forty-four pages long with thirty-nine different chapters. He begins by asserting that one must make a distinction between learning to read and write and being educated. There are great advantages to the former obviously, but being able to read and write does not make one a good man, and Mayhew agreed that this was the purpose of education. (This was the point on which he later attacked the claims of the Ragged Schools that they had reduced juvenile crime by educating the poor.) However, the system of education at Westminster and elsewhere can never produce the good man: "the chief object and tendency of all our instruction," he says "is the formation of good scholars, rather than good men."[42]

Mayhew's social criticism as usual is perceptive. But the next part of his argument is more dubious. The purpose of education will be better achieved, he says, by expanding the individual's intellectual capacities and making him happy. This is as good a way as any, but the difficulty is in determining what is happiness and what causes it. Mayhew makes some rather breathtaking assertions in his effort to do so. Man has instinctively both sympathy and altruism, he says, as well as a capacity to reason or to see the relationship among things. What is needed through education is an expansion of these innate capabilities, the fulfillment of which will bring happiness.

Next he takes up the subject of happiness. It is of three kinds, he says: material or physical; mental or intellectual; and moral or emotional. The "laws" governing these three areas of human activity should be the subject of education but "in the present system every-thing is taught but this, so education is a curse" (10). Instead, May-hew would build a curriculum around natural philosophy, which will help fill the need for *mental* happiness as well as inculcate "the sense and profound love of truth" (11); "mental philosophy" by which he means psychology, particularly the associations of thought and feeling which "give rise to a feeling of beauty" (15); and "moral philosophy," the natural extension of this which will show the "laws" that govern our behavior toward others and will teach us both the happiness that comes from gratification of our beneficent desires and the misery from our malevolent ones and "that Man's greatest happiness lies in the happiness of those around him" (18). In summing up his thoughts on what to teach, he argues that history and languages are only periph-eral to the goals of education. Rather we need to learn prudence through "the inculcation of a knowledge of the relations between la-bour and capital" (by which he apparently does not mean political economy but the moral principle that you must work to gratify de-sires) and the scientific laws governing the material, mental, and moral worlds. In addition we should have some practical application of these principles in subjects that Mayhew calls "artistic," and, fi-nally, sounding very modern indeed, all should be trained in one such "art" (20–22).

In the context of English education in 1842 Mayhew's ideas are certainly in the right direction if the justifications for his suggested reforms in curriculum are vague and presumptive. In his later re-marks on education the element that recurs is the need to expand the curriculum to include more immediate and more relevant subject matter. The rest of his educational writings try to exemplify how this might be done.

This is also the subject of the second half of the treatise *What to Teach and How to Teach It*. Here Mayhew has some excellent remarks scattered amidst turgid prose and philosophical padding. The basic problem in teaching is securing the attention of the student and mo-tivating him or her to maintain that attention and concentration over a sustained period of time. (These are not the exact words he uses, of course.) First the attention must be aroused and Mayhew argues that the current method of doing this—rewards of prizes versus punish-ment by the rod—is utterly pernicious. The child is "being punished for the teacher's failure to gain his attention" (29). Instead of this self-defeating method, the child's curiosity should be aroused and

Mayhew lays out the process by which this is done. First a novelty is suggested by the teacher. This is followed by surprise in the child, leading to wonder, then curiosity, then attention and the result is learning. Children's natural curiosity is thus used to sustain attention. Rather than immediately satisfying their curiosity, let them do so themselves by practical experiments (we learn by doing), the expression of which idea becomes the object of Mayhew's first two children's books.

The next sections analyze the way in which learning is made pleasurable. Mere rote learning as was the present method induces no pleasure, for the child must understand what he is doing to enjoy it; relying on mere memory engenders only "folly," but inducing "talent" can be achieved by strengthening a child's ability to see the relationships among things. Rather than by memorization, the matter taught may be impressed on the mind by the "liveliness" with which it is presented and received. Such "liveliness" of impression results when there is an emotion connected with the matter, particularly curiosity. Further we are more likely to remember matter associated with perceptible objects for we learn more by sight than by hearing. Thus Mayhew argues for the effectiveness of audiovisual aids in teaching. Finally, we should teach goodness not by precepts but by action. The pamphlet breaks off at the point at which Mayhew is returning to his first point, the relation of reading and writing to education.

Mayhew's criticisms of the current system are just, and his ideas about the circumstances under which children really learn something are quite in keeping with modern educational thought. His first principles are shaky and vague, and he has no practical suggestions as to how to arouse curiosity (we now talk about "motivation") about the specific subjects, which, as any teacher knows, is the real nub of the problem. But he must be credited with the basic soundness of his general ideas on education.

Two years later he began another publication in parts, *The Prince of Wales's Primer,* intended as an example of the ideas in *What to Teach.* The purpose of the book is to teach a child to read by means of the principles of syllabification, prefixes, affixes, and roots. In other words, rather than by rote memorization, which was the current mode of teaching reading, the child would learn the principles of his language and thus find pleasure in the process, according to Mayhew's theory. Only one number of the series was issued, which included an illustrated alphabet in rhymed couplets, followed by a series of simple words and sentences classified according to their linguistic structure. All are exemplified by moralistic tags and tales, such as "Chil-dren should be mild and meek, quick to hear and slow to speak." This presumably taught "moral philosophy," thus fulfilling the intention behind the normal use of the Bible as the book from which children learned to read. The last item is an adaptation of Robert Southey's poem "The Old Man's Comforts," whose moral is that if you are a good child you will be blessed by God in old age.[43] In early 1851 an advertisement for "The Classic Spelling Book" appeared on the covers of *London Labour and the London Poor*. This was the same project only here the whole plan is outlined (the spelling book apparently was never issued) and specifically addressed to the working classes.

We cannot know why either *What to Teach* or *The Prince of Wales's Library* were not continued, nor why the "Classic Spelling Book" did not appear as announced. Such failures are the norm in Mayhew's career; in this case he may have sensed he had not found the right form for either of his works.

The same problem of balance exists in his four books written for children between the years 1854 and 1864. Not only is there a disjunction between subject and reader but in addition there is a problem of integrating two different goals: preaching conventional moral lessons and the more innovative desire to encourage individual initiative in learning through natural science. Unfortunately the form Mayhew chooses in which to serve these purposes—the conventional success story of rags to riches, though with an intellectual bent—does not lend itself to stories that involve mostly talk and very little action.

Mayhew's children's books should be viewed in the context of both his own educational theories, as laid down in *What to Teach,* and the state of children's literature in England at the time he was writing.[44] We think of the Victorian period as the golden age of children's literature, *Alice in Wonderland, Peter Pan, The Wind in the Willows* forming the classics of the genre. But this movement came late in the period; most historians see it beginning no earlier than 1860. Though we can see the movement toward the rich fantasy literature for children that marks the latter half of the period as well as the increase in informative tales as early as the 1830s, religious and moralistic stories dominated early Victorian children's literature because adults believed that what children read affected their characters for life.

All of Mayhew's children's books look back to that tradition; all preach—and that is the right word—conventional morality of filial obedience, religious humility, self-sufficiency, and perseverance. Yet this is not their sole concern. They are also shaped by Mayhew's own interests and thoughts about education. The parts of his children's books determined by these elements look forward, very far forward indeed, even into the revolution in textbooks in the twentieth century. The dated, overt moralizing and the modern emphasis on learning about the natural world through experience and experiment combine uneasily in these works and, coupled with Mayhew's uncertainty about what and how much a child can absorb, are responsible for their inadequacy.

The four children's books fall into three types. The first two, *The Story of the Peasant-Boy Philosopher* (Owen Ferguson, an early astronomer) (1854), and *The Wonders of Science; or, Young Humphry Davy* (1855) are moralistic tales which also impart a great deal of information about mechanics, astronomy, chemistry, and physics. As such they are almost unique in the Victorian period before 1860. Children's nonfiction books of any sort were rare during the period, and books on science for children even rarer. The Reverend J. G. Wood wrote a very popular children's series on the natural history of the seashore, the garden, and the country (his *Common Objects of the Country* sold 100,000 copies in 1858), but not until the 1880s were there equivalent children's books on electricity and chemistry. Mayhew was preparing new ground with these works and, in light of that, his inability to hit the right note is perhaps inevitable. He deserves recognition, however, as a pioneer.

The third book, *Young Benjamin Franklin* (1861), is based on the same principle, but the lessons it teaches are moral. The pursuit in this book is not after the secrets of the natural world but rather "the right road to human happiness." As such it is an enlightening book about Mayhew's theories, most of which we have met before, but it is also old-fashioned and dated.

The fourth book, *The Boyhood of Martin Luther* (1863), is again something new in children's literature. Though it is written with the same moralistic intent, it is a "little historical novel" about a real person but written for children. Saints' lives and hero stories are one of the oldest types of educational literature, but in the past most of the stories were more fiction than fact. Though Mayhew makes rather free with some of the facts, there is more fact than fiction in his fourth children's book and hence it looks forward to the increased interest in biographies of "eminent persons" for children at the end of the century.

All four of these works teach the same moral: the boys in each are born in lowly stations and all, through perseverance, hard work, and good character, become eminent successes. The subtitle of each work spells it out: Ferguson is a "poor lad" who becomes "acquainted with the principles of natural science"; Humphry Davy is "the Cornish apothecary's boy, who taught himself natural philosophy, and eventually became president of the Royal Society"; Benjamin Franklin's story shows "the principles which raised a Printer's Boy to First Ambassador of the American Republic"; and Martin Luther's tells of "the Sufferings of the Heroic Little Beggar-Boy who afterwards became the Great German Reformer." In addition, all these works exemplify the principle of "self-help," that is, that by doing things themselves rather than having them done for them, these wonderful boys achieved wonderful things. This idea is most clearly presented in the preface to *Humphry Davy:* it is "my belief that our present system of education begets in the minds of youths too great a sense of dependence, and too little reliance on their own powers, so that it is thought by a lad on leaving school to be impossible to learn anything without the help of a master to teach it." Mayhew wanted to show, on the contrary, that "some of the greatest minds the world has yet seen have been self-taught."[45]

Mayhew expressed belief in the notion of self-help throughout his life. It lies behind his criticism of philanthropy, his insistence on charging interest on penny and shilling loans to the street folk, and his most peculiar attitude toward German universities, of which more is said in the next section. The principle of self-help, a kind of moral and social version of laissez-faire, was a strong Victorian sentiment, one present long before it became associated with Samuel Smiles's work of that name, published in 1859, only a few years after Mayhew's first two boys' books.

In their attitudes about self-help Smiles and Mayhew have interesting similarities, though there is a strong class difference in all they wrote. Smiles's first work was on child care, and he argued, like Mayhew, against a mere cramming of book learning as opposed to learning from the observation of nature and people. Children's curiosities should be aroused from actual experience, he wrote, making them desire to learn on their own.[46] The similarity of these ideas to Mayhew's, though the latter's are more philosophically based, shows the general currency of such thoughts. The two men may also have known each other. R. G. G. Price says Mayhew suggested the idea of the greatly successful series *Lives of the Engineers* to Smiles,[47] but Smiles himself credits the idea to the son of the engineer George Stephenson, whose biography he had written.

The Story of the Peasant Boy Philosopher. Mayhew's own "biographies," however, are imbued with his educational philosophy. The first two are intended to "excite a taste in youths for natural science, by means of the feelings of wonder and admiration."[48] In this way their "active" intelligence will be excited and they will both profit from and remember what they learn. These ideas come right out of *What to Teach.* In addition, in *The Story of the Peasant Boy Philosopher* Mayhew wanted to impress his youthful readers with "the eternal duration of the spiritual forces." Thus a minister tells the lad who has constructed a pulley on his own that "the machines, boy, are of the earth, earthly; but the forces that quicken them come from the Great Fountain of all power, and turn mind to Heaven, filling it with higher and nobler thoughts" (113).

The boy Ferguson is first moved to experiment with natural forces by watching a pulley lift a roof off a cottage. His curiosity piqued, he begins to put together his own machines. With the help of various "teachers"—his father, the minister, a miller, a blacksmith, and finally a sailor—the boy makes his pulley, and then a clock and a watch. The steps of all these processes are given in detail with diagrams. Throughout, the boy's thoughts and words are highly artificial; the interest is not on realism but on the lesson being taught. Through the old sailor's description of navigation, the boy is turned finally to a study of the stars and through various intermediaries becomes a pupil of an astronomer with a telescope. The work ends with what Mayhew claimed was a first: a "proof" for the immortality of the soul based on natural science. It goes like this: ideas have no connection with the body obviously; they were put in motion by the Prime Mover. Since it is a scientific principle that once in motion an object cannot be stopped except by an external object, ideas cannot be stopped by the death of the body which has no connection to them. Thus they go on forever; they are "immortal."

The Wonders of Science. *The Wonders of Science; or, Young Humphry Davy* is more narrowly a book about science per se, and perhaps that is why it was also published in America and stayed in print for a number of years. The format is the same; the young Davy must support his family, but while apprenticed to an apothecary, he is moved by the story of a mine disaster to his first experiments (Mayhew made free with the facts here). Like Ferguson, he is helped by various "teachers"—a medical man and an older friend who finally makes the right connections for him and propels him on his career. But in the meantime he discovers by experiments—which are all detailed and illustrated at great length in the text—the properties of heat, which lead to his invention of the safety lamp; the properties of light, reflection, and color, with a few final examples of how photography works.

Young Benjamin Franklin. To the student of the work of Henry Mayhew as opposed to the history of children's literature, *Young Benjamin Franklin* is the most interesting of his children's books. It is a kind of summation of many of his ideas about life and human society, although expressed in a theoretically simplified form appropriate for a young reader. In the mouth of the fictional Uncle Benjamin and through the many footnotes that stud the book, Mayhew expressed his opinions about a wide variety of subjects: the value and necessity of work; the value of moderation in all things; the differences among the pleasures of the ' senses, the intellect, and the moral self; the use of public opinion; the "law of human suffering." In addition, there are thoughts on the works of Charles Dickens, of Shakespeare, Rabelais, and Charles Lamb; the nature of wit; paintings; prison conditions; the census; and the psychology of the four humors. Many of these ideas Mayhew touched on in one work or another, sometimes at length, but some are expressed only here.

In his preface Mayhew announced the intention of the work: "to give young men some sense of the principles that should guide a prudent, honorable, generous, and refined gentleman through the world."[49] He wants to give to all boys "what I myself felt the want of more than anything, after leaving Westminster School" (vi), and the work is based on his opposition to the notion that "to manufacture a wise man is necessarily to rear a good one" (viii).

To this end he freely adapts parts of Franklin's autobiography (to which he gives conscientious reference in long notes), inventing the tutorial figure of Uncle Benjamin, "the expounder of the Franklin philosophy," and adding various scenes from London prisons in 1856 taken from *The Criminal Prisons of London.* Uncle Benjamin lectures too much; unlike the earlier science books, this one cannot offer many practical suggestions to induce self-help in moral growth. The book is tedious to read and probably unbearably so for a youth. Nowhere is Mayhew's failure of form in a child's book more apparent than in *Young Benjamin Franklin.*

The story begins with young Ben's desire to go to sea and his "weaning" from this desire, followed by Uncle Benjamin's five lessons on life and his further exposition of where happiness lies. His lessons include the precepts that men must choose "work, beggary or death" and that we must "save or be a slave." He and young Ben take a tour of all different types of people from the drunkard to the entomologist, Uncle Benjamin rigorously refusing to express an opinion other than that one must balance work and play. Before Ben is allowed to choose his future path, he is further instructed in the various "pleasures of the senses," which are necessary for happiness but must be kept in moderation; the "pleasures of the intellect" (here Mayhew inserts most of his footnotes of literary and artistic criticism); and finally the "moral pleasures," particularly the unselfish ones of gratitude, esteem, regard, admiration, and veneration. To test the theory that a balance of all these three types of pleasure are necessary for human happiness, Uncle Benjamin takes Ben on a tour of a poorhouse, an orphanage, and a jail (Tothill Fields) where people live in misery because of the lack of such a balance in their lives. Thus Ben learns the law of human suffering: "it is the rule of life, that more are born to want and suffer than to feast and be merry" (508) and hence we must be tolerant, grateful, and helpful, responsive to "the still, small voice" of conscience which Mayhew defines as the world of opinion and our desire to look well in the eyes of the world. The moral: "labour thriftfully at your business, have graceful amusements, and do your duty." After consulting Mayhew's grand chart of work from the opening pages of volume 4 of *London Labour and the London Poor,* young Ben Franklin chooses to be a printer because he likes reading. It is an anticlimactic ending.

Mayhew's literary judgments in the footnotes between pages 250–300 are perceptive and worth a note before moving on to a discussion of his final children's book. In his comments on both literature and painting Mayhew displays his preference for interpretative suggestion rather than realistic accuracy and detail in art. The same preference appears in his theories of description as stated in the preface to *The Rhine.* He recognizes and lauds Dickens's genius, chiding him only for his sentimentalizing of the lower classes and his tendency to overwrought humor. He finds the suggestiveness of Rembrandt far superior to the precision and inclusiveness of narrative painting or the particularity of detail in Pre-Raphaelite painting. Truth, he says, is not a matter of piling up accurate detail; we must perceive the connections and relationships among details for the truth to be apprehended. This idea is related to his objections to rote learning and memorizing in education; it is related to his passion for classification and discrimination that marks all of his work, but particularly *London Labour and the London Poor*. It is related to his intention from the beginning of his social surveys to find the "laws" of relationship among the myriad details he was uncovering about life and labor in London.

The Boyhood of Martin Luther.   About Mayhew's last children's book *The Boyhood of Martin Luther* there is little to say. He did some field work into Luther's childhood, and this led to his 1200-page book on the Germans discussed below. The "little historical novel" itself has limited interest. As an experiment, he tries using in dialogue "only such words . . . as are of Anglo-Saxon origin,"[50] but the result is not successful. The speeches are stiff and artificial. The book, like *Young Benjamin Franklin,* centers on the question of "what is the boy to be?", but Martin, unlike Ben, has no supportive relative. Instead he has a brutal father. Mayhew suggests, though he does not follow the suggestion very far, that much of Martin's subsequent life was the result of his early struggle with his father. Mayhew's book follows the boy Luther through all his early trials and sufferings, suggesting in the series of events and accidents that lead him to take holy orders a *"design* on the part of some person unknown" (315). Though the book is strongly anti-Catholic, it lacks the virulence of his other anti-German feelings, which are the subject of the next section.

Travel Books

It is hard to know what to say about Mayhew's three books on Germany. They are prejudiced and unrelieved in tone, ill-mannered and unrelenting in sentiment. They are a surprise to the student of Mayhew who has constructed from his social surveys and the reminiscences of his early friends an appealing picture of an easy-going, tolerant, concerned man. None of these traits appear in these books. Why? What happened?

It is not lack of information that mars these books. Mayhew was not a tourist; he spent a number of years in residence in Germany. The length of stay produced much firsthand information but it did not produce a deep insight, only a strong disgust for the "life and manners" of the German people. Perhaps the length of stay even contributed to this reaction; forced to live away from the city and friends he knew and unable to engage in the work he did best, the bitterness of exile may have colored his judgments. But that can only be part of the explanation. The rest of it lies in elements of personality and situation that we simply know nothing about. In trying to understand and account for these uncomfortable books, how we long for the "life and letters" Mayhew's son Athol was supposedly writing of his father.

Mayhew went to Germany at least twice; once in late 1853 or early 1854, when he stayed at Coblenz, returning to England late in 1855. The second time was in 1861, when the family lived in Eisenach for two or three years. Both of these foreign residences were necessitated by Mayhew's financial problems. The first followed the failure of *London Labour and the London Poor* and the second the collapse of "The Great World of London" and Mayhew's editorship of the *Morning News*.

The tradition of living in Germany to save money was strong in England. Mayhew himself remarks in *German Life and Manners* that the English residents in the town he was staying in were there in order to live cheaply. Such a reason for living in a place is not the best motivation for enjoying the differences of culture and custom.

Certainly Mayhew's difficulties in accepting the manners and customs of a foreign society are not unique. Experience of a foreign culture is "educational," the cliché goes, precisely because it challenges the traveler with unfamiliar ways of doing familiar things and different ways of thinking about shared human concerns. Every day if not every hour the traveler comes up against situations that are "foreign": familiar foods are cooked differently; beds and bedding are not the same; manners are difficult to interpret; systems of education are confusing; religious observance can be opposed to his or her own beliefs and practices. All of these differences are also the very reason to travel: the excitement of experiencing new things, the expansion of emotional and mental horizons, the challenge of the new and the different culture. The combination of excitement and challenge plus the constant need to readjust to different modes of living create the strain of traveling. It can be exhausting to confront, understand, and absorb the myriad of differences large and small. (Mayhew like many travelers expresses his discomfort at these differences by constantly referring back to how things are done at "home.") To live abroad exacerbates these problems. It is also possible that the more sustained contact will make acceptance of the foreign easier. But most "exiles," however happy in their new home, will confess that there is at least one thing about their adopted country that "they have never got used to."

The perennial popularity of travel books is due in part to the dual challenges of traveling: books about foreign places both appeal to the desire to experience the different and eliminate the strain of dealing with that experience on an everyday basis. The travel book was a well-established literary tradition by the nineteenth century. Its roots may be as far back as Homer's *Odyssey,* but the modern travel book is a product of the eighteenth century when it was one of the most popular genres, as Swift's satire on the tradition in *Gulliver's Travels* indicates. In 1851, a few years before Mayhew's books appear, the publisher Murray's list of forty-nine titles in his Home and Colonial Library included twenty-one books of travels and accounts of strange countries.[51] Throughout the period, travel books were perhaps second in popularity only to novels.

The characteristics of the genre were thus well established by the time Mayhew wrote his German books. In the eighteenth century most were compendiums of information about monuments, scenery, customs, and costumes. Mayhew's first travel book *The Rhine* is in this tradition. In the nineteenth century, however, under the impetus of romanticism, "factual information was increasingly relegated to a new genre, the guidebook, while narratives of travels and tours began to emphasize the personal response of the traveler to exotic landscapes, peoples, and experiences." When Mayhew was writing, "the personality of the traveler had become as important as the material he was writing about, and travel literature was moving into the domain of autobiography."[52]

The popularity of the travel book perhaps prompted Mayhew to take advantage of his enforced exiles in Germany to produce something that would make enough money to allow him to return to England more quickly. His three books included the conventions that a mid-Victorian audience would expect: picturesque descriptions of architecture, scenery, local conditions, economics, agricultural production, and the moral condition of the people. *The Rhine* (1856) consists of the first two, with periodic attacks on the relics and decoration of Catholic churches scattered throughout, while *The Upper Rhine* (1858) reverses the emphasis, with attacks on local conditions, economics, and the condition of the people interspersed with descriptions of architecture and scenery. *German Life and Manners As Seen in Saxony at the Present Day* (1864) is a two-volume, 1200-page diatribe against all things German with only a few intermittent positive notes.

In traveling or living in a foreign country, the attitude with which we approach differences of custom, of behavior, of life style determines a good deal of the nature of the experience. The successful traveler is the one who manages to keep an open mind, to have few hard and fast ideas about the "right" way to do things, who can be intensely curious and extremely flexible. He also needs to be able to make candid judgments about what he sees. Because of the personal nature of the nineteenth-century travel book, only such a good traveler is likely to write a travel book that strikes the right balance between curiosity, even passion for things different, and a critical eye that evaluates justly and discriminates informatively. The best travel books of the period—George Borrow's books on Spain, Dickens's pieces on France and Italy, Darwin's *Voyage of the Beagle*—all have this critical balance of involvement and distance as well as a lightness of touch essential for popular literature.

Mayhew's travel books fail to find this balance. The exact nature of the failure—prejudice, intolerance, rigidity—is so unlike the Mayhew of *Punch* or *The Greatest Plague of Life* or *London Labour and the London Poor,* that we are reduced to describing the books without explaining them. Given his background in comic journalism, we might expect that his antipathy to the Germans might be expressed in one of the wry, comic travelogues satirizing the oddities of the foreigner, such as Mark Twain's *Innocents Abroad,* or, more relevant, the *Punch* illustrator Richard Doyle's *Foreign Tour of Messrs. Brown, Jones, and Robinson* (1854), or Thackeray's *Kickleburys on the Rhine* (1850), two Victorian comic travel books that make fun of the Germans' pretensions, drinking, and pedantry, but that are also satiric of English and other tourists. The comic travel book is an established type of travel literature. While it pokes fun at differences, it usually concentrates on the trivial with a light tone that implies that both traveler and native have their ridiculous side. But Mayhew was too personally repelled by the German bourgeoisie, too incensed by the differences from English manners to treat their culture comically.

Everything we know about Mayhew would make him, we think, an ideal traveler: his delight in incongruity, his easy-going bohemian early years, his sense of humor, his great compassion for men and women very different from himself; his unwillingness to make judgments without sufficient evidence; his respect for the neutrality of scientific method. All of this goes for nought when he travels. Since his intermittent remarks on Paris and the French are as negative as those on Germany, we must assume his comments grow out of a general attitude about foreigners and are not simply due to an unlucky choice of subject in the Germans.

The Rhine and *The Upper Rhine.*   The books *The Rhine and Its Picturesque Scenery* (1856) and *The Upper Rhine; the Scenery of Its Banks and the Manners of Its People* (1858) are companion volumes, though it does not seem that Mayhew had in mind the second when he wrote the first. They describe the sights a traveler would encounter on a trip up the Rhine from Rotterdam to the Lurlei pass, and then to the source in Lake Constance. Such a trip was a common part of an English tour of the Continent. Both books, though by different publishers, have twenty-two engravings taken from drawings by Birket Foster, a minor but prolific illustrator of the period. These engravings are in the romantic landscape tradition; there are no illustrations of costume, people at work, or urban street scenes.

The first of the two is essentially descriptive of the main sights on the trip up the Rhine and informative about history and legend surrounding various monuments and locations. It is the most balanced of the three books. His anti-Catholicism apart (the relics in churches show "priestly trickery"; the decoration in the Cologne cathedral, a "bit of empty medieval pomp," is an "insult" to Christ, who accepted a beggar's role), he seems to have enjoyed the Rhine trip and to have had several positive contacts with local people. The book is not successful as a travel book, however, because there is no sense of personality in it, or rather the personality of the narrator is colorless and conventional with only a few individualizing traits. This renders *The Rhine* closer to a guidebook than a travel book, though it is too extended even to be a good guidebook. The long series of descriptions are wearing to read. The lack of personality is characteristic of all Mayhew's descriptions, however. In his short passages of description in his social surveys the absence of a clearly articulated narrator is a "scientific" advantage. The extension of this descriptive mode to 386 pages does not work; it cannot sustain the interest of the reader.

In *The Rhine* Mayhew uses the descriptive method he used in "The Great World of London"; he gives the reader a picture of the various places as they appear or might appear on a representative day. He also follows the nineteenth-century travel book convention of comparing what he sees to English equivalents so that in describing Dutch villas he says "these villas are called *'lusts,'* or pleasure-houses, and are built in that metropolitan-rustic style which prevails about Peckham Rye and Clapham Park."[53] In *The Rhine* this device is used for descriptive analogy only, but in the next two books it becomes a moral judgment on the Germans. The book also has footnotes on etymology and other technical matters that are characteristic of Mayhew's work.

The Upper Rhine is quite a different book. It is a study of the "domestic manners of the Prussians" with "interpolated Rhenish Scenes" in the manner of the first book. Over two-thirds of the 448 pages are given to the "domestic manners." Mayhew includes a six-page preface to this work in which he outlines his method of description and the purpose and moral of his book. He sees three methods of description: first, a rendering of the exact properties of a scene; second, a comparison of the object or scene to some known object, as by simile or metaphor; third, "the highest and most artistic of all," a setting forth of "the effects or feelings produced" by the scene or person. Mayhew opts for the first, not "the cataloguing" style of science, but rather the presentation of the *"one* particular quality by which [the object being described] is immediately apprehended in the mind".[54] This is the same criterion he used to attack narrative and Pre-Raphaelite painting in *Young Benjamin Franklin;* the artist needs to select details to give a true picture. Though the theory makes sense, Mayhew's commitment to a "neutral" descriptive style adds to the uniformity of surface which is part of the tedium of the book.

There are other difficulties with *The Upper Rhine*. Perhaps because he had lived in Germany for a number of years, spoke German, and had a reputation as a keen observer of the social scene, Mayhew and his publishers felt he was qualified to write a book analyzing the German character. It was a good bet, but something in Mayhew or his situation prevented the release of his talents. The very conception of *The Upper Rhine* (and *German Life and Manners* is based on the same idea) as outlined in the preface demonstrates the difficulty. Though he says he limits his description to the middle classes, not knowing the aristocracy and not choosing to cover the lower classes, his preface makes clear the general application of his findings. The purpose, he says, is to test "the manners and opinions of the people of the Rhenish capital, according to the ethical and political standards of our own country" (v). It is not inevitable that such an approach will make him a closed and intolerant observer. However, since he begins with the assumption that "Englishmen can say with justice that there is no nation, either past or present, which will, for a moment, admit the comparison with their own" (ix), and then compares each facet of German life to how things are at home, the result is predictable. Mayhew's basic charge against the Germans in both *The Upper Rhine* and *German Life and Manners* is that they are not English. Treated comically, this would be an amusing satirical point, but here and throughout Mayhew's books on Germany every observation is made with teeth-gritting seriousness. The first line of the text of *The Upper Rhine* states it in a nutshell: "The surest way to make an Englishman love his country is to send him out of it" (1).

Mayhew also makes clear the extent of this judgment in his preface to *The Upper Rhine*. "It has long appeared to the author, that travelling southward from England is like going backward in time" (vii). Thus the Germans are in the Middle Ages, the French as well, and the Spaniards are barbarians. Only the English meet the test of civilization, which Mayhew equates with "home-feelings and a desire for comfort" (103). He gives two reasons for the Germans' uncivilized and barbaric lives: one, the lack of a free press, which would act as "a moral court of judicature, where the public acts of all men are daily tried" (xi–xii), and two, the Germans' lack of energy in mind and body. Mayhew attributes the second to a defective organization of their brains: "if the brains of a large number of Englishmen were to be compared with those of the Prussians, the Deutschers would be found to have the motor ganglia at the base of the cerebrum imperfectly developed" (131–32). (This is not a joke but meant literally.) Or later, "an English workman must *necessarily* be more quick-witted than the scholastic professors of Germany" because of his heredity. "British veins may be said to contain the essence, as it were, of all the noblest tribes the world ever saw" (351–52).

With these general ideas operating, Mayhew attacks German beds ("the most exquisite instruments of torture" [11]), their "barbaric" stoves; their smell; the "slovenly" housewives, the "obscene" men, the "shameless" women. He is revolted by their eating raw herrings;

he finds German beer compared to English "wretched physicky wash" (73). Their food is too sour and too unvaried; they have no table manners. "The most savage and selfish of all a Prussian's animal enjoyments consists in his overweaning indulgence in his pipe" (115). The women have ugly voices; the people are gawky and ungraceful. Their wedding feasts are "disgusting." There are "more dwarves and more idiots [in Germany] than in any other part of the globe" because they swaddle their infants (271). The Prussians have no nobility, no justice, no chivalry, no sense of equity, no manly courage, no sense of fair play, no honesty, no sympathy with the poor. They are intolerant, religiously tyrannized over by scandal-ridden clergy, superstitious; they worship dolls. He even attacks them for what Samuel Smiles thought was the most important virtue, thrift: "like all slow-witted people, the Prussians are an almost miserly race,—they will save something out of the smallest weekly pittance" (438). His anti-Catholicism, present in the first book, here is uncontrolled: "How long, indeed, will the great lesson of Protestantism be wasted on Papists, and priests persist in degrading Religion down to the muck and mire of the world; or in using that which should serve to wean men from earthly things and treasures, that 'moth and rust corrode,' as a showy snare and instrument of a mere worldly power?" (83).

The one positive trait Mayhew gives the Prussians is their superior love of music. We might expect, given his own early desires to be a chemist and the impossibility of getting training as such in England, that he would also be sympathetic to the German educational system, particularly the universities which were known to be superior in the teaching of natural science. Several German universities had chemical research departments of the highest order, and throughout the nineteenth century many British chemists spent time at a German university.[55] Mayhew, however, denied any positive qualities to German education, basing his argument not on a study of the curriculum or investigation of the educational system but only on what he believed to be the total ignorance and stupidity of the people. He attacks several times throughout the book the remark Richard Cobden, the radical politician, made in Parliament that "every baker in Germany can serve you with bread in Latin, as well as in his own language." He also utterly denies the statement of the distinguished English scientist, Sir Charles Lyell, that there was superior teaching of natural philosophy and science in German universities (which was true). "Be assured, then, reader, that the most distinctive feature of the ordinary

Prussian mind is its *utter ignorance upon all scientific matters"* (327). Mayhew goes to the extreme of Victorian sentiment about self-help here and denies the value of formal schooling at all: in England "almost every man among us is aware that he has to *educate himself,* and that the knowledge which he acquires at school, or indeed which he gets out of books, avails him little or nothing as a means of 'making his way in society' " (351). While in other contexts he had advocated educational self-help, he had never except under this impetus of attacking the Germans denied the value of school and books.

From these examples, and they are taken almost at random, we can see that whatever accuracy of observation might lie behind an individual judgment, the tone of Mayhew's books is created by overstatement. It is not just that the wedding feasts are excessive; they are "disgusting"; the German populace is not just unknowledgeable about scientific matters but have "utter ignorance"; "all" German women have ugly voices, and so forth. The lack of balance undermines whatever value Mayhew's observations might have.

German Life and Manners.   *German Life and Manners as Seen in Saxony at the Present Day* (1864) continues this mode for two volumes. In a perverse way it is a *tour de force;* it would not seem possible to sustain such hostile feelings over so many pages. Mayhew dedicates the book to his wife in a long and affectionate preface and the book contains a much larger personal component than either *The Rhine* or *The Upper Rhine.* We get glimpses of Mayhew family life for the two or three years they lived in Eisenach. But the tone of disgust prevails. There is no point in a chapter-by-chapter summary of this book; the pattern established by *The Upper Rhine* is continued and in fact portions of the first book are reprinted in the second. Nonetheless, in the interest of completeness, a general impression of the book follows.

Mayhew went to Germany in the early 1860s, probably 1861. Given his feelings about Germany, it is surprising he returned to live there. Probably only severe financial hardship would have forced him to do so. But he also had a publishing project in mind. He wanted to write a history of the early life of Martin Luther. (One of the interpolated descriptive sections of *The Upper Rhine* had contained a minihistory of young Luther.) To this end he visited the sites of Thuringia associated with Luther's early life. The initial chapters of *German Life and Manners* describe his researches and *The Boyhood of Martin Luther* relates the results. In the process of the investigations, however, "we could not help contrasting the misery and squalor which we found to prevail on every side in Saxony, with the comparative comfort and decency of folk in the same grade of life in England." Therefore, he decided to write a book "to let our countrymen know how much better housed, better fed, better paid, better cared for, and better treated, were English workpeople than the labouring population abroad."[56] (However, he does not deal with the laboring population in Saxony but only with the middle classes.)

In this preface he extends his judgments to all Europeans: "There is an inner life pervading the heart of England, graced with home feelings and affections, which makes our national character, in a measure, a sealed book to foreigners. On the Continent, however, all is external existence and outward display . . . so vainglorious is [an ordinary foreigner], you can read him 'all through' in a few quiet half-hours" (1:xi). It is not an approach nor an attitude that is likely to produce sympathetic insight into a foreign culture.

The first volume is divided into sections covering village life, town life, fashionable and domestic life, married life, and the beginning and end of German life, ending on a section on school and university life. A continuation of this latter section opens the second volume, which also includes ancient life and customs, legendary life, and ends on English life in Saxony. The book concludes with two chapters, "Why is Germany so poor?" and "The Moral of a Long Tale."

Within this framework Mayhew attacks the German bourgeoisie from every angle. Their houses are unhealthy because they are overheated and overcrowded, and as a result they smell worse than "the fetid atmosphere of the hold of the old hulks at Woolwich" (1:59). But before he gets too far into the particulars, Mayhew feels called upon to justify the work. He asserts that "we never saw such wretchedness, such squalor, such rude housing, such meanness in beggary, such utter want of truth and friendship in the terrible struggle to live, in the darkest dens, nor among the least luckless of the vagrants congregated in the British metropolis, as are to be found even in the families of the middle-class citizens of Saxony" (1:116). He denies that this is exaggeration, and sensing that his readers may wonder why, if he can't say anything good, say anything at all?

We answer, why should we have troubled our head about the poor of London, if we had not some sense of human dignity in our heart—some wish to make the well-to-do think better and kindlier of the ill-to-do; and some desire to teach even the wretched themselves how virtue and friendship and the decencies of life, can be maintained as well by the humblest as by the proudest. So now we tell you, in all frankness, that our single purpose here is to hold such a plain-speaking looking-glass in the face of these starving, cringing, swaggering German folk, that they shall see themselves in the same despicable guise as an English gentleman beholds them; and feel how much they have to achieve—how much they have to learn—how much they have to alter, before they can pretend to take rank among the civilized nations of Europe; or before even their nobles and their professional gentry can aspire to live as comfortably, as decently and as honourably, as even a working engineer with us. (1:117)

I have quoted this justification at length because it gives the fullest expression in Mayhew's own words to his intentions for his book and the attitudes on which they are based. The justification he gives is a little naive. It is unlikely that the Germans would admit the justice of this one-sided portrait. Even the few positive remarks he has to make about the universities and a few private individuals soon become negative observations. The true audience for the book was the English as the preface indicated. When in 1865 the publishers issued a one-volume condensation of *German Life and Manners,* "every passage in the least degree calculated to offend the most fastidious taste" is omitted, including the whole section at the end of volume 2 where Mayhew directs his hostility toward pretentious English tourists in Germany.

In volume 1 he again dwells on all that he found disagreeable and uncomfortable in living arrangements in Germany. He says the people have no self-reliance because of the feudal class system. Yet despite his assertion that his purpose in writing is to make mankind "soften down the cursed petty class distinctions of the world" (1:163), he is offended by the pretensions of the German merchants. In England there are true "merchant princes" because of the size of their enterprises. He finds it unacceptable that his daughter should dance at a ball with shopmen and store owners. He is irritated and annoyed because craftsmen also have their own gardens and make their own sausages: "A man like ourselves, who happens to be somewhat of a scientific and experimental turn of mind" finds "this mixture of agrarian and civic life . . . most temper-trying," and this "made us, over and over again, wish that the economical divisions of labour had travelled as far as the heart of Germany" (1:179). Intermittently he reminds his readers that he is only speaking of

Rhenish and Saxon communities in Germany, but such a qualification is usually undercut. In the hotels all over Germany at which he stayed "we never yet saw the German gentleman or lady, officer or nobleman, who knew how to take their food, or to conduct themselves at dinner with more decency or grace than an English publican or stage-coachman" (1:184).

Some positive remarks occur occasionally as when, after a long series of passages berating the taste and style of German ballgowns, he remarks that at a dance "we have seen barbers, and bootmakers, and butchers dressed as neatly and unostentatiously, and found them dance as well, and behave as politely as even gentlefolks with us; for, to be candid, the artizan and lower classes of Germany are as far ahead of our people in this respect as the German gentlefolks are behind our gentry in the same quality" (1:249). Perhaps if Mayhew had been able to write about the working classes of Germany, he would have produced a more sympathetic account. With the lower classes of London he never felt his class position threatened, and this enabled him to give voice to their point of view. The German middle-classes' claim to be equal to him is seemingly what triggered his more extreme reactions.

Mayhew continued his analysis with a section on excessive drinking among Germans, their arranged marriages, their openness in the expression of strong feelings: "when men publish their grief, or their religious sentiments, or indeed their love, they really feel little if any such emotions" and what he calls the "public love-making" in Germany demonstrates ipso facto that no love exists and "is at the same time positively loathsome, on account of its violation of all the rules of social decency" (1:438).

It is, however, in the discussion of German universities that we see most clearly the way in which Mayhew's preconceived attitudes color his observations. As stated above, Mayhew had many criticisms to make about English education. When other critics of the English system wanted a counter-example, they usually turned to Germany. But in *The Upper Rhine* Mayhew denied the superiority of German universities outright. He is more circumspect in *German Life and Manners*. Essentially he credits their reputation ("the schools of Germany are famous throughout Europe, and, we believe, justly so" [1:539]), but by adopting the English belief that the real purpose of education is to turn out gentlemen, he is able to use even their superior schools as evidence of German inferiority. Because they encourage "scholasticism" at the expense of all else, the schools turn out mere pedants rather than gentlemen. Thus the traits that the schools encourage reflect the nature of the German people: patient, plodding, tunnelvisioned. "They lack the originality, the invention, the spirit, the fire of English and French minds" (1:540).

Though he may learn more about language and natural science, the German schoolboy participates in no manly sports; thus even children are limited and obsessed by mere intellectual study. "The entire German race is but a nation of schoolmasters and scholars, they are always either learning or teaching; and the Lord defend us from passing a quiet evening with a real live German professor, for he is a bore of the largest possible calibre . . . His skull is as full of soporific sporules as a poppyhead, and he is a spouting engine of forty-ass power at least" (1:544). So much for the superiority of German schools.

Having given German education "its due," Mayhew moves into a description of student life in Jena where he spent some time researching the topic just before returning to England. Needless to say, he is quite negative about German students and student life compared to that of England. He admits that "the best minds of every country are invariably derived" from University education (2:72), but the "greater worth" is "the moral tone that the young men of the land thus acquire" (2:74). This insistence, which is his justification for the condemnation of German schools, brings forth the only positive remark we ever found him make about his own experiences at Westminster: "we nevertheless learnt at that school the creed of an English gentleman, *i.e.* to consider honour and dignity of far higher worth than even life or money, and to believe that the old chivalrous faith of helping the weak and waging war against the unjust was not a mere feudal folly" (2:74).

It is here the German schools fail. What is learned is drunken sentimentality rather than manly virtues, a "boyish, lackadaisical sentimentalism concerning the Fatherland . . . spread by means of the pot-valiant pot-house songs sung upon such occasions" (2:76). They are all drunken talk, no action. He patronizingly excuses their childish swordplays, drinking bouts, and ignorance of sports since the students at this university tend to be from the lower-middle classes. But when the boys become men and continue their scholastic, sentimental talk, Mayhew's scorn is unmitigated. Finally, "fine philologues they may be—acute critics, too, concerning everything that belongs to scholarship; but upon such matters as depend upon muscular train-

ing, or, indeed, upon that polite and honourable education which
constitutes the chief dignity of our own country, they are either children or boors compared with the sportsmen and gentlemen of England" (2:173).

Volume 2 of *German Life and Manners* draws to a close with a section on "English Characters on the Continent," which, except for a
long section on an English circus in the mode of *London Labour and
the London Poor,* is equally critical of the pretensions and stupidity of
most English tourists. In that way, if no other, the book is balanced.
Two English women lived with a high official of Eisenach, and Mayhew had a number of favorable things to say about the English and
German women in this establishment, though he does not miss the
chance to use their good traits to show up the general low quality of
the rest of life in Eisenach. When the English ladies leave and the
German wife of the official dies, the Mayhews withdraw "from the
ordinary society of a place where there is no such thing as friendship,
where the ladies are as unrefined as English barmaids, and the gentlemen have the manners and tastes of English publicans" (2:497).

The volume closes on a summary of all Mayhew's negative judgments: the Germans lack energy, they are miserly, and ill-fed. They
are servile and hypocritical; their government meddles in everything;
the people are ruled by the police; the judiciary is inept and corrupt
(unlike the English equivalents where "the probity, the fairness, the
honour and wisdom of the judges constitute one of the finest institutions of the land" [2:658]); they lack the control and educative
value of a free press.

It is not the accuracy of Mayhew's basic observations that is the
problem in these books; in some cases he was wrong, in some cases
he was undoubtedly right in what he judged to be "the facts." What
he made of what he experienced is what is important, for this determined the shape and tone of his books on Germany. At the very least
he did not make interesting books of his years in Germany; page after
page of predictably negative judgments are tedious, and with the
unrelieved sameness of the judgments, the reader soon suspects something is wrong with the observer rather than the subject. The point
of the book is blunted; it says more, finally, about Mayhew's failure
to penetrate sympathetically a foreign culture than about the middle
classes of Germany in the mid-nineteenth century. The causes of this
failure are rooted in a personality that is still a mystery to us.

Chapter Three
The Social Surveys

Henry Mayhew began his major work in late 1849. To understand the shape, direction, and achievement of his surveys, we should know something about the period out of which they arose.

The years between the passing of the First Reform Bill in 1832 and the Great Exhibition in 1851 were ones of economic and political change, and partly because these changes had in some cases negative results on human lives, it was also a period of social unrest. Indeed in 1848 there were revolutions in France and Austria, and while there was no violent overturning of the government in England, there was civil discontent and much fear on the part of the ruling classes that there would be a French-style revolution in England.

In any period of social change different complex forces contribute to the shift from one way of life to another. The situation in England in the early Victorian period had come about gradually as the country developed from an essentially feudal or agriculturally based society, where the aristocracy controlled the wealth and the power through its ownership of the land, to a modern industrial society where the wealth and the power are basically in the hands of the industrialists who own "the means of production" and the financiers who provide the money or "capital" to develop the industry. A corresponding set of social relationships went along with these economic organizations. Class position and duties were relatively clear in feudal times. Though the aristocracy had the power, an "aristocratic code" of loyalty, service, and reward went along with the power and theoretically kept it from becoming tyrannical, though there were very many exceptions to this. Indeed much literature of the medieval and Renaissance periods centers on the abuse of power in the hands of those who did not respect the feudal code. With the gradual transfer of power to the industrialists and financiers—the bourgeoisie—a new code governing class relationships was needed. However, instead of being based on ethics, the new code came to be seen as determined by a series of impersonal and immutable scientific "laws" that worked like the laws of natural science.

The first promulgator of these economic "laws" by which the middle classes were to govern their conduct and use their power was a Scotsman, Adam Smith, whose *Wealth of Nations,* published in 1776, developed the doctrine of laissez-faire ("let it alone") that was to govern the thinking of English political economists, and hence the lives of all Englishmen, throughout the nineteenth century. (It is still very much a part of our lives today.) Smith argued that the economic development of a nation depended on its industrial production and not its agricultural production (goods rather than food) and that the ability to increase the wealth of the nation depended on maintaining the delicate balance between the cost of producing the goods (the wages for workers, the cost of the raw materials, the cost of the machinery and plant, the profit for the capitalist) and the price for which they could be sold. Left alone, without any interference, this balance would work perfectly to the advantage of all, just as the "law of gravity" worked.

Coupled with this "law" was one "discovered" by another Scotsman, the clergyman Thomas Malthus, who at the turn of the century argued in *Essay on the Principle of Population* (1789) that the wages of labor must be at a subsistence level because any betterment of the working classes' conditions resulted in an increased work force, which, because of the competition for jobs, drove wages down again. The lower wage reduced the work force again by limiting the size of working-class families. Wages then rose; the family size and the work force rose; wages fell. This truly vicious cycle continued eternally. Thus, since any birth control other than abstinence was immoral, Malthus gloomily concluded that it was a "law" that the working population will always be forced to live at a subsistence level.

In theory the Smith and Malthus laws made sense. The capitalist was encouraged to minimize his costs in the hopes of increasing his profit, and to do so he was justified by Malthus's theory in keeping his workers' wages at the lowest level. The lower his costs were, the lower he could make the price of his finished goods and the more competitive they would be on the open market (this was why it was important to get rid of protective tariffs). To benefit the labor force, the goods on the market would be more plentiful and hence cheaper. The nation also could export what it didn't need for its own consumption and hence increase the general wealth. All benefited.

But the result for many of the working class was pernicious. They lived in squalor and ignorance, and men, women, and children all worked under cruel conditions. The visible results were crowded slums with neither running water nor waste disposal of any kind; young children maimed and emaciated from working long hours in factories and mines where not even minimal safety precautions were taken; a population of workers degraded to ignorant brutes by their work, their living conditions, and their only "leisure" activity— drinking.

As if these results were not bad enough, two other factors contributed to the visibly brutal condition of the working classes in the 1840s. First, there was a depression in the late 1830s and early 1840s and several bad harvests drove up the price of bread. Second, the change from a feudal-agricultural base to a capitalist-industrial base corresponded to the development of modern technology. By building new and better machines and by more efficient and cheaper means of production and distribution, costs of the capitalist could be reduced, but only if he eliminated the workers whose jobs were made redundant by machinery and improved methods of mass production. What was to be done with this "surplus" labor? Theoretically, increased demand for the cheaper goods would create new jobs. But in the 1830s and 1840s England had to face the fact that apparently this had not happened. The "law" of supply and demand said nothing about the many workers unable to find jobs; it seemed that they, like old unwanted machines, were just to rot—or starve—away. Many (how many no one knows) did just that. And it was their fate along with the subsistence living conditions of many of those who survived that lay behind the reform movements of the 1830s and 1840s.

Of course, much argument and debate centered about exactly what the situation was and why and what ought to be done. The working-class Chartists wanted political power for their class through the vote. The middle- and upper-class reformers, many of whom were in Parliament, had various suggestions: free trade, education, religious conversion, government interference. But three steps were necessary to deal with the problem as a whole; first, an investigation to establish the facts of the "Condition of England," as Thomas Carlyle phrased it in his seminal pamphlet *Chartism* in 1839. Second, the facts being clear, the "philosophers" or social theorists could discover the "laws" that determined the working of wages and capital, and finally, knowing these laws, the government could take the appropriate action—if any was called for. This orderly proceeding is certainly the best way to go about social reform, and the belief in its possibility survived long into the century, providing among other things the underlying rationale for Mayhew's social surveys at mid-century. But in practice it could not work this way. It was not possible to wait for the "laws" to be discovered before the government took action; the "facts" as they were uncovered were frequently too dreadful and demanded immediate redress. Thus, the energy of the 1830s and 1840s was devoted to step one—uncovering facts piecemeal—and step three, legislating in the same way to remedy specific local situations. For example, the investigation into women and children working in factories in 1832 led later to the so-called Ten-Hours-Bill in 1842, which set legal limits to the work day and introduced other changes.

By far the greatest energy went into step one, discovery of the facts. In that area Mayhew made his contribution, though throughout the seven-year period that he devoted, off and on, to his social surveys, he always intended to move on to step two. But for him as for others, there were just too many "facts" to uncover. We must note, too, that by the word *fact* the Victorian social investigator had a somewhat different understanding than do we. Although they, like ourselves, tended to equate "facts" with "figures" or statistics, a science that was still in its infancy at the time, they differed from us in the large number of things they believed could be statistically quantified as well as in their view of what conclusions one could draw from statistics. We still need to be reminded that "statistics can lie" or at least can be manipulated to demonstrate different things. Mayhew and his contemporaries had little or no sense either of the complications or limitations of statistics. In the 1840s and 1850s the many debates over the relationship of education (or lack of it) and crime, for example, frequently centered on imperfectly collected, understood, and interpreted statistics. Mayhew later thought he could determine how dirty London streets were by multiplying the number of horses times the number of streets in London. In addition, "statistics" sometimes seemed to have a broader meaning to the early Victorians than that of arithmetical numbers. Frequently included in statistical reports were descriptions of places and people, descriptions that we now think are more subjective than mere numbers, but that many Victorian social investigators (including Mayhew for the most part) considered as unbiased as their numerical tallies.

The task of discovering these facts or figures was undertaken by all manner of groups and individuals: bodies such as the newly formed statistical societies of Manchester and London, medical men such as Dr. James Kay-Shuttleworth (*The Moral and Physical Condition of the Working Classes Employed in the Cotton Manufacture of Manchester* [1832]), and civil servants like Edwin Chadwick (*An Inquiry into the Sanitary Condition of the Labouring Population of Great Britain* [1842]). The government's more extensive and official investigations were under the aegis of royal commissions (originating in the House of Lords) and select committees of the House of Commons, which published their findings in blue covers, the well-known "blue books."

There was in addition an artistic response. Thomas Hood's poem "Song of the Shirt," which bewailed the plight of the underpaid seamstress, published in *Punch* in 1843, became notorious. Mrs. Gaskell's *Mary Barton* (1848) looked at the problems of living in Manchester from a working-class point of view, while the suave young Disraeli's *Sybil* (1845) turned the blue books of parliamentary investigation into art. In addition, there were many minor novels and short stories dealing with similar perceptions of the Condition-of-England.

In journalism the same fervor was evident. Not only did established journals like the venerable *Times* enter the investigatory fray by sending reporters to Ireland in the mid-1840s to report on the effects of the potato famine, but new publications sprang up to respond to the need for information. Not all of these were as dry as the statistical society publications or as rabble rousing as the *Red Republican,* a radical socialist weekly. Many attacked the authorities through satire as did Mayhew and his *Punch* friends.

Yet despite all the investigative activity of the government, the newspapers and journals, the novelists and poets, the church, the statistical societies, and individual citizens, the total picture never really became clear. Information was spotty. Not all trades and industries reacted the same way, nor did all workers. Wages fluctuated according to the state of the economy, as did prices, and most workers only got paid when they actually worked. As a result of the fragmentation of information, throughout the late 1830s and 1840s, more and more informative surveys were undertaken and published. Englishmen were subjected to one shocking revelation after another regarding situations in individual industries, institutions, particular slums, and towns. But because no satisfactory explanation or solution emerged, the average man of goodwill, who certainly wanted the suffering of his fellowman to be alleviated, was somewhat at a loss as to what to think or to do. The orthodox economic thinkers, the laissez-fairists, argued that any "interference" on behalf of the workers by the government would only make things worse for everybody by upsetting the market balance. Still, it was not right, the man of goodwill thought, that children working in factories should die of what looked like old age at fourteen or that a man could not feed his family without himself, his wife, and all his children working fifteen hours a day. Maybe some further investigation, some new revelation would point the way to the cause and cure for England's economic and social ills.

It was in the context of this frustration and desire that Henry Mayhew and the *Morning Chronicle* began their social survey of the condition of the working population in England in 1849. The editorial announcing the series stated that "it is proposed to give a full and detailed description of the moral, intellectual, material, and physical condition of the industrial poor throughout England" (18 October 1849).

To us, over a hundred and thirty years later, it seems naive to think that a newspaper could possibly uncover the true facts of the living and working conditions of all people throughout England, particularly when the government with all its superior resources of staff and money had only been able to do so piecemeal. Even more surprising is the fact that Henry Mayhew set out almost single-handedly (he had some assistant writers, some stenographers, and help in working up statistics) to determine the true facts about "London labour and the London poor." It is as if one solitary reporter for the *New York Times* took upon himself to determine the living conditions and the working history of every kind of trade—skilled, semiskilled, unskilled, and illegal—in New York City, and all as a prelude to discovering the "laws" that determined the economic interrelationships of the entire city; to do this in a few months' time; and to write up the results of each day's work for publication the next day.

Yet the belief that this was possible is characteristic of the Victorian age in its enthusiasm and its earnestness, not to mention its amateurism, as well as its protestant belief in the power and responsibility of the individual to engage in good works. More important to our concerns is that Mayhew's belief that he could uncover all the facts about the condition of London's lower classes (and thereafter through examination of these facts discover the "laws" that governed the economic community) inspired him, a lazy if brilliant man, to a seemingly superhuman expense of energy. Without that belief it is unlikely he would have found his true vocation, nor would he have produced any work of the first order.

"**Labour and the Poor.**" The *Morning Chronicle* project to examine "Labour and the Poor" in England theoretically grew out of a trip Mayhew had made as a reporter to one of London's slum areas south of the Thames where the cholera epidemic of 1848–1849 had been very bad. A terrible, usually fatal disease spread by infected water, cholera turns its victims into wizened, blue corpses. People noticed that the worst outbreaks of the disease seemed to be in the slums. Thus the well-meaning thought cholera too might be connected to the Condition-of-England question. Even as they hoped to understand the causes of economic distress by collecting masses of empirical evidence, they had a sense that the same kind of information about the slums might uncover the "laws" governing the spread of cholera. Some such idea lay behind Mayhew's trip in late August or early September to Jacob's Island.

But in a way reminiscent of other investigations, the immediate theoretical impetus to Mayhew's journalistic assignment was put aside in the horror of the specific facts uncovered. Jacob's Island was in early Victorian England almost a literary symbol; in 1838 Dickens had used it as the final retreat of the murderer Bill Sikes in *Oliver Twist,* and in his later preface to the novel he angrily insisted on the accuracy of his representation of the place. After Mayhew's revelations and as a direct result of them, the slum again emerged as symbol in another novel of social protest, Charles Kingsley's *Alton Lock* (1850).

In his report, published 24 September 1849, Mayhew only mentions cholera in passing; instead he dwells in graphic detail on the situation at that moment in the "houses" of the slums with the implicit moral that something must be done to change the situation NOW.

What he found was that the only drinking water came from a ditch that was contaminated by the refuse from the tanneries and that ran red in some places and olive green with scum in others. It was also a common privy. A dreadful effluvium arose from this polluted water and entered all the houses, which were old and decrepit and hung over the ditch. The houses were damp and poorly maintained. One inhabitant told Mayhew that "Neither I nor my children know what

health is, . . . But what is one to do? We must live where our bread
is." Mayhew referred to hearing stories "that made one's blood
curdle."

A couple of weeks after his report about Jacob's Island in Ber-
mondsey, the *Morning Chronicle* began its multi-series on "Labour and
the Poor." Mayhew later claimed that it was his idea; the editors of
the *Morning Chronicle* said it was theirs. Probably it was a combination of both.

The project was divided into three parts. Reporters—or "correspondents" as they were called—included Angus Reach and later
Charles Mackay from the manufacturing districts; Alexander Mackay
followed by Shirley Brooks from the rural areas. Mayhew reported
from London as the "Metropolitan Correspondent."

The articles or "letters" began 19 October and one appeared every
day, alternating among the three different areas—manufacturing,
London, and rural. For about three months nearly the whole of the
Morning Chronicle, next to the *Times* the most prestigious daily newspaper though without its circulation, was devoted to these reports.
After the first of the year, however, when Parliament was again in
session, the "Labour and the Poor" series appears less often. Mayhew's
contributions ended sometime in the last months of 1850; the series
as a whole continued intermittently for another six months or so. The
major force of the articles, particularly Mayhew's on London, which
were almost immediately famous, lasted the half year between October 1849 and the spring of 1850.

When he began his investigations, Mayhew was just short of
thirty-seven years old. He had behind him a long career of writing in
various modes: drama, journalism, fiction, and educational theory,
but nothing had had lasting success. He had spent many years in educating himself about natural science, particularly chemistry. He had
helped found several magazines, but none had given him a permanent
place. He had had altercations with his father. He had married and
had two children and had managed to quarrel with his father-in-law.
His bankruptcy had left him barely solvent. In other words, looking
at his situation in October 1849, there was little to indicate that
Henry Mayhew was on the brink of his major work.

In the next two years Mayhew produced, at an impressive speed
and with an astonishing energy, thousands of words of investigative
reporting into various London occupations and hundreds of portraits
of lower-class men and women. Three things motivated him to this

output. One was a fascination with the subject, particularly as it developed from a general survey into a collection of personal biographies of lower-class men and women. Second was his sense that he might make an original contribution by applying his amateur training in scientific methodology to the relatively new field of social investigation. Finally, the *Morning Chronicle's* prestige and circulation gave him something he had not had before: a good deal of extra help and support. He was well paid, according to Sutherland Edwards, and had "an army of assistant writers, stenographers, and hansom cabmen constantly at his call."[1] This support freed him from the administrative responsibilities of accounting and organizing, which temperamentally he could not handle and which had probably been among the reasons little of his work had flourished.

Before describing the way in which Mayhew's letters on London's labor and the poor developed into the long series of personal biographies that both his contemporaries and modern readers recognize as his major achievement, we might pause to discuss the state of social science and its relationship to journalism in 1849. There was not at this time a very clear idea of the social sciences as sciences. Mayhew's desire to apply the methodology of the natural sciences to the study of social problems was one of the first such efforts. As he said later in 1850, "I made up my mind to deal with human nature as a natural philosopher or [as] a chemist deals with any material object; and, as a man who had devoted some little of his time to physical and metaphysical science, I must say I did most heartily rejoice that it should have been left to me to apply the laws of the inductive philosophy for the first time, I believe, in the world to the abstract questions of political economy."[2] Sociology, a word coined in the early part of the 1840s by the French philosopher Auguste Comte, was almost exclusively theoretical. Like many of his contemporaries, Mayhew had come to believe that in matters of human organization the data had to precede the theory. Though the government, other institutions, and many individuals were collecting these facts, the only way to publish the results was in a book or pamphlet. There were no professional journals to speak of, though those of the statistical societies were laying the groundwork for this new kind of publication. To publish results quickly and distribute them widely there were only newspapers. In this context Mayhew and the editors of the *Morning Chronicle* were making a natural and reasonable decision.

Newspapers in Victorian England also were different than they are today. First of all, they looked different; there were no pictures or illustrations, and the front page was a series of classified advertisements. Furthermore, lacking modern teletypes and press services, depending on the mail or courier for distant reports, there was less "international" news. Lacking telephones, the reporters had to bring in their stories and so there was less local news. The newspapers thus had room for long verbatim accounts of Parliament and other bodies. When Parliament was in session, for example, the paper printed the complete record of the proceedings day by day, thus becoming a kind of *Congressional Record*. The readers of early Victorian newspapers expected this kind of leisurely treatment of any important subject.

Of course, publishing a work of what was essentially social history in a daily newspaper put restrictions on the format and the shape of Mayhew's reports. But these restrictions were fewer than we might think. It does not appear that the length of his reports or perhaps even the number of informants quoted was curtailed by the format. On the other hand, the newspaper context probably contributed to the way he finally came to report his interviews. Because of the limitation on space, he collapsed the interviews into long, "biographical" narratives in which his questions are subsumed into the answers of his informants. This mode of reporting also made the narrative more readable and hence more effective than the more orthodox question-and-answer format of the blue books.

Another element of Mayhew's work was determined by the journalistic need to publish every few days. We can see him learning to be a social historian through experience. He began his investigation into "Labour and the Poor" in London with a fairly clearly articulated intention and direction. In his initial letter he announced that he would be mainly concerned to determine the rate of wages among the working population of London, but he also intended "to learn, by close communication with them, the real or fancied wrongs of their lot." He categorizes the "poor" in various conventional ways and says he intends to begin with "the poorly-paid—the unfortunate—and the improvident. While treating of the poorly-paid, I shall endeavour to lay before the reader a catalogue of such occupations in London as yield a bare subsistence. . . . At the same time I purpose, when possible, giving the weekly amount of income derived from each, together with the cause—if discoverable—of the inadequate return. After this, it is my intention to visit the dwellings of the unrelieved poor—to ascertain, by positive inspection, the condition of their homes . . . [and] to calculate the interest that the petty capitalist reaps from their necessities."[3]

He was not able to be so complete, however. The first two months of his work for the *Chronicle* are inconsistent in what they claim, attempt, and achieve. But gradually in terms of his investigations yet quickly in terms of actual time, Mayhew sorted out what he had to do and made significant strides toward knowing how to do it. By late January 1850, just four months after his visit to Jacob's Island, he had the format of his social surveys essentially in place. It is an impressive achievement, particularly when we realize that he had no models, little professional guidance, and that his subject was one of the most obscure and inarticulate of all—the life and work of the lower classes. Under the pressure of publishing frequent reports, the development of this sorting-out process became part of the record of his work, sometimes directly when he tells us of his changes of mind and plan, but more often indirectly as the mode and direction of his articles shift.

One way to begin a discussion of Mayhew's work as Metropolitan Correspondent is with the general title "Labour and the Poor." What does this title tell us about the projected series? What was meant by the two key terms and what if anything was the relationship between them? Mayhew did not spell out the answers because he was not completely sure of them himself. But we can tell something of what he had in mind by looking at what he did and did not survey. He certainly did not include as "labour" any of the professional or subprofessional groups, or even the poorly paid and overworked clerks of various sorts. He also did not intend to include servants, who comprised a full 20 percent of London's labor force at this time, though their exclusion from his survey may have been due mainly to the difficulty of collecting evidence from such a decentralized group of individual workers and employers.

What he did seem to mean were the traditional London trades. In the early nineteenth century London was the greatest artisan center in the world; it included the building, clothing-making, and food trades as the most numerous, followed by furniture-making, precision instrument-making, printing, tanning, currying, engineering, and ship-building, traditionally the oldest, most highly skilled, and most important of all the artistan's occupations.

But though the title of the series puts labor first, it was really poverty that motivated the series, that shaped its definitions, and deter-

mined its scope, and while he never tried to define "labour," Mayhew
spent a good part of his opening letter trying to arrive at an adequate
notion of "poor." All he came up with, however, was the lack of necessities, which lack resulted in pain, as opposed to the lack of lux-
uries which resulted in mere discomfort. He also categorized the poor
as either willing, unwilling, or unable to work.

Probably because the series was generated in something of a rush
and not completely or even partially thought out in advance, no list
of occupations to be examined appears, nor was there given any specific system by which material was to be collected, checked, and reported. Nonetheless, Mayhew's original intentions do emerge from
his early articles and some of his subsequent comments. As he stated,
his plan was first to collect systematically from each of the trades in
London the facts or statistics about costs and wages and to elucidate
their "attitudes and feelings" about the causes and cures of their current situation. To achieve the first, he planned to use whatever
printed material was available—government reports, Board of Trade
figures, the census reports, any individual pamphlets and books that
came to hand—plus whatever original figures he could collect from
employers and workers. To achieve the next part of this goal he
hoped to visit the working and living quarters (in a good many cases
this would be the same lodging) of some representative workers
whom he would find through sources who knew each trade well. He
would describe what he saw and report what the workers told him in
answer to his questions.

This plan, or something like it, was rendered obsolete almost immediately by what Mayhew found when he actually began to collect
his facts. Only the first few letters follow this outline conscientiously
and, as the series developed, one part of it—the interviews—began
to dominate.

After two initial letters describing the contrasts of London physically and statistically and laying down a few general guidelines ("My
vocation is to collect facts, and to register opinions" [2, 23 Oct.
1849]), Mayhew began his investigation with the weavers in Spital-
fields, an area in East London which had long been famous for its
weaving trade. The invention of the power loom in the 1780s and the
eventual mechanization of the craft during the first two decades of the
nineteenth century had destroyed the trade of hand-weaving, a fact
well known to Mayhew and most of his readers. He reported the statistics and visited a few poor weavers in their homes. But here at this

very early stage occurred the first of several changes in his direction caused by the discovery of some new information.

The weavers explained why the quoted wages for their labor did not reflect their true condition: they were paid only when they worked, and they did not work all the time. Thus the wage for one job, which took them a week, would probably have to support them and their families for perhaps two or three more weeks until they could get another job. What did they do if the money ran out and they were still out of work or "at play," as the men ironically referred to unemployment, a word and a concept not yet in existence. They went to the London docks and tried to get jobs loading or unloading ships; they moved, in other words, from the highly skilled trade of weaving to the unskilled heavy manual labor of dock work.

The systematic thing to do at this point was for Mayhew to file this piece of information away and to continue in his investigation of the weaving trade. But he couldn't do it; he was too interested in this new aspect of the labor scene. He wanted to follow it up immediately. And he did. He dropped the investigation of the weavers, for good it turned out, for he never came back to it, and began instead an investigation of the labor connected with the London docks. He followed the same procedure with which he had begun the weaver survey, collecting printed documents, personally visiting the docks, and interviewing various men in different kinds of dock work. This survey extended for two articles and then itself led to a further break in systematic presentation when he tried to investigate the "low" lodging houses where many of the dockworkers lived and which were sometimes also the habitations of thieves, beggars, runaways, and prostitutes, and the owners of which sometimes served as fences for stolen goods. Mayhew reports that he was taken for a government spy when he visited one and had to beat a quick retreat.

Anyone who has done research of any sort knows that this kind of discovery is typical of investigations into unknown territory. It is not that it happened this way that is significant in our understanding of Mayhew's work but rather that because of the format in which he was publishing his results, these sudden shifts of direction and the corresponding abandonments of other investigations are not hidden away in notebooks but have themselves become part of his work. When we read the letters of the Metropolitan Correspondent in "Labour and the Poor" and to a lesser degree *London Labour and the London Poor* we are reading two related but different documents at the same time: one, the record of "labour and the poor" in London at mid-century as it appeared to one brilliant observer, but also, two, the record of the failures and successes of that observer in seeing, comprehending, controlling, and reporting on a complex and sometimes confusing set of exciting daily experiences. "Labour and the Poor" thus is partly a social record and partly an indirect intellectual autobiography. Mayhew himself acknowledged as much in late November when he wrote, "This unsystematic mode of treating the subject is almost a necessary evil attendant upon the nature of the investigation. In the course of my inquiries into the earnings and condition of one class of people, sources of information respecting the habits and incomings of another are opened up to me, of which, for several reasons, I am glad to avail myself at the immediate moment, rather than defer making use of them till a more fitting and orderly occasion." And later in the same article, he promised that "when I come to the second part of my inquiry, I may be able to state the results rather than the details of the present investigations" (12, 27 Nov. 1849).

During that first investigation into the docks, Mayhew arrived at the mode by which his best and most important work would be reported: that is, his description of specific scenes in London, which are among some of the most evocative pieces about the city in the nineteenth century, and his interviews, which, in the unique way he evolved of reporting them, became one of the main sources of our limited knowledge of the thoughts and feelings of London's poor at mid-century.

Mayhew covered laborers at the London and St. Katharine docks, but he did not survey all kinds of dockworkers at this time. Two months later he returned to the subject and surveyed the dockworkers in the coal trade and in June 1850 he touched on others in the course of his investigation into the timber trade. He intended to complete his survey of dock work, however, for periodically during the next year he referred to an upcoming survey of "longshore workers" in the process of completion but which never appeared. Probably Mayhew and his associates were trying to pull together the general information about dockworkers but the pressure of time and other interests just got in the way and the work was never finished.

Certainly the investigation that he took up next soon absorbed every bit of energy he had as well as made increasing demands on the resources and space of the *Morning Chronicle*. Why he moved from dockworkers to tailors and needlewomen is not clear. Perhaps he had met some out-of-work tailors on the docks or in the low lodging houses, and they gave him contacts or information. However it happened, Mayhew's investigation of the exploited or "dishonorable" portion of this trade, made up of underpaid pieceworkers, was the most influential in his own lifetime of anything he ever wrote, and undoubtedly on the basis of this investigation his contemporary reputation rested.

The London clothing industry was divided into four main categories: tailors who made men's jackets, suits, trousers, and so forth; needlewomen or seamstresses who made shirts, blouses, underclothes, etc.; dressmakers, and boot and shoemakers. It was one of the oldest and largest trades in London. Since the sewing machine had not yet been invented, all the work was done by hand. The well-established shops were in the West End of London; for the most part these shops hired the best workers who stayed on for the duration of their working lives and were paid a regular, reasonable salary of around sixpence an hour, a wage established by custom and the standards of their "society," an early form of union. There had been some fluctuation of the wages of the workers in this "honorable" trade, but by and large they were not "poor" as defined by Mayhew.

Customarily, if a man wanted a suit or a woman a dress, he or she would have it made to order by one of these shops. But, along with the rise of the factory system in England, there grew up a new kind of shop, the forebear of our own clothing stores, where clothes were not made to order but were bought ready-to-wear. Many government uniforms were also made by this system of production. These large firms could sell clothes more cheaply because they could produce goods in a kind of crude mass production. They also engaged in some elaborate advertising to gain custom. One firm had a man parade in a seven-foot hat, which subsequently became for Carlyle in *Past and Present* a symbol of England's substitution of the showy fake for the real thing. These ready-to-wear firms flourished during the early part of the nineteenth century. Frequently located in the East End of London, they became known as the East End trade.

There was an ugly underside to this development of cheap, ready-to-wear clothes. Since it was not necessary to use good and hence well-paid workmen or workwomen—the customers buying ready-to-wear clothes valued cheapness rather than workmanship—many of the owners of these firms had inferior workpeople make up the clothes off the premises by the piece. A workman would be paid a certain price for a finished garment. Theoretically this worked to the advantage of both the employer and the employed. The former had to pay only for work done, and, if as was usual, the worker worked at home and even furnished his own needles and thread, the overhead for the employer could be reduced significantly and the price of the finished product reduced even more. In theory, the employee also had an advantage, for he could work at his own speed and if he was a fast worker he could make more money. If such a worker was on a fixed salary, he would have no chance to increase his wages by working harder, faster, or longer.

But in practice it usually did not work this way. There was the problem of distribution. How were individual workers to get the garments from the shops? They were not paid for their time in picking up and delivering or hunting out work. So a system of "middlemen" developed whereby one individual collected the contracts and "subcontracted" them whole or in parts to other workers. He or she took a share of the garment price for this service. This system, Mayhew learned eventually, resulted in incomes for pieceworkers, though not for middlemen, lower than the subsistence wage that Malthus had predicted as the bottom line.

It worked something like this. Say a West End firm custom-made a pair of foot-guards trousers for eight shillings. If one worker in the West-End trade custom-made three such trousers a week, he would be paid his regular wage, about twenty shillings, the rest of the price of the trousers going to his employer for overhead and profit. In the piece system it worked differently. Say the East-End firm wanted to sell the same trousers ready-to-wear at seven shillings. A middleman would get the contract for the trousers at, say, five shillings a piece, and he then contracted them out again for, Mayhew learned, sixpence a pair (twelve pence made one shilling). Or he might contract out different parts of the garment, the seams to a distressed needlewoman for twopence, the hem to another for one pence, and so forth. Frequently the worker had to provide his own thread, not to mention candles and other items in his home. At the end of the week, the employer had a profit of six shillings on the three pairs of trousers, but the middleman had thirteen-and-a-half shillings simply for acting as subcontractor. The worker had one-and-a-half shillings minus whatever he had had to supply on his own. It is not hard to see who suffered nor to understand why the original employers could insist that they paid perfectly fair wages and, by closing their eyes as to how they got their garments made, react with surprise at Mayhew's insistence that the workpeople lived in squalor and degradation caused by overwork and underpay. When Mayhew answered the inquiry of the foreman and the principal of a large "slop"[4] clothing firm from whom he had sought information about how he found the workpeople generally, he said "I told them I had never seen or heard of such destitution. 'Destitution!' was the exclamation. 'God bless my soul you surprise me!' [the foreman and principal replied]. 'And I think it but right, gentlemen,' I added, 'to apprise you that your statement as to prices differs most materially from that of the workpeople' " (6,6 Nov. 1849).

The description through interviews of the various ways in which the workpeople in this "slop" trade kept body and soul together became Mayhew's total effort for over a month. He tells the story unsystematically but with vivid detail, authorial restraint, and great effect. It shocked the nation and rocketed Henry Mayhew to fame. As a recent commentator on "the sweated trades" has remarked, "Outwork, as it existed in the nineteenth century, was in fact one of the least acceptable of the many disagreeable aspects of private capitalism. The principle that 'labour' was a mere factor of production— one more item in an impersonal list of costs, to be acquired in the cheapest market without any regard for its human dimension—was perhaps put into practice more obviously in the outwork system than anywhere else."[5]

After a month of interviews reported in increasing length which uncovered the lives of tailors engaged in "slop" work, plus army clothing makers, plain needlework women, cloakmakers, stay stitchers (who only sewed stays into clothes), shoe binders (who sewed uppers to lowers), stock or necktie makers, upholsterers, and needlewomen engaged in a variety of occupations, Mayhew took a break to collate his material and to make plans for a couple of large meetings of tailors by which he hoped to collect even more information. In the two-week hiatus he interviewed the various hucksters who sold provisions, domestic hardware, and paper products on the street. The buyers of these street-sold goods were almost exclusively the poor workers and nonworkers. Mayhew said the purpose of this investigation was to find out if the poor were overcharged for their necessaries as well as underpaid for their work. Over a week and a half four articles on these street folk, who would later be the subject of *London Labour and the London Poor,* appeared in the *Morning Chronicle.*

While Mayhew was writing these reports he was also collecting information from interviews and other sources that allowed him to form a picture of the relationship between the West End or honorable trade and the East End or dishonorable slop trade given above. In Letter 16, 11 December 1849, he returned to the tailors, reporting in the two subsequent articles on two large meetings, one of East End tailors at the British and Foreign School and the next of some two thousand West End tailors in the Hanover Square rooms. After the report of this meeting Mayhew left the clothing workers and went back to the docks.

The reaction to Mayhew's interviews with the East End tailors and needlewomen was extensive. Partly it was preconditioned by a widespread "iconology of the seamstress" to use the phrase of T. J. Edelstein. Mainly due to "The Song of the Shirt" by Hood, throughout the late 1840s there had been an image of the noble but pathetic sempstress in all forms of art—popular theater (Mark Lemon wrote a play called *The Sempstress* in 1844), painting (the subject of Edelstein's article),[6] and literature. Mrs. Gaskell makes her working-class heroine Mary Barton a poor seamstress. Mayhew's revelations in 1849, which include a sympathetic but abbreviated investigation into the number of seamstresses driven to prostitution by low wages, rode the crest of this popular reaction. Edelstein uses Mayhew as an example of anti-sentimentality about seamstresses. Still it is likely that the strong and widespread outrage caused by his revelations came from an audience already prepared for what he found.

Different meetings were held and several schemes debated on how to alleviate the destitute condition of the workers Mayhew found at the bottom of the subcontracting system. A fund for immediate relief was started by the *Morning Chronicle* into which poured hundreds of pounds. Charles Kingsley and his group of Christian socialists set up a primitive collective called the Working Tailors' Association run by the tailors themselves. In behalf of this organization, which hoped to draw customers away from the ready-to-wear firms that sold clothing produced by slop workmen, Kingsley wrote his famous pamphlet *Cheap Clothes and Nasty* (1850) which was made up primarily of quotations from Mayhew's articles. Kingsley also introduced some of Mayhew's material into his novel *Alton Locke* which was published later in the same year.

The reaction largest in scope was undoubtedly the Female Emigration Society formed by two upper-class philanthropists, Sidney Herbert, one of the owners of the *Morning Chronicle,* and Lord Ashley, the future Lord Shaftesbury. These two men collected money over the next several months to help needlewomen of impeccable character emigrate to Australia where the two reformers thought they had a better chance of finding work and husbands; for Herbert and Lord Ashley clung to the idea that the cause of the distress of the tailors and needlewomen had to be found in the established doctrine of supply and demand: if wages were low it was because there were too many workers competing for too few jobs. Thus the solution was to get rid of the "excess population" by sending them to the colonies. Mayhew, on the other hand, though at this point he said nothing about it publicly, had begun to doubt that supply and demand were working as they were supposed to do in the matter of wages. The way the famous and rich philanthropists took the limelight away from him at the highpoint of his career may have contributed to his ironic comments about philanthropy in the *Comic Almanac* of 1851.

In the "Labour and the Poor" series itself, however, nothing of either the Female Emigration Society or Mayhew's irritation appears. Instead the Metropolitan Correspondent spends the next month reporting on his further investigations of dockworkers, this time concentrating on the coal trade and the longshoremen who unloaded the coal barges and loaded the ballast which filled the ships on their return trip to the northern coal ports. In this series of articles Mayhew becomes involved in the question of drunkenness in the lower classes. He is led to this first because of the amount of drinking done by dock laborers with the predictable effects on their health and their families, and second, because of the method of hiring and payment of ballast heavers. These workers were contracted for and paid by public-house (or bar) owners, and traditionally the ballast heavers were expected to spend money on beer at the public house in order to curry favor with the publican-employer.

From the time of his meetings of tailors, Mayhew had tried to gather some of his information at meetings. He felt the large number of statistics collected this way plus the immediate correction of exaggerated stories by others present would help assure some accuracy in the statements. In pursuit of this story of the ballast heavers' miserable lives, he held two meetings, one with the men and one in early January 1850 with the wives of these workers. The women described in vivid detail the hardships brought about by the publicans' control over hiring and paying.

This dramatic meeting is a good example of the combination of a journalistic mode and a "philosophical" or scientific goal. The interviews are full of personal details concerning how these women tried to support their families on small sums of money, and of the brutality and humiliation resulting from a drunken husband. As such, they are interesting historical documents. But they also read as effectively as if they were from a novel by Charles Dickens. The decision to attack the system of hiring ballast heavers by having women describe the worst results of the practice was inspired. Dickens did the same kind of thing in *Bleak House* where the brutalized lives of the brickmakers are underlined for the reader by the experiences of their wives. Thus Mayhew's personal combination of journalist and amateur scientist gave shape here as elsewhere to his work. The power of his writing in turn explains why the readers of his initial articles in "Labour and the Poor" responded so strongly and with such shock to information that was not new. The particularity and extensive detail in Mayhew's report interviews plus the number of them made an impression that lasted.

We could cite many examples of this power, but one will have to stand for the rest. The statement is that of the wife of a poor dockworker:

To show the temptations that beset the poor, I give the statement of a woman known to all her neighbours as a very thrifty housewife, and an active, industrious woman. Her children's, her own, and her husband's clothing, scant and old as it was, all showed great care-taking; her home was very tidy. A few years back, a little after Christmas, she and her husband . . . had been out all day, penniless, and returned to their room a little before dusk, without having earned a farthing. The wife was then suckling her first child, which was two months old. She felt very faint, and the only thing in the house on which she thought it possible to raise a penny was a glass tumbler—"that very tumbler," she continued, "which you see on the table. Everything but that had gone to the pawn-shop. Well, it cost 5½d., and I went to—— and tried to sell it for 2d. I couldn't sell it at all, as the dealer had too many of such things. I then went to a neighbour and said, 'Mrs. B—, for God's sake lend me 2d. on this glass, for we're starving.' 'Mrs.—,' said she, 'I'm sure you should have 3d., but I haven't 3d., nor a halfpenny.' Well, when I'd gone back it was dark, and my husband had gone to bed, such as it was—for we had neither blankets nor sheets left to cover us—as the best way to forget he was hungry and cold. We hadn't a bit of fire nor candle, but there was a bit of light came from the lamp in the street through the window. I sat down by the fire, that wasn't in, to suckle my child—poor little Bill! he's a fine lad now—and I found I had hardly any milk; and what would become of the child? All at once a thought came into my head, and I said to myself, 'Yes, I'll cut my own throat, and then little Bill's'—and I determined I would. Then I said to myself, 'No, I won't; for if I can cut my own throat, I know I can't cut the child's; so it'll be little use, I'll go to the waterworks, and jump in with him in my arms.' I got up to do it, and then another thought came on me, and I laid down the child on that chair, and I shook my husband and said, 'You villain, I'll cut your throat, I will,' and he jumped up and seized hold of me, and then I felt how bad I'd been; but one's passion must have some vent, so I seized that very kettle you see there by the spout—the gas rather lighted it—and I smashed it on the floor; it was the first thing that came to hand—and broke a hole in it that cost me 2½d. to get mended. After that I felt calmed a bit, and began to see how wicked I'd been, and I fell down on my knees and cried like a child, for I was thankful to God I'd been preserved. Then I went to bed and prayed never to feel the like again." This statement was made with perfect simplicity; it came out incidentally, and the poor woman had no reason to believe that it would be printed. (24, 8 Jan. 1850)

In mid-January Mayhew finished his survey of the dockworkers for the time being. He turned next to an investigation of "houses of refuge for the destitute poor" because, he said, the winter months were when these places were open. This subject engaged him for the rest of January and took him into cursory reports on vagrancy, another look at low lodging houses, and a series of interesting interviews with vagrants, beggars, petty thieves, and prostitutes.

These refuges were related to the workhouse and were usually under the jurisdiction of the Poor Law Board of Guardians. Many workhouses had a "casual ward" which served as a temporary accommodation for workers on the move. Many of these casual wards became meeting places for professional vagrants, as well as thieves and other marginal types. In London there was also a "refuge for the houseless poor," which opened its doors when the temperature reached freezing. The clients were admitted after dusk and forced to leave in the morning. Mayhew wrote a very moving description of the homeless waiting for the doors to open as seen from a balcony above, later reprinted in volume 3 of *London Labour and the London Poor*.

To look down upon them from the main staircase, as I did, was to survey a very motley scene. There they were—the shirtless, the shoeless, the coatless, the unshaven, the uncouth, ay, and the decent and respectable. There were men from every part of the United Kingdom, with a coloured man or two,

a few seamen, navigators, agricultural labourers, and artizans. There were
no foreigners on the nights that I was there; and in the returns of those
admitted there will not be found one Jew. . . . To attempt to give an account of anything like a prevailing garb among these men is impossible,
unless I described it as rags. As they were washing, or waiting for a wash,
there was some stir, and a loud buzz of talk, in which "the brogue" strongly
predominated. There was some little fun, too, as there must be where a
crowd of many youths is assembled. One in a ragged, coarse, striped shirt,
exclaimed as he shoved along, "By your leave, gentlemen!" with a significant emphasis of his "gentlemen." Another man said to his neighbour, "The
bread's fine, Joe; but the sleep, isn't that plummy?" Some few, I say,
seemed merry enough, but that is easily accounted for. Their present object
was attained, and your real professional vagabond is always happy by that—
for a forgetfulness of the past, or an indifference to it, and a recklessness as
to the future, are the primary elements of a vagrant's enjoyment." (26, 15
Jan. 1851; 3, 408)

By now he had recognized, at least unconsciously if not openly,
that the real strength in his work for the *Morning Chronicle* lay in the
reports of the interviews he conducted with individual workers. These
reported interviews, at first intended as the "data" which supported
the generalizations he was making about the condition in each occupation he took up, had during the tailor and needlewoman investigations gradually usurped not only the whole interest of the reader—
and one suspects of the investigator himself—but also the space in
the newspaper. These accounts bring reader and poor face to face. We
can sense the questions Mayhew probably asked in the following example but the woman speaks for herself:

"I have got no home, sir," she [a shoe-binder] said. "My work wouldn't
allow me to pay rent—no, that it wouldn't at the price we have now. I live
with this good woman and her husband. The rent is half-a-crown a week,
and they allow me to live with them rent free. We all live in this one room
together—there are five of us, four sleep in one bed; that is the man and the
wife and two children, and I lie on the floor. If it wasn't for them I must
go to the work-house; out of what little I earn I couldn't possibly pay rent."
(35, 14 Feb. 1850)

We do not know exactly how Mayhew turned the interviews into
these lengthy "monologues." Possibly he shaped their structure, for
some begin with a biographical background which then turns into an
account of the present situation of the given subject, complete with

what figures are available. He said that "hardly a line will be written but what a note of the matter recorded has been taken upon the spot" (2, 23 Oct. 1849), but it is unlikely that a verbatim account was consistently kept. At several of his meetings the newspaper account notes that a shorthand reporter was present to take down a transcript of the proceedings. (Shorthand reporters, of whom Charles Dickens was one before he became a novelist, were mainly used to take verbatim accounts of the proceedings in Parliament.) If they were present at the meetings, they may very well have been present during individual interviews. At the very least the presence of these shorthand writers indicates that Mayhew and his colleagues were aware of the problem of accuracy, and they made efforts to assure it throughout the series. (The controversy over Mayhew's accuracy is treated in detail in the final chapter of this book.)

Mayhew used most of his space in the six and a half letters on houses of refuge for his interviews and a meeting of vagrants. These interviews are among the most sensational as opposed to pathetic and moving that he did. They are perhaps suspect in terms of their specific accuracy, for most of the subjects were outside the law in one way or another and had good reason to fudge the truth of their lives or to brag about their exploits. Nonetheless, the atmosphere in these houses of refuge, in which impoverished skilled workers, the weak or disabled, runaway children, hardened criminals of all sorts, beggars (legitimate and phony), hobos, and the dispossessed were all thrown together, is undoubtedly accurate.

In February Mayhew, his articles now appearing twice a week, returned to the skilled workers, still focusing on the clothing industry, with an investigation of boot and shoemakers. These five articles plus three on toymakers made up his work for February 1850.

He brought to his new investigation his understanding of the "honorable" West-End Trade and the "dishonorable" East-End trade, as well as of "slop" workmanship in general, subcontracting or "chamber-mastering," and the use of cheap child labor. Hence his articles on the boot and shoe trade are more orderly than those on the tailors. He begins with three pieces on the honorable trade and follows this with two on the "slop" trade. Perhaps because the shock of discovery and the reaction of a surprised outrage are missing here—Mayhew found a pattern already uncovered in the tailors' series—the articles as a whole lack the compelling interest of the former ones, though individual interviews have interest. Important for Mayhew's future development, however, was further statistical evidence that the decrease in wages for both West End and "slop" workers was apparently not the result of an excess of workers. Rather an influx of French imports, plus some cheap northern goods, had forced the price of English shoes lower in order to compete. Because bread prices were also low, this lowering of the price of shoes frequently resulted in the lowering of wages, which in turn resulted in a lower standard of living for good workmen and the enslavement of lesser workmen to the "slop" subcontracting system. All this evidence against the supply-and-demand explanation of low wages was gradually accumulating. In just a few months Mayhew would feel sufficiently informed to offer his own explanation of the causes of low wages. (The interview with a "very intelligent 'closer' " in which these ideas are aired was one of those Mayhew later claimed the *Morning Chronicle* had censored. Bootmakers in London were traditionally radical in politics.)

At this point he essentially left the clothing workers for good. At the end of the year there were two short articles on dressmakers and milliners and one on journeymen hatters by the Metropolitan Correspondent but how much Mayhew had to do with these articles is in doubt.[7] For now he took a selective glance at some toymakers in London because they were small in number and thus provided a good "fill-in" while he pursued a larger topic of prison labor.

He broke the subject of toymakers into those for the poor, superior toymakers, and doll makers. In the last article he reported what was to be one of his favorite interviews, probably because of the oddity of the occupation, that with the dolls'-eye maker. Little of any general significance emerged from these letters, but they contain a number of interesting interviews, one with a toy-theater maker and one with a worker who made penny wooden toys to be sold to the poor.

Beginning in March, Mayhew started a new investigation, an extensive look at the merchant marine. He seems to have been moved to this subject by a bill currently being debated in Parliament as to the method of payment for sailors. The proponents of the bill wanted the government to regulate such payment through a board. This would, they hoped, eliminate the bribery, harassment, and outright fraud that was currently the norm in the trade. Mayhew's knowledge of the problem may have come from his informants on the docks. If so, it is a good example of how his work evolved, one investigation shading into another, though the points of contact are not always evident to the casual reader.

Mayhew asks the sailors for their opinions about the method of payment, but he seems by the nature of his questions as a whole to be more interested in a general picture of life on sea and on land. He focuses on the abuses felt by the sailors in both contexts. This is perhaps natural, not only because of his sense of being an investigative reporter who is uncovering the details of his society in all areas of "the poor," but also because his interviews were with the sailors themselves. They, like most of us, tend to dwell on grievances when catching a sympathetic ear.

This leads to a consideration of a truly remarkable aspect of Mayhew's social surveys. Though, as indicated above, there had been any number of investigations into living and working conditions in England during the fifteen years before Mayhew began his work, and though the form of Mayhew's reports owes some debts to these earlier investigations, his surveys differed from their predecessors in one fundamental way. Though the government select committees took testimony from workers, it was combined with that from "authorities"—philanthropists, clergymen, doctors, and officials of various kinds. There was thus a broad spectrum of facts and opinions, but partly because the information of authorities always carries more weight and partly because of the inarticulateness of the lower classes, not to mention outright prejudice against their having anything reliable or meaningful to say, the sense of lower-class life escaped most if not all of the earlier investigations.

In Mayhew's survey for "Labour and the Poor" this is not true. Part of the reason for this is the broader scope of his questions and the detail in which the answers are reported. But equally important is that at least as far as the interviews go, expression is given exclusively by the members of the lower classes themselves. Mayhew gave his survey over to the words of the workers.

He did not intend to do this at the beginning. Early in the tailor survey he tried to get corroborating information from employers and middlemen but, not surprisingly, he found the ones most suspect singularly uncooperative, and so he pretty much abandoned any effort to gain their evidence. Instead, in the general informational and statistical articles that he gave preceding each investigation, he tried to redress the balance by including as many official facts and figures as he could. This is the aspect of his surveys that needed to be worked up during the various hiatuses in the early surveys. But his contemporary and modern readers have both tended to ignore these general histories of each trade and instead have poured over and marveled at the interviews with the workers. Disraeli said in *Sybil* that England was comprised of "Two Nations," the rich and the poor, between whom there was no communication. In Mayhew's interviews contact was made.

Theoretically he could have interviewed clergymen, doctors, and do-gooders in the same depth as the workers: he does refer periodically to information from anonymous well-placed sources. But he was really just one man trying to investigate the whole of London's poorer workers, and he had to limit what he covered. He chose the lives and opinions of the workers, and that was both an historic decision and the source of his importance to us. Since his fellow reporters for the "Labour and the Poor" series from the manufacturing and rural districts made the opposite decision and took little note of workers' thoughts and feelings, the decision to do otherwise was clearly Mayhew's, not newspaper policy.

He did not ignore official opinion. While management was uncooperative, the "authorities" generally were not. In *London Labour and the London Poor* he acknowledges the help of the Home Secretary, Lord Grey. Mayhew used government sources but the weight of the reports is in a variety of lower-class informants. By 1851 he was fully aware of the significance of this aspect of his work. In the preface to volume 1 of *London Labour and the London Poor* he said his purpose in this was "to give the rich a more intimate knowledge of the sufferings, and the frequent heroism under those sufferings, of the poor."

So, like the other series, that on the merchant marine contained many personal histories of sailors on both sea and shore. After three articles devoted to "seamen afloat," which included interviews with sailors on the Australian, South American, African, West and East Indian routes, Mayhew had to interrupt this survey to collect data about seamen ashore. As a fill-in series he began an investigation of the Ragged Schools, which soon landed him in a hot controversy and provoked the first significant negative response to his work.

Education for the lower classes at mid-century was essentially nonexistent. However, there was some feeling that part of the reason for what appeared to be an increase in the rate of crime, particularly "juvenile" crime, in the 1840s was the result of this lack of education. Though not specifically designed for the purpose of reducing juvenile crime, Ragged Schools were part of an early Victorian concern that was motivated by the belief in the connection of crime and ignorance. In 1844, with the blessing and guidance of Lord Ashley among other well-known philanthropists, the Ragged School Union was founded to administer a series of evening schools where poor children could learn to read and write.

Mayhew had scoffed at the notion that reading and writing per se had an effect on morals in his pamphlet *What to Teach and How to Teach It*. So he began the three-part series on the Ragged Schools for "Labour and the Poor" with some predisposition against the claims that had been made for the schools. His whole series was by and large an attack on the Ragged Schools conducted through interviews. Since the crime rate had apparently gone up after the founding of the schools, he argued not only that the schools had had no effect on the crime rate but that, by bringing together the different members of the lower classes indiscriminately, had actually contributed to crime: boys with criminal activities corrupted whatever innocent boys also attended.

We do not have to spend much time uncovering the hidden assumptions and fallacies in Mayhew's deductions here, except to note that such broad generalizations based on raw figures were by no means uncommon for the period. What is of note is that Mayhew failed in this series to protect himself and his claim of objectivity in the way that had become normal for him, namely, to try to find examples of all different aspects of opinion.

The reaction against Mayhew's articles, however, was as unreasonable as his initial attack. The *Morning Chronicle,* which editorially supported the Ragged Schools, reported various meetings of Ragged School boards, who responded in one way or another to Mayhew's charges. The culmination of this was a letter from the secretary of the Ragged School Union to the *Morning Chronicle.* It was printed in full, as was Mayhew's answer. The Secretary responded to Mayhew's charges by attacking the reporter—his accuracy, his interviewing, and above all his intentions.

Mayhew tried to answer all this in Letter 49 (25 April 1850). He introduced testimonials by some of his colleagues who had been with him during his interviews and who affirmed his honesty and denied that he had led witnesses or suppressed information. After sifting the evidence, we have concluded that though Mayhew was biased, his bias did not show itself in the manipulation of the interviews. Rather it turned up in the uncritical deductions based on questionable statistics and in the one-sidedness of the letters on the Ragged Schools themselves. Within weeks Mayhew was to be embroiled in another controversy over criticism of the model "Sailors Home," but this time he gave voice to both sides, and so could with justice claim that he was not supporting one side or another but was just "reporting the facts." His attitude toward the Ragged Schools was less disinterested, and to some readers who wanted to ignore the implications of all Mayhew's reports, this series was an easy way to discredit him.

The second controversy over the Sailors Home was part of Mayhew's continuing survey of the merchant marine. After a letter on the "Coasting Trade" up and down the British coasts, a group of three letters during late March and early April surveyed the accommodations for sailors "ashore." Mayhew was interested in the various levels of boardinghouse, from the respectable Sailors Home, which he, following his informants, thought was too rigid in its rules and hence discouraged rather than encouraged sailors to frequent it, to the notorious dives where thieves, prostitutes, and con men preyed on sailors on the loose after months if not years at sea and with all their pay in their pockets. Mayhew described how the "crimps" or touts for unreliable boardinghouses lured the unwary sailor into the dens by capturing his gear and taking it away. Again the testimony in the interviews was sensational; yet there was no public outcry similar to that against "slop" clothing makers, except when Mayhew seemed to be attacking the Sailors Home, which like the Ragged Schools was a middle- and upper-class charity. Perhaps the readers were worn out by or too accustomed to revelations of exploitation and misery. Yet the muted response to these tales of human suffering, especially when compared to the energetic response to his criticisms of the Ragged Schools and the Sailors Home, suggests another explanation. The middle and upper classes were moved by distress that they could identify with just as they were angered by attacks on institutions they created. And it was much easier for Mayhew's readers to identify with the skilled workmen or even more, the distressed women shirtmakers, however down and out they were, than with the rough sailors.

After completing his investigations with a discussion of charitable institutions for sailors, Mayhew made a major shift in the structure of his investigations. This was another step in the development of his perceptions of the labor situation in London. He had always wanted his work to be "scientific," by which he meant inductive in method—drawing general laws governing the economy from a mass of particular facts, first collected by himself. From the beginning, however, he realized that it was going to take a very long time—years—to collect all the data. Nonetheless, he still wanted to theorize and in various ways throughout the next two years, he made stabs at deductions from the "facts" he had accumulated.

In the *Morning Chronicle* he begins this theorizing by formulating a classification that will bring all types of work into an orderly pattern. In his third letter he could only say that the poor could be classified "according to their employments, under three heads—Artisans, Labourers, and Petty Traders" (26 Oct. 1849). Now his categories were artisans, laborers, and servants. Artisans he decided to classify further according to the material they worked on, which included not only raw materials (wood, metal, glass, etc.), but also provisions, animals, and so forth. He intended this more refined method of organization to shape the rest of his investigations. He was going to begin with "the workers in wood" and treat every single aspect of this classification before moving onto the next group of workers in metal. But because of his dispute with his editors, Mayhew did not get to the metal workers.

Before he could begin this new way of proceeding, Mayhew and his associates needed some time to pull together various reports and documents. He turned to another group to fill the space, the "outdoor workers." He had looked at the hucksters earlier. Now, from 16 May 1850 through 13 June 1850, four and a half articles appear made up of some interesting but abbreviated interviews with various "street showmen and performers," a large group of itinerant entertainers who either individually or as part of a group made a living in the streets of London. Many were legitimate performers, but some used their meager activities as a cover for begging. These four letters would in 1856 provide the basis for the first half of volume 3 of *London Labour and the London Poor*. While involved in preparing the material on the workers in wood, the Metropolitan Correspondent reported on talks with performers of feats of strength and manual dexterity, clowns of various sorts, drums and pipes players, other musicians and vocalists, street artists and exhibition keepers.

By the second half of June, Mayhew was able to begin his more "scientifically" organized survey with a "general survey of the timber trade" followed by an article on dock laborers at the timber docks. From that he moved to the construction industry, treating sawyers, carpenters, and "moulding, planing, and veneering mills" in four letters. Next he turned to furniture makers, a skilled trade that was suffering from the same system of subcontracting as the clothing workers. In discussing the "slop" side of cabinetmaking Mayhew reported a number of powerful personal histories. The final three letters treated turners (who worked lathes), ship and boat builders, and finally coopers (who made wooden barrels).

As we can easily see, the general scope of these thirteen letters appearing over three months was much larger than that of the earlier investigations into the clothing workers and the merchant marine. Mayhew must have sensed that the amount of detail in his initial interviews plus the number of such interviews in each subdivision of each trade had rendered impossible his goal of covering "Labour and the Poor" in London in any inclusive way. And so with this new series he made a choice which, while perfectly reasonable from the point of view of investigative reporting or "scientific" study, had the effect of limiting the appeal of his surveys. By starting with a larger segment of the work force in mind—all the workers in wood—Mayhew was forced to limit the number of interviews he reported, and probably the number he conducted as well, and in some cases to reduce the breadth and depth of the individual interview itself, though there are still a number of compelling "biographies." Thus he tended to undermine the elements in his work that have the greatest value— the sympathetic, detailed, to some degree rambling interviews with worker upon worker.

We cannot blame Mayhew for doing this. Yet we can regret his movement from a narrow range that, because it went deep, allows us to glimpse the human dimension of the lower classes, to the broader range more typical of modern surveys, whose scope is achieved through the use of standardized questions. In such works we lose the individual to the larger picture. Had Mayhew continued in this way, we would never have had *London Labour and the London Poor*. But as it happened, such condensation and generalization did not fit his genius and in *London Labour and the London Poor* his mania for detail and curiosity about lower-class lives was unchecked.

One aspect of the articles on the workers in wood has considerable interest. In the course of them Mayhew finally rejects the laissez-faire explanation for low wages and articulates other reasons wages had fallen in the London trades. At the beginning of the series he attacks the middle-man system at length. He sees it as the main cause of low wages: "Whether the middleman goes by the name of sweater, chamber-master, lumper, or contractor, it is this trading operative who is the great means of reducing the wages of his fellowmen. To make a profit out of the employment of his brother operatives he must obtain a lower-class labourer" (58, 27 June 1850). He expands and develops this idea throughout all his investigations into the workers in wood. He also deals with the effect of machinery on employment. Finally, by comparing the statistics regarding the number of London carpenters and the rate of their wages, he saw there was no cause and effect among the demand for workers, the number of carpenters available, and the rate of wages. If the decrease in wages was not here or elsewhere the result of an "excess population," to what was it due? Through his experiences in investigating the "dishonorable" part of each trade where piecework prices had been substituted for a set wage Mayhew thought he had the answer. In piecework, when wages were lowered, workers were forced to get through more work to earn the same wage. "Underpay makes overwork," as Mayhew put it. The initial reduction could come from a number of sources: limited markets, a sudden influx of immigrants like the Irish who came to England during the potato famine in 1846-1848, a desire to reduce costs. The individual worker could get through this extra work by "scamping" (inferior or incomplete work), by using his family, or by subcontracting. But this was not the end of it. By managing to get through the extra work for lower pay, a worker *insured* that the price per piece would be permanently lowered. Every time he agreed to work for less, he drove down his wage and that of others further: "overwork makes underpay."

At this point in time Mayhew felt he could say nothing about the implications of his explanation for low wages. He was cautious about general application of his findings: "almost every craft suffers from some system of labor peculiar to itself" (66, 22 Aug. 1850). Nonetheless, wages depended as much on the distribution of labor as the supply and demand of it. Moreover, his verbalization of these unorthodox ideas in the pages of the *Morning Chronicle,* a staunch supporter of the conventional view, was a brave step and undoubtedly exacerbated his situation at the newspaper.

Mayhew later said that he refused to do the series on the metal workers because of his argument with the *Morning Chronicle* editors over their editing out of his reports various statements critical of free trade. Certainly the editors and Mayhew had come to a parting of the way. But even though he did not embark on the workers in metal, he did begin a new series of five articles on the transit workers. Per-

haps this was because a survey of transit workers was a narrower enterprise than the metal workers would have been. Also there had been
several government investigations of the subject a few years before so
there was plenty of documentary evidence if he did not have the time
or the inclination to conduct original investigations. There certainly
is a good deal of official material in this series, and Mayhew himself
considered it incomplete. Nonetheless, there are as usual a few interviews of note, particularly the reminiscences of a hackney coachman.

The five letters include a survey of ominibus drivers, conductors
and time-keepers, hackney coachmen and drivers, carters and porters,
and a single article on the water transit system—watermen, lighter-
men, and steamboatmen. At this point, almost a year to the day after
he had started his investigation of "Labour and the Poor" as Metropolitan Correspondent, Mayhew was finished. Eight more articles appear from mid-October to mid-December and there is some evidence
that Mayhew was involved in the research if not the writing of these
last contributions from the Metropolitan Correspondent.

He and the *Morning Chronicle* parted on bad terms, intensified by
various public statements on both sides about the other's culpability.
The hard feelings might account for the failure of Mayhew's contributions, particularly those on the tailors and seamstresses, to find a
final, permanent form. They are still today not completely available
except in the microfilm rooms of major research libraries, though Caliban Books of London plans to reprint them in six volumes.

London Labour and the London Poor.   At the same time that
Mayhew was breaking off his relationship with the *Morning Chronicle,*
he was making arrangements to continue his work in a publication of
his own. This project began in December 1850 and Mayhew gave it
a title that was close enough to that of the *Morning Chronicle* series so
that the public would recognize its connection but just different
enough to indicate its variant form.

He saw this publication as a continuation of his survey of London
occupations organized according to the system he devised toward the
end of the *Morning Chronicle* series—workers in wood, in metal, and
so forth. On the cover of one of the early numbers he printed a detailed breakdown of this system of classification.

The format of *London Labour and the London Poor,* however, was different from that of "Labour and the Poor." In the first place, it was
to be a serial publication published by Mayhew, printed by a commercial printer, and distributed through booksellers and other regular

outlets. Serial publications of all sorts had been very popular from the beginning of the century, and Mayhew used the form consistently.

The weekly parts of *London Labour and the London Poor,* about eighteen pages each, came out with a distinctive cover, and sold for twopence. Each part contained a woodcut of one of the street sellers described in that number and engraved after a photograph by the early Victorian photographer Richard Beard. (Unfortunately the original photographs have disappeared.) The page was divided into two columns of print with various subheadings which broke up the sea of black type. As usual with serial publications of this sort, the parts were intended to be bound into a volume when complete.

The most important differences in this mode of publication were the reduction in resources in terms of money and staff, as well as ease of access, and the professional stature lent the reporter by his association with a major daily newspaper. Mayhew had only the reputation earned while at the *Morning Chronicle* to gain him the cooperation of official bodies, access to documents, and help in finding informants. His reputation was considerable, however, and he had made many important contacts among the working classes and their friends in his year at the *Morning Chronicle.* But because he had to do almost everything himself, though he did have some helpers, and because he became increasingly fascinated with London street life, he never continued the survey of London occupations.

Mayhew carried forward with him some strengths he had developed while at the newspaper, as well as all the knowledge he had gained about the labor scene in London. Thus *London Labour and the London Poor* had a few similarities to his contributions to "Labour and the Poor." Most significantly, in both works he used the interview— "street biographies" he called them in *London Labour and the London Poor*—as the main evidence. The form of these biographies is similar too, his questions being absorbed into the answer and the whole presented as a continuous narrative.

One other similarity between the "Labour and the Poor" articles and *London Labour and the London Poor* has a negative effect on the reader's ability to comprehend *London Labour and the London Poor* as a whole. We have seen how the earlier articles reflected the necessarily unsystematic way Mayhew discovered his topics and developed his methods of control. The pressure of several publications a week and the failure to ever go back and reorganize leads to a confused picture, though individual details remain clearly etched in one's mind. *London*

Labour and the London Poor begins with a stronger general control, but midway in volume 1, for reasons discussed below, the control slips. It becomes hard to get a "fix" on the whole of *London Labour and the London Poor.* The unwary reader is not likely to be aware of this because he reads *London Labour and the London Poor* in a very impressive book form which connotes a finished work. This book format is misleading, however, for the volumes are simply unrevised reprints of the numbers that were written and printed week by week. The four-volume series again essentially records the evolution of Mayhew's investigations and opinions rather than a finished product.

Mayhew could not begin his survey of London workers immediately in the first number of *London Labour and the London Poor,* he said, because he needed time to collect the data, a familiar excuse. So, just as he had done twice before, he turned to the people who made a living in various ways in the streets of London. He planned to spend six months on the street trades, he said initially, and then move on to the "Producers."

There were several advantages for Mayhew in this decision. First of all, he had already done many of the interviews. Secondly, there was very little published information about this "occupation"; therefore little had to be worked up. Mayhew himself was the expert simply by virtue of his having collected the facts. Not only did this make meeting the weekly deadline for copy easier but also he could feel he was contributing something really unique.

There was, furthermore, a literary and journalistic tradition behind a survey of street life that assured an interested audience much as the "iconology of the seamstress" had done for his previous series, though Mayhew probably did not consciously think of writing in the tradition of London "low life" sketches when he turned to the street folk at the beginning of *London Labour and the London Poor.* This tradition stretched back over a hundred years to the broadsheets and lives of criminals that were such a lively trade in earlier periods. In the Victorian age the interest in the subject was as intense as ever. Much of this curiosity was about crime itself. But the term "low life" covers other individuals outside the social norm—the professional vagrants, the harmlessly mad, and people who have bizarre occupations and unconventional lives. Part of their fascination is due to their apparent liberation from the conventions that tie the readers down—social class, family, responsibility. We are attracted by their "otherness" and by the freedom it seems to give them. "High life" is equally fascinating for the same reasons, and it has its own literary tradition, the "silver fork" school that in our age has become the best-selling novels of Hollywood, of the "jet set" and of the *Vogue* model.

Throughout the two decades that preceded Mayhew's survey of street life many articles and books had either described "low life" or used it as a piquant background for a fictional account. Even the most respectable newspapers carried a large number of long accounts of "horrible" and "dreadful" events. The most famous of the purely fictional works was Pierce Egan's *Life in London* (1821) which recounted the various adventures of two wild Regency bucks, Tom and Jerry, in many different areas of London and with many different types of people. Dickens's earliest efforts, the *Sketches by Boz,* have many pieces in the same tradition, and his later journals *Household Words* and *All the Year Round* also contain articles on the more unusual corners of London life. His novels feed on the same tradition. The French series by Eugene Sue, *Les Mystères de Paris* (1843), which was very popular in England, had many accounts of low life, and G. W. M. Reynolds issued the *Mysteries of London,* modeled on Sue, from 1844–1848. Even Charles Knights's *London* (1841–1844), a publication for the evangelical Society for the Diffusion of Useful Knowledge, had some descriptions of low life. As the century wore on, there were many books with titles similar to *Curiosities of London Life* by Charles Manby Smith, 1853.

The most important characteristic of this literary-journalistic tradition is the tone of many pieces of low-life reporting. Much is outrightly sensational. Within this response, however, are subtler elements: shock at the more ugly and dehumanizing aspects, outrage at the social injustice involved with any group on the periphery of the law, and curiosity about the details of day-to-day life. There is a sense of superiority that the "other" is not us. But there is also that element of wonder, even of envy of the seeming liberation from job, family, church, state.

Readers of *London Labour and the London Poor* will recognize this tone in Mayhew's interviews with and descriptions of patterers (itinerant salesmen who sell goods by keeping up a clever spiel), costermongers, even vagrants and beggars, all the types who loved, in the words of one of them, "to shake a free leg." This mixed feeling on the reader's part, an "attraction of repulsion" as John Forster said of Dickens's feelings about the slums, is certainly one of the driving forces behind the achievement of *London Labour and the London Poor.*

Mayhew did not consider himself in this tradition, however, because he was trying instead "to apply the laws of the inductive philosophy" to an investigation of a neglected (they were not even counted for the most part in the census) and hence unknown segment of society, whose importance to the lower classes Mayhew came to respect more and more. His intentions thus for *London Labour and the London Poor* put that work squarely in the mode of the "social scientific" "Labour and the Poor" articles. He hoped that his new work would be even more "scientific," for in his prospectus for *London Labour and the London Poor* he said his intention was to present his earlier material "so condensed and revised as to be made bookworthy."[8] The subject of the street folk got in the way of his goal. The closer he looked at them the more he saw. He was not only a camera, as his colleague Charles Mackay said, but also a microscope.[9] With no outside controls, no editors or institutional limits, the "fill-in" series expanded to over one thousand densely printed pages.

Street vending in London was probably as old an occupation as the city itself. It had been made famous in words and pictures by the eighteenth-century collection *The Street Cries of London*. Street people of various sorts turn up in much nineteenth-century literature from the blind beggar that upset Wordsworth so much in Book 7 of *The Prelude* to the Artful Dodger and beyond in the novels of Dickens. They were a permanent part of the journalism of low life, the comic stage, and the whole of urban literature of the Victorian period.

They had an important economic role in the lives of the London working classes also. They were the main if not the sole source of food and domestic goods for much of the working population. Costermongers (from *costard,* a kind of apple), who sold vegetables, fruit, or fish, carried these goods into neighborhoods devoid of shops. Also they would sell very small quantities of food, which was crucial to many working-class families who lived from weekly payday to payday, and even more so to the pieceworkers and others who lived from day to day, sometimes hour to hour. These groups had the money to buy only what they needed at the moment. Many of the street sellers, especially in 1850 when Mayhew was writing, had themselves been skilled or semiskilled workers, and for various reasons—an injury, lack of work, a desire to be outside—had turned to street selling.

The sellers usually worked alone though an established costermonger might have a boy helper. The costermongers and other sellers of food who sold a few apples or watercresses from a tray bought their

goods early every morning at the various London markets—Farring-
don for watercresses and other green stuff, Covent Garden for fruits
and vegetables, Billingsgate for fish, Leadenhall for meat and poultry.
After arranging the goods in their barrows or on their trays, they
would trek through various streets until it was gone. Then they deducted the "stock money" to buy the goods for the next day, and
what was left was their wage. On Saturday night—payday for the
regularly employed—there was a large outdoor market where many
vendors congregated. Mayhew described the scene at this market
early in *London Labour and the London Poor*. Traditionally some costermongers had fixed stands, but in the year between Mayhew's first survey of the group and the beginning of *London Labour and the London
Poor*, legislation had been introduced under pressure from shop owners that could be used to force street sellers to move. The penalty for
failure to do so was the loss of the wheelbarrow and the stock.

In addition to food, nearly every other conceivable item was available somewhere on the streets of London. The investigation and enumeration of this rich variety of goods is the subject of volume 1 of
London Labour and the London Poor, in which Mayhew goes to extraordinary lengths to catalog each type of street seller in existence in
1850.

Beyond the sellers there was an enormous body of other activities
among the street folk: the familiar old-clothes man who bought
goods rather than sold them; some groups who neither bought nor
traded, but who "found" goods which they then sold—old cigar
butts, dogs' dung (used in the tanning industry), pieces of coal that
had fallen from carts, and so on. And there were all the performers
and entertainers whom Mayhew had looked at briefly in the latter
part of "Labour and the Poor."

Much common prejudice existed against the street folk at this
time. In the popular mind they were associated indiscriminately with
the rest of London low life—thieves, conmen, prostitutes, and beggars. Undoubtedly there was some overlap. Many street folk lived on
the edge of financial disaster every day and a turn to petty crime
would not be surprising when disaster hit. Furthermore, the street
folk lived in many of the same neighborhoods as the criminal elements, and so there was proximity even if there was no actual mixture of the two groups.

This whole element in the lower classes was frequently thought to
have few moral restraints, little intelligence, and to be of a biologi-

cally-determined violent nature. They were called "the dangerous classes" because people feared that at the least opportunity the whole lot would run amok and storm the bastille of Victorian peace and prosperity. Mayhew's general comments sometimes support these prejudices, though the "data" of his interviews just as often undermine them. But finally he refused to accept the biological determinism he himself advocated as an explanation; as early as the third number he says "I am anxious to make others feel, as I do myself, that we are the culpable parties in these matters,"[10] a moral he repeated throughout London Labour and the London Poor.

This varied and extensive world then—some 40,000 people by his calculation in a city of two and a half million—was the subject he took upon himself as a short six-months survey while he pulled together his material on the various trades.

He began the first number of his new periodical with an effort at generalization, linking those who made their living in the streets with "wandering tribes" of different sorts throughout the world. It was not a very good theory, and it had the bad effect of suggesting that the street folk were a separate, barbaric race.[11] But this effort only took up two pages, and then Mayhew came to his real subject, the London street folk. He demonstrates his initial control over his subject by detailing at this early point, before the data of the interviews, a six-part classification of street folk into sellers, buyers, finders, performers, artisans, and laborers. He then subdivides each of these six categories into the various types of goods dealt with. He follows the initial outline of sellers, buyers, and finders more or less systematically in the first two volumes. The third volume, not written until 1856, covers the performers pretty much in the order in which he lists them initially, though the survey is unfinished. He was not able to investigate the artisans and laborers before the project stopped.

After this outline Mayhew begins his survey with the costermongers and has some fifty-five pages of general information about them. This section is made up of statistics, historical texts, immediate descriptions, general observations of his own and of an unnamed "expert" source, and finally direct quotations from his informants. There are also two extended statements by a coster boy and a coster girl.

General topics covered in this prelude are the character of costermongers in general, the elements and conditions of their personal lives, their various activities when not working, their opinions about politics, religion, and other things, how they conduct their business, and their place in the economy. These topics are not developed in this order necessarily, and there is some repetition and overlapping. The highlights of this fifty-odd page general discussion are the many quotations of the costers themselves, such as that from the boy who tells Mayhew "the worst of hair is . . . that it is always getting cut off in quod [jail], all along of muzzling the bobbies" (1: 36). There are also good descriptions of the markets, a gambling game, even the obscene entertainment at a "penny gaff" (a storefront theater) which seriously offended Mayhew, but of which he gives a lengthy though general account. In the manner of his investigations for the *Morning Chronicle* he visits and describes the homes of three costermongers: one who is in comfortable circumstances, one who is struggling, one who is destitute.

This opening section of Mayhew's survey of the street sellers contains a large variety of information. As usual, we have to be careful in using his statistics and in crediting individual witnesses, some of whom are introduced in as casual a way as when "the person whom I was with brought to me two girls, who, he informed me, had been forced to go on the streets to gain a living" (1: 60). But the general picture of a hard-working, sometimes unreliable, essentially ignorant population emerges convincingly. Their words, opinions, and experiences give us a glimpse intense in depth and detail of a part of Victorian London life that was inarticulate in its own day and lost to us in our own, except for Mayhew's work.

The picture continues to gain density and resonance in the succeeding sections of *London Labour and the London Poor*. Mayhew starts to examine each individual sub-section of the general category of street seller, that is, the fish sellers (1: 61–78), the fruit and vegetable sellers (1: 79–120), and so on. In this more detailed look at the various street sellers Mayhew for the most part maintains the same format for each discussion. As in the *Morning Chronicle* series he begins with a general survey of the "trade," including a history, whatever statistics are available, a description of the market, and any other general characteristic that he runs across, for example "forestalling" at Billingsgate, a system which is used to save money by buying in large quantities. Frequently there will be a long interview with a well-informed and articulate member of the "trade" about the business in general. Another summary appears at the end of each major section.

These final summaries contain the statistics for each group as well as Mayhew's methods of arriving at the final figures. For example, at the end of the large section on "street-sellers of eatables and drinkables" he gives five pages of statistical summary, beginning with the estimate that "in summer there are, in addition to the 10,000 costers before mentioned, about 3,000 people, and in winter between 4,000 and 5,000, engaged in the eatable and drinkable branch of the street-traffic" (1: 208). In addition, he tries to estimate for each class of seller in this group the total capital, so that the three hundred who sell hot eels represent £339-10-0 in capital and take in yearly £19,448. Here as elsewhere the context of the figures gives a picture of the relative numbers and earnings of the different groups.

After his general introduction, Mayhew again divides the topic, this time into the different categories of fish or vegetable or whatever kind of seller it is, that is, wet-fish, sprats, oysters, etc. Though usually some statistics are included, each of these sections is primarily taken up by a long "representative" interview or street biography of one of the sellers. These biographies along with the descriptions of various scenes dominate the volumes of *London Labour and the London Poor,* providing its tone, its interest, and its value.

In volume 1 Mayhew covers the street sellers of fish; of fruits and vegetables; of game, poultry, rabbits, butter, cheese, and eggs; of trees, shrubs, flowers, roots, seeds, and branches; of green stuff (watercresses, bird food, turf); of eatables and drinkables; of stationery, literature, and the fine arts; and of manufactured goods. He does this with a number of digressions, either to related topics that he discovers in the course of his investigation or else various comments and observations by himself. Both these kinds of digressions also appeared in "Labour and the Poor" and are another link between the two works.

Examples of the first kind of digression, the related topic, in volume 1 include a section on the Irish, the result of his seeing many impoverished Irish street sellers of oranges, watercress, and other marginal products; descriptions of the literature and songs sold by the patterers, and what amounts to a whole subsection on the patterers as a class. Other lengthy interruptions concern low lodging houses, which he discusses in two different places, in the second of which he reprints interviews from "Labour and the Poor" and the account of a meeting of vagrants. He also has a long section on the blind as street sellers.

An example of the second kind of digression comes at the end of the section on costermongers. Mayhew affirms the general belief in the costermongers' amorality and ignorance and their "dangerous" threat to the state. But he insists again that it is not their fault but that of their "betters" who have utterly ignored them, given them no education or healthy entertainments. This moral, repeated periodically in *London Labour and the London Poor,* is a reflection of what he later said, in his German travel book, was his purpose in all his writing; to reconcile the classes by showing that differences in status and worldly position were a matter of God's providence and hence nothing to feel superior about. He thus preached tolerance between classes and self-help within them. He himself tried to start a self-help group, "The Friendly Association of London Costermongers," which would provide the services of a savings and loan bank, an insurance company, legal counsel, a police force, a school, and a social manager all combined. In 1851 the organization was dormant for lack of funds and soon after collapsed when the secretary embezzled the few pounds that had been donated. In the same connection Mayhew reported on a meeting of costermongers he had held while he was still at the *Chronicle* to which he said some one thousand street sellers came.

At the end of the section on patterers Mayhew included a number of pages of his own conclusions about the London street folk. He makes a distinction here among those bred to the streets, those who take to the streets by choice, and those driven to the streets. He repeats his assertion that it is his readers who are responsible for the benighted nature of these people.

Mayhew's interviews in *London Labour and the London Poor* are more inclusive than most of those in "Labour and the Poor." He reports a wide variety of side remarks and expansions by his informants and an equally wide range of topics: family history, previous life, experience of the trade past and present, personal characteristics and opinions, and the figures about earnings. For the most part these interviews are reported as though spoken by the subject, but occasionally Mayhew himself will summarize the information. In these cases, however, he nearly always inserts into the summary some quotation from the subject; for example, "at thirteen years old she was sent to prison (she stated) 'for selling combs in the street' (it was winter and there were no flowers to be had)" (1: 136).

The sheer numbers of street people quoted either briefly or at length is impressive. There may be five hundred or more, though the same informant may be used more than once. Mayhew in his preface said he had had contact with "some thousands of the humbler classes in society." Every reader will have his or her own list of favorite interviews and descriptions. Most readers will include the coster-lad (1: 39–40), who tells Mayhew "I have heerd a little about our Saviour,— they seem to say he were a goodish kind of man; but if he says as how a cove's to forgive a feller as hits you, I should say he know'd nothing about it"; the pitiful flower girl (1: 136); the eight-year-old watercress girl (1: 151–52), who says "No; people never pities me in the street—excepting one gentleman, and he says, says he, "What do you do out so soon in the morning?' but he gave me nothink—he only walked away." Or the ham sandwich seller (1: 177–78), most of the patterers, especially the street stationer quoted at length (1: 267–69), the crippled seller of nutmeg grinders (1:329–33), who is "unable even to stand and cannot move from place to place but on his knees, which are shod with leather caps, like the heels of a clog, strapped around the joint," and the tinware seller (1: 355–58).

The system of classification Mayhew was using begins to break down in the section on sellers of stationery, literature, and the fine arts. There are several reasons for this. First, this was material that he had not covered in "Labour and the Poor" in any depth and hence he had to grapple in the printed pages for control over new material. In addition, these sellers were an interesting, frequently intelligent, and by definition articulate and verbal group. Mayhew had more material, and most of it new, to deal with; as a result much of it got into the pages of *London Labour and the London Poor* in a "raw" form.

The next section, on the sellers of manufactured articles, also presented problems. There were a bewildering array of goods, the mere enumeration of which takes several paragraphs: metal goods (cutlery, needles, jewelry, medals, children's gilt watches, tinware and dog collars), crockery and glass, textiles (soft wares, tapes, lace, japan table-covers, braces, hose, waistcoats), and finally the many different kinds of chemical goods (blacking, black-lead, French polish, grease-removing compositions, plating balls, corn salves, glass and china cement, razor-paste, crackers and detonating balls, lucifer matches, cigar-lights, gutta-percha heads, flypapers and beetle-wafers, and rat poison). There was also a group of unclassifiable sellers of walking sticks, whips, tobacco pipes, snuff boxes, cigars, sponges, wash leathers, spectacles and eyeglasses, dolls, roulette boxes, rhubarb and spice, rat-catchers, combs, money-bags, and coat studs. Mayhew's system of classification was good, but not precise enough to bring this large variety under control. The lack of a clear organization is further indicated and the reader further confused by the inconsistent type used to indicate the various divisions and subdivisions. For example, the section on women street sellers has a title in type size indicating it as a major division, which it is, according to the table of contents. But the section on children street sellers which follows and which is also listed in the contents as a major section is introduced in the text with small type indicating it as a minor subdivision. This typographical difference is one more way in which the unrevised weekly publication manifests itself in the final volumes.

Mayhew's conclusions about the street sellers and his sense of what he is doing appear again in the early pages of volume 2 as well as in the "preface" which he wrote for volume 1 when it was issued in book form in June 1851. In this preface he described the way he expected volume 2 to develop; he would not only include the street buyers, finders, performers, artisans, and laborers, but also Jews, Italians, and other foreigners. In book form volume 1 is also dedicated to Douglas Jerrold, perhaps in recognition of his influence on Mayhew's social conscience, perhaps as tribute to his fighting social commentary. The 1851 volume 1 also includes an index and a list of errata but not "Answers to Correspondents."

What picture of the street sellers emerges from this first volume? As a whole these people demonstrate an amazing capacity to make the most of very little, to shift for themselves, to survive under sometimes terrible conditions. They are some of the liveliest, most colorfully articulate people we meet in Victorian literature. They have a rich sense of humor, and they do not complain much about the hardness of their lives. There were important differences among them, and Mayhew's classification of those who are bred to, take to, or are driven to street selling reflects his recognition of this. Yet even he qualifies this view: "There are many grades of vagrants among us, and . . . though they are all essentially non-producing and, consequently, predatory, still many are in no way distinguished from a large portion of even our wealthy tradesmen—our puffing grocers and slopsellers" (1:322).

From our perspective, thanks to the detail and particularity of Mayhew's work, we can see discriminations among the sellers that he does not point out. The "upper classes" of street sellers include most of the keepers of stands for "eatables and drinkables," as well as many of the sellers of more sophisticated paper products like books, or the more unusual or complicated manufactured goods like eyeglasses. On the other hand, at the very bottom of the social scale are the poorest—frequently women and children—who sell watercresses, oranges, matches, tapes, and other "small wares." The costermongers are essentially the "middle class" in this society and can move up and down the scale. Finally, outside class in a way, are the patterers both "running" and "standing." They considered themselves, as one put it, "the haristocracy of the streets" because of their abilities, or as the patterer expressed it "the hexercise of our hintellects" (1:213).

Volume 2 opens with several pages of introduction, but the subject matter is still the street sellers, and Mayhew does not get to the next group for 100 pages. In the beginning he asserts through statistics the economic importance of the street sellers. He estimated that there were around 40,000 of them, and they did around three million pounds in business a year. So that "however unsatisfactory it may be to the aristocratic pride of the wealthy commercial classes, it cannot be denied that . . . a large proportion of the commerce of the capital of Great Britain is in the hands of the Street-Folk" (2:3). Because of this, he felt it grossly shortsighted to try to eliminate street sellers (40,000 people would have to go on relief) and suggested setting up marketplaces in different neighborhoods where sellers could have a regular pitch and where the authorities could check for short weights and other illegal activities. Mayhew's suggestion was not taken up then, but has subsequently become part of the urban scene in London as well as other large cities. His continued support of the working classes and, more important, his belief in their ability to determine their own lives are indicated by the way he described the governing committee of these "poor men's markets": the power would be shared equally among the shareholders (presumably middle- and upper-class philanthropists), the street sellers, and consumer advocates in the person of working men who would represent the customers. In such a committee the lower classes would outnumber their "betters," a highly unusual situation in any Victorian philanthropic project.

The three final divisions of street sellers covered in volume 2 are those who sell secondhand articles like metal objects, cloth, curiosities, and other miscellaneous items; those who sell live animals, mainly birds and dogs, and those selling "mineral productions and natural curiosities" like coal, salt, sand, and "purl," a drink sold to river men from boats. The last is really a disgression rather than an integral part of the survey of street sellers.

These final pages on the sellers continue in the same mode as the previous ones, including loosely related topics on secondhand shops, with an excerpt from one of Dickens's early pieces; a section on the old clothes exchange in London's East End; an account of the wholesale business in old clothes; and a further one on the use of secondhand garments. There are also two good descriptions of the markets for secondhand clothes and other objects—Petticoat Lane (still a thriving market in east London) and Rosemary Lane—and two evocative interviews with the crippled bird-seller and the street seller of birds' nests, both of whom are also represented by engravings. The final statistical summary gives the total figures for the sellers, whom Mayhew numbers now at 43,640 (2:97).

According to his initial classification in both the opening of volume 1 and the preface he wrote at the end of that volume, there were, in addition to the sellers, five other divisions of street folk. From everything he had said up to this point, we expect the rest of volume 2 to be devoted, with the same thoroughness and detail exercised on the sellers, to the five remaining categories. This is not how volume 2 develops, however. Mayhew spends only fifteen pages, the equivalent of one weekly part, on the buyers, breaking the survey in two in order to include a thirty-page discussion of the East End Jews. After this come fifty pages on "finders," among whom he initially includes the refuse collectors.

The buyers and the Jews are linked because, as Mayhew says, "the largest, and, in every respect, the most remarkable body of [street buyers] are the buyers of old clothes" (2:103), a trade almost exclusively in the hands of Jews and one that was iconographically identified with them. (A political cartoon once pictured Disraeli as an old-clothes man.) In the seventeen pages Mayhew devoted to the Jews he gives a brief history of their presence in England, a description of their street trades, a survey of the old-clothes men, several sections on various types of Jewish street sellers, and concludes with a discussion of their religion, amusements, charities, and education. He is impressed by the way the Jews take care of each other, but most of his information comes from secondhand sources. There are only two interviews with street Jews.

He next turns to the "street-finders or collectors." This group is linked to the preceding short survey of buyers because, with a few exceptions, he considered both "of the lower sort, both as to means and intelligence" (2:103). The street-finders—the bone-and-rag grubbers, who searched leftover garbage heaps for old bones and rags to sell to rag and bottle shops; the "pure" finders who collected dogs' dung to sell to tanneries; the cigar-end finders who scoured gutters and streets for butts of cigars to make into "new" cigars, and the mudlarks who rummaged in the shallows of the Thames for loose pieces of coal which had fallen from barges—are among the most bizarre of all Mayhew's subjects. The descriptions in this section include some of rag and bottle shops like Krook's in *Bleak House* by Dickens and marine shops, which bought old metal, drippings, bottles, and rags.

At the end of this major section Mayhew included a statistical chart (not published in 1852), which shows "the quantity of refuse bought, collected, or found, in the streets of London" (2:462–63). The chart allows us to see at a glance what numerous and varied materials were available for street buying or finding—everything from fish skins to cigar ends. Combined with representative statements from different buyers and sellers, this chart presents us with a unique glimpse of a remarkable substratum of Victorian society.

After he finishes with these "street-finders," Mayhew moves to the refuse collectors, and here his organization breaks down. The refuse collectors he lists here include the dustmen who collect household waste; scavengers who clean the streets; the nightmen who empty cesspools; chimney sweeps and crossing sweepers (men, women, and children who stood at curbside to sweep refuse away for pedestrians for which service they were presumably tipped).

Mayhew recognizes in his opening remarks about the finders that the refuse collectors are not really street folk. He says they are connected by having "pursuits carried on in the open air." In addition there is an associative link. Readers of Dickens's *Our Mutual Friend* know that there was a great deal more to "dust" than kitchen slops. The "dust heaps" could be a mine of valuables, and every dust yard had its complement of sifters who went through the garbage for coins, silver, or whatever of value they could find. Thus, dustmen were "finders" of another sort.

Mayhew's text and table of contents show the confusion in the unfolding of this part of his work. Volume 2 from page 159, where the subsection "Of the London Dustmen, Nightmen, Sweeps, and Scavengers" begins, is disorganized, repetitious, and chart-ridden. The table of contents (provided over ten years after the writing of this portion of volume 2) tries to clarify its shape. It makes separate sections of "street-finders or collectors" in which group it includes only the pages on the dustmen. The contents page then gives as the next section "the streets of London" with page numbers including Mayhew's 150-odd page survey of the conditions of the streets, the scavengers, and the rubbish carters. The next section is on the chimney sweeps who have nothing at all to do with the streets but are connected to the "refuse collecting trade." The contents page does not mention the sewermen and nightmen to whom Mayhew devotes forty-nine pages before he was forced to stop his work on *London Labour and the London Poor*. The contents page ends with the section on crossing sweepers, probably written by Augustus Mayhew in 1856.

The 1862 table of contents thus itself represents the volume inaccurately. Since the text for the volume was not changed at all from the 1851 edition, disparities in type and shape remain. Mayhew gives all the refuse collectors a typographical subtitle that suggests they are subdivisions of the street finders, and his introductory comments to that section include them as such. But the discussion of this group got out of control. Partly this was because there was a plethora of official information about refuse collection from various sources: parish records, government reports, and considerable evidence adduced by private groups since sanitary reform was one of the biggest public concerns throughout the period. Mayhew's pages are filled by charts and by lists of figures. He did not have the inclination or the time to digest and summarize most of this forest of figures. For one of the few times in his work, the interviews are buried under the statistical data.

Further confusing the orderly development of this part of volume 2, Mayhew inserts in four different places his conclusions on the causes and cures of low wages and some thoughts about the general economy. He had been working these ideas out on the covers of *London Labour and the London Poor,* the "waste pages" as he put it, and was in a few months to begin to codify them systematically in a serial pamphlet *Low Wages*. This last project was ended after the publication of four of a projected nine numbers.

The subject of this section, however, is the dustman and nightmen, the dredgerman who work in teams to pick up what they can find in the river (Lizzie Hexam's father in *Our Mutual Friend* is an exaggerated type of river hunter: he "dredges" for dead bodies), the sewer-hunters who look for "lost treasure" in the sewer system, and other refuse collectors. Though in some ways their work is as strange to the reader as that of the "pure" finder or the mudlark, theirs was an established trade. They worked in gangs and some were contracted for by the parish. The men got reasonable wages by and large. However, Mayhew discovered that even in this trade there was a tendency to hire cheap casual labor which drove wages down and impoverished all the work force. The articulation of his conclusions about this aspect of the trade and the data and calculations that lay behind his conclusions led to the various discussions of political economy in these final pages of volume 2.

Many of the ideas expressed in these pages about political economy had been formulated in some way in the late articles in "Labour and the Poor." Mayhew was forced to repeat them here, expanding his discussion a little, because he did not want to make any generalizations about the economy in the absence of complete data. In each case the discussion is in the context of a specific trade. This was inevitable, given that Mayhew was publishing his work as he went along. We sense again that we are reading a diary of a social survey rather than the survey itself.

He begins with an effort to provide a statistical description of the amount of dirt that accumulates and needs to be removed each year from the streets of London. In the process of doing this he makes some of his more idiosyncratic calculations, such as that on how much dirty streets cost in terms of clothes washing, and the amount of horse dung produced each day. This last has been quoted over and over again as an example of his crazy statistics, but here, as was frequently the case, Mayhew was using official figures (and says so), a fact that none of the amused critics pointing to the quaintness of this figure have indicated.[12]

After this survey of the dirt on the streets, he turns to the question of how it is to be removed. He summarizes the possibilities and turns to the first one, scavenging, the cleaning of the streets by contract labor. The other ways are by machines, by paupers on welfare, or by "street-orderlies" employed by private philanthropists. When he comes to the subsection on "Of the Working Scavengers under the Contractors," he reminds his readers that this long work on the street folk was really subsidiary to his real project: "I have now to deal with what throughout the whole course of my inquiry into the state of

London Labour and the London Poor I have considered the great object of investigation—the condition and characteristics of the working men; and what is more immediately the 'labour question,' the relation of the labourer to his employer, as to rates of payment, modes of payment, hiring of labourers, constancy or inconstancy of work, supply of hands, the many points concerning wages, perquisites [money or goods added to the regular wage], family work, and parochial or club relief" (2:216). In the course of describing all these details about the scavengers Mayhew also discusses the difference between the "nominal" and the "actual" wage, the way in which "overwork makes underpay" (which he had treated before in "Labour and the Poor"), the uncertainty of the effect of the repeal of the Corn Laws (which resulted in lower bread prices) on workers, the differences between large (standard) employers and small ("cutting") employers in all trades and in the scavengering trade in particular, and the effect of the government using pauper labor on the wages of the regularly employed. He concludes with a discussion of the use of "street orderlies" who kept cleaning the street throughout the day versus scavengering either by contract or paupers once a day.

In this series of discussions Mayhew comes to several different conclusions about the rate of wages. First, the stated wage (the "nominal") wage probably never reflects what the worker actually gets (the "actual" wage). To arrive at the latter one must deduct all the charges against the workers and add any perquisites. Second, the rate of wage is determined by several different things, none of which is a strict supply and demand: "The mere number of labourers in a trade is, *per se,* no criterion as to the quantity of labour employed in it; to arrive at this three things are required:—(1) The number of hands; (2) The hours of labour; (3) The rate of labouring" (2:222). Third, the artificial creation of overwork is usually found in the employment of "small" masters, the "drivers" and "grinders" who force men to longer hours or faster work (2:233). Competitive contracting also tends to lower wages because contractors will not reduce their profit margin to make a low bid but are more likely to reduce the wages of their employees. Finally, any worker who works for below the standard wage—either by choice or because he or she is forced to—contributes to the lowering of wages throughout the trade. These workers who undercut the standard wage include "scurf" scavengers who compete for jobs by working for less, pauper street cleaners who are forced to work for nothing by the Poor Law Boards, and street orderlies, a group paid by philanthropists. Mayhew approves the street-orderly system but only if the workers are paid the standard wage: the "street-orderly system is incomparably the best mode of scavaging, and the payment of the men by the '*honourable*' masters the best mode of employing the scavengers" (2:275). In the course of this discussion Mayhew has some rather hard things to say about the effects of the Poor Law in making people hate work. He also includes a comprehensive list, without comment, on all the ways that have ever been proposed to remedy low wages (2:254–56).

The next large group are the rubbish carters who take away the dirt collected by street cleaners and from buildings and chimneys. Mayhew as usual begins with a general description, heavy on the statistics of the trade, ending with interviews with regular rubbish carters employed in the standard trade. When he turns to the "casual" workers in the rubbish carting trade, he is led into a discussion that repeats much of the material given in the previous pages, especially those on the effect of casual labor on the working classes.

He begins by explaining what gives rise to casual labor: brisk and slack seasons and a surplus of workers. The latter phenomenon had always interested him, and in these twenty-two pages Mayhew sums up all his findings and thoughts about this subject. He had already touched on this in his more general discussions in "Answers to Correspondents" during the preceding year and had been waiting perhaps for an opportune moment to introduce the material into the permanent pages of *London Labour and the London Poor*. He hoped to do the whole thing properly in his series *Low Wages*.

With considerable detail Mayhew deduces that the absolute number of workers had not increased significantly and that the supposed "surplus population" was artificially created by "an alteration in the hours, rate, or mode of working, as well as in the mode of hiring" (2:322). He had discussed before most of the ways in which this was achieved: by increasing the work day or by forcing workers to do more work for the same pay. This was in turn achieved by piecework, by "scamping," by reduction of wages, by "strapping" (increased supervision), by subcontracting (which had been the curse of the clothing trades), or by the replacement of workers by machinery. In all of these ways, management sought to "economize" on labor; as Mayhew said on the covers, where he allowed himself far greater freedom of opinion than in *London Labour and the London Poor* proper, the approved orthodox practice of cutting costs to save money for investment resulted in *"the greatest possible good to the employer, and the greatest possible evil to the employed"* (22, 10 May 1852).

Even if there were numerically more workers in some occupations, these were not necessarily due to "surplus population." Apprentices could be used more than normal; women and children, traditionally not part of the labor market, were now employed in many places, and there were some foreign workers.

Mayhew's final conclusions were uncompromising: "I am led to believe that there is considerable truth in the statement lately put forward by the working classes, that only one-third of the operatives of this country are fully employed, while another third are partially employed, and the remaining third wholly unemployed . . . Adopt what explanation we will of this appalling deficiency of employment, one thing at least is certain: we cannot *consistently with the facts of the country,* ascribe it to an increase of the population beyond the means of labour" (2:322–23).

After the discussion of the causes of casual labor Mayhew moves to the effects of such labor in general. He has a sense of the psychological effects of the uncertainty of work associated with casual labor; it leads, he says, "to improvidence, recklessness, and pauperism," an interesting trio since it suggests pauperism is a frame of mind (2:325). As an example of this cause and its effect, he calculates how much beer drinking increases among out-of-door workers during wet weather.

After this short discussion, Mayhew repeats the points he had made just a few pages before about the way employers could cheapen labor. He goes into a little more detail and includes a number of quotations from various informants, including some of his own from "Labour and the Poor." He discusses the "domestic system," where workers use their homes (and their families) for their work, the "middleman" or "contract" or "lump" or "small master" system (all the terms are used to describe the same process in different trades). About the latter he concludes that "in every trade where there are *small* masters, trades into which it requires but little capital to embark, there is certain to be a cheapening of labour" (2:311). He closes with an examination of the types of cheaper workmen available: the unskillful, the untrustworthy, and the inexpensive—workers who will live on less or else have supplementary incomes.

At this point Mayhew's "political economy" is about as complete as he was to make it. When he turns to the remaining groups of refuse collectors—chimney sweeps, sewermen, and nightmen—he describes the trades without drawing any more conclusions. Each section begins with a general history and survey of the conditions of each group, followed by one or two interviews with representative workmen of the different parts of each trade. Much of the information in the section on crossing sweepers came from parliamentary investigations into child labor. The conditions detailed no longer existed since there had been legislative reform which abolished the practice of sending "climbing boys" into the chimneys to clean them. There are two interviews with current sweeps and one with a "knuller," as the cheap, inferior sweeps were called. The final section is a digression on the statistics of fires in London.

The sections on the sewermen and nightmen are much the same, only there is even less human interest and even more charts and figures. Mayhew considers the different kinds of sewage, the quantity and the nature of the sewers and street drains, plans and management of sewers, and finally methods of cleaning. Here he includes a few short statements by the flushermen who cleaned out the sewers and a digression on rats in sewers. In the last number of *London Labour and the London Poor* written in 1852 but not published until 1861, he compares the cesspools of London and Paris, and includes one interview with a cesspool-sewerman. At this point he had deviated a considerable degree indeed from the London street folk, not to mention the subject of "labour and the poor."

The material written in 1852 stops at this point. Before seeing what he did in 1856 when he returned to the project, we need to look at the opening pages of volume 4 of *London Labour and the London Poor,* which Mayhew wrote at the same time that he was investigating the refuse collectors for volume 2.

The appetite for learning about low life which played a role in Mayhew's increasingly detailed survey of the street folk brought about another shift in *London Labour and the London Poor.* In the beginning, as we have seen, he intended to get back to the working men quickly. Yet correspondents urged him to continue to investigate London low life by looking at thieves and prostitutes, groups he had touched in passing at several points in both "Labour and the Poor" and *London Labour and the London Poor.* He resisted the topic, saying as late as March 1851 that he had no intention of making any investigation of this aspect of London life. Five months later, however, in August 1851 he began an "extra" volume of *London Labour and the London Poor* to deal with "those who will not work" or the criminal classes in London. He charged twice as much for the weekly parts of this "extra" volume because of its supposedly limited interest. The parts appeared alternately with those of volume 2.

Mayhew did not survey either prostitutes or thieves before the collapse of *London Labour and the London Poor;* he provided only the first thirty-seven pages of the "extra" volume. The rest of what became volume 4 was written by other, less talented men: Horace St. John contributed an historical survey of prostitution in 1852; in 1861 the survey of London prostitutes was done by Bracebridge Hemyng, that on thieves and swindlers by John Binny, and that on beggars by Andrew Halliday, all minor journalists of the period.

The first number of the "extra" volume—which Mayhew did write—has interest in terms of his developing position on the subject of labor. In this number he finally evolved a system of classifying the total population of England in terms of work. This classification system, which he takes mainly from John Stuart Mill's *Principles of Political Economy,* was his final statement on the relationships among the population in terms of work. In the two years that had passed between the first "Labour and the Poor" articles and the opening number of the "extra" volume Mayhew had refined his initial distinctions with great thoroughness so that seemingly every conceivable occupation—legal, illegal, or merely nominal—found its place on a chart. It is where, were he writing up the results of his investigations instead of reporting on them as he went along, he would have started. Even this final classification does not have the pride of place it should but is only part of an "introduction" to the non-workers or criminal classes.

Mayhew begins his classification of workers with an analysis of "facts"; they are meaningless by themselves and need to be seen in relationship to each other in order to achieve meaning. (By "facts" he means primarily quantifiable material.) Thus, before collecting all the data about those who "won't work," he feels he must relate that class to the rest of the population. This he proceeds to do, after another sideswipe at Prince Albert's method of classification at the Great Exhibition and at the system used to classify workers in the official census. Mayhew uses instead John Stuart Mill's division of labor, giving it his own labels: *enrichers,* those who produce "exchangeable commodities or riches"; *benefactors,* whose productions are "permanently embodied in human beings"; *servitors,* who confer "some temporary

good upon another." From these divisions of Mill's Mayhew discriminates a fourth group who do not produce anything useful directly
but are only *auxiliaries* "who are employed in aiding the production
of exchangeable commodities." In this group are Mayhew's revolutionary revisions of traditional political economy. He insists that the
capitalist is such an "auxiliary" just as is a bricklayer's helper who
carries the bricks to the man building the wall.

Nowhere is Mayhew's elevation of labor over capital more strongly
stated: "Mr. Mill's mistake in ranking the Employers and Distribu-
tors among the Enrichers, or those who increase the exchangeable
commodities of the country, arose from a desire to place the dealers
and capitalists among the productive labourers, than which nothing
could be more idle, for surely they do not add, *directly,* one brass farthing, as the saying is, to the national stock of wealth" (4:28).

If the capitalists are only auxiliaries to the real producers, labor,
then what are we to make of the wealth of one and the poverty of the
other? Mayhew sees the issue. He concludes by drawing attention to
this unequal distribution of wealth, but he will go no further. "If the
poorer classes require fifteen millions to be added in charity every year
to their aggregate income in order to relieve their pains and priva-
tions, and the richer can afford to have the same immense sum taken
from theirs, and yet scarcely feel the loss, it shows at once how much
the one class must have in excess and the other in deficiency." But
"it is for others to lay bare the cause, and, if possible, discover the
remedy" for this situation (4:35).

Mayhew's whole classification is an impressive effort. He recognized himself that any task like this was bound to be incomplete at
first and qualified his divisions himself immediately after printing
them. Nonetheless, within the elaboration of this system, both in
paragraph and in chart form, there are many important points. For
example, he asserts almost in passing that housewives are "workers"
and so foreshadows one of the tenets of the radical feminist movement
in the latter half of the twentieth century: "I look upon soldiers, sailors, Government and parochial officers, capitalists, clergymen, lawyers, wives, etc., etc., as self-supporting—a certain amount of
labour, or a certain desirable commodity, being given by each and all
in exchange for other commodities, which are considered less desirable to the individuals parting with them, and more desirable to
those receiving them" (4:9–10). In the chart he includes again the
various divisions of operatives he had made in other places by the

material they worked on, by the way they worked and so forth. The two pages devoted to the classification of cheats and thieves is a mine of slang terms, such as "snoozers," those who sleep at railway hotels and decamp with some passengers' luggage or property in the morning, or "flatcatchers," those who defraud by pretending to find some valuable article.

When he comes to introduce the subject of the "non-workers" more generally, Mayhew advances some observations on crime which he will elaborate later in *The Criminal Prisons of London*. He defines the class as those "who object to labour for their living" (as opposed to those who can't), and his first distinction is between those who are habitual or professional criminals and those who are accidental or casual criminals. Mayhew thus argues against the contemporary way of classifying criminals in terms of the criminal act. He substitutes a classification by the "character of the people committing the crimes." The "extra" volume was to deal only with the professional class, which he sees as endemic in society—there will always be those who object to working for a living. He describes generally the different types of thieves and prostitutes and concludes with a set of statistics from the metropolitan police for 1837 showing the number of these professional criminals. Mayhew uses these figures to try to arrive at the total number of people in Great Britain who "won't work."

The first subsection of this group is the prostitutes and Mayhew has a short introduction to them in which he defines prostitution as "the using of her charms by a woman for immoral purposes" (4:35). He has Horace St. John begin the historical survey of prostitution to lay down "the invariable antecedents which excite the moral disgust in every act of prostitution" (4:36). At this point Mayhew's role in this survey ends permanently, though he will take up the question of the criminal classes in general and prostitution specifically in *The Criminal Prisons of London*. Unfortunately, he never interviewed individual members of those classes, a loss to social history.

So ended *London Labour and the London Poor* in February of 1852. When Mayhew took up the project again in 1856, his only intention was to finish the survey of the street folk. He had apparently abandoned permanently the grand survey of "labor and the poor." He seems to have got his brother Augustus to write the equivalent of one number on London crossing sweepers while Mayhew himself expanded his *Morning Chronicle* articles on street entertainers.

Augustus contributed a number of lively interviews, written in his brother's style. He later used his experiences in his own novel *Paved with Gold* where the gangs of children who combined crossing sweeping with gymnastic acts provide a part of the action. There are no statistics in his section, however, and the classification is of the simplest sort: able-bodied and afflicted adult crossing sweepers, and boy and girl crossing sweepers.

Henry Mayhew may have intended a similarly condensed survey of street entertainers, but the simplification involved in such a procedure was not in his style. His material on London workers always expanded in the process of investigation. The street entertainers were no different, though, as in the section on crossing sweepers, there are no statistical summaries such as Mayhew gave on every other branch of the trade, probably because he was not able to finish this investigation. He was writing up his interviews at the end of 1856 when his publisher died. This is also why he never covered the last two of the original six categories of street folk—the street artisans and street laborers. Even the street entertainers are not complete, for the proprietors of street games are omitted as are many of the showmen.

Volume 3 as it was eventually published does not begin with the street entertainers but rather with a section loosely connected to that of the refuse collectors and probably intended as part of that survey. It may have been that this opening section on "The Destroyers of Vermin" was to conclude volume 2, being a natural extension of a discussion of refuse and in no way a natural preface for entertainers. The section includes a fascinating ten-page interview with the Queen's rat catcher, Jack Black, and one with a flypaper maker. It contains a number of digressions, one Augustus said he wrote describing "A Night at Rat-Killing" (where dogs competed to see which could kill the most rats in the shortest time and betting was heavy) at a London tavern and an interview with the proprietor of "one of the largest sporting public-houses in London." There are in addition entomological discussions of the different types of vermin— rats, flies, bugs and fleas, black-beetles, and crickets. Mayhew also reprints essentially unchanged an interview he had during the *Morning Chronicle* series with a poor toymaker who also made mouse traps.

There is no general introduction to the street entertainers, only a headline for the general category immediately followed by one for the first subsection, street exhibitors. The text begins with a monologue by a performer of Punch shows and includes a Punch script. All of the interviews in this section—and the whole 115 pages devoted to the street exhibitors is made up of interviews—are lengthy and informative. The subjects were intelligent and articulate, most of them real craftsmen who enjoyed talking about their lives and work and whom Mayhew clearly liked and respected. They have had varied lives and they are not as beaten down as many of Mayhew's other subjects. The whole section with its long pieces on Guy Fawkes performers, various scientific exhibitions, acrobats and other circus performers, is among the most interesting and informative in the whole of *London Labour and the London Poor.* The same is true for the street biographies produced of the "street musicians," a number of whom were blind, and all of whom had life stories worth telling. One, the poor harp player, had such an affecting tale of woe that when his story was originally told in "Labour and the Poor" he was the recipient of a number of private donations of money. The street artists and an unfinished section on exhibitors of trained animals completes the 1856 half of volume 3.

Most readers will enjoy this part of *London Labour and the London Poor* perhaps more than any other single division. The whole problem about Mayhew's "accuracy" is not as important here either, for neither he nor his subjects had axes to grind. The inevitable errors of memory and transcription and the details of dates and places are not significant to the total picture. Mayhew creates character through gesture, evocative idiosyncracies of speech, peculiar emphases, and so on.

Nonetheless, the reader does have to be cautioned about the time of this picture of street life. A good deal of the material originates in the early 1850s during the "Labour and the Poor" series. Mayhew did not revise the material he used from these earlier pieces nor did he indicate when he was using earlier sources. Some interviews he updated by returning to the subject, as with Old Sarah, the blind hurdy-gurdy singer, but without detailed comparison it is not always possible to tell what in any given interview dates from 1850 and what from 1856. None of it comes from 1861 when Volume 3 was first published. The engravings for volume 3 were probably made in 1856, though that is not clear. Some may be earlier (Old Sarah) and some later. The engravings in volume 4 date from the early 1860s.

With the unfinished interview of the exhibitor of birds and mice Mayhew ends his survey of street entertainers, of the street folk, and of *London Labour and the London Poor.* How the volume reached its final form is a puzzling question. Mayhew seems to have been in Germany from late 1861 to late 1863, a period of time that covers the publication of the four volumes. He probably did not supervise the editorial arrangements for the four volumes, which may account for the inaccuracies of the tables of contents and advertisement, as well as the chaos of the last half of volume 3.

Volumes 1 and 2 are identical in text to the 1851–1852 weekly parts. The first half of volume 3 represents the material Mayhew had pulled together in 1856, but there is no evidence of an effort to do more than reprint the manuscript as it stood in its incomplete form. Perhaps the editors added the titles and tacked the "Destroyers of Vermin" which was meant for volume 2 onto volume 3. They made other mistakes. The uncompleted volume 3 was half as long as volumes 1 and 2. How to make it more consistent in length? The solution was to reprint a series of selections—some 100-odd pages— from Mayhew's 1849–1850 articles as Metropolitan Correspondent. These selections were given the general title in *London Labour and the London Poor* of "Skilled and Unskilled Labour."

Such a plan made good sense. But the incomprehensible part is not that the editors chose to finish volume 3 with reprints of material that was twelve years old, but the articles that were chosen. They represented neither Mayhew's most famous articles as Metropolitan Correspondent (those on the clothing workers) nor his best. Despite the title, volume 3 includes practically no skilled workers at all— only a few "slop" cabinetmakers. Instead this section is made up of pieces from the survey of dock laborers, transit workers (which Mayhew had said was unfinished), and vagrants.

The choice of these particular *Morning Chronicle* articles might have been governed by a desire to put in one place all the material Mayhew had collected on the "longshore workers," a general topic he had frequently referred to in the *Morning Chronicle*. Or since in the classification of workers in the "extra" volume he had one section on "carriers," which included both dockworkers and transit workers, these two surveys were put together in *London Labour and the London Poor*. There is not, however, even a headline in volume 3 to indicate that this was the reason. Moreover, the final selection is even more unrelated; the volume closes with the reprint of a newspaper account of a meeting Mayhew held with ticket-of-leave men in 1856 in connection with his investigations into the London prisons. Probably the availability of proof or copies of all these earlier works was what determined the selection rather than any editorial or "philosophical" concerns.

No editing was done when these materials were reprinted. There are some minor word changes, and blocks of copy were shifted around, which actually results in a more confusing text than the original. Nothing new was added, not even a line to indicate the source of the material in this section. Everything about the second half of volume 3 in fact suggests hurry and carelessness. In one place two consecutive letters are reversed when reprinted and as a result the discussion makes little sense. The section on vagrants is chopped up with pieces from several different letters shuffled together in what seems a completely random manner. One wants to believe that this was the doing of anonymous editors and not of Mayhew himself, for it is hard to think he could be so indifferent to the final form of his own work.

The next year, 1862, the other contributors finished their interviews with the professional criminals for the "extra" volume, which was then published as volume 4 of *London Labour and the London Poor*. Why Mayhew did not come home from Germany where he was so miserable and finish these books himself is not known. Perhaps his finances would not allow it. There is no record of his thoughts about this final publication of his life's major work. We hope he had some satisfaction from the publication, but it came too late to bring him either fame or fortune.

The covers of *London Labour and the London Poor* and *Low Wages*. When Mayhew began *London Labour and the London Poor* in December 1850, each weekly part appeared in a distinctive cover or "wrapper." He used the inside pages of these covers each week for a correspondence column which he titled "Answers to Correspondents." He allowed himself considerable freedom of expression in his remarks in these "waste" pages as he called them. He felt he could give his opinions here because the wrappers were not a permanent record in the way the text was.

Because his work was never finished, however, these "waste" wrappers are essentially the only record we have of Mayhew's methods and intentions, his thoughts and opinions about his experiences, as well as his personal interests and biases. It too is an incomplete record, and one very hard to come by. Many of the opinions and ideas first expressed on the covers are also integrated into the second half of vol-

ume 2 of *London Labour and the London Poor,* and into the unfinished
Low Wages and *The Criminal Prisons of London.* Some idea of the scope
of his "Answers to Correspondents," however, gives a sense of the in-
terplay between Mayhew and his readers.

The subjects under review in "Answers to Correspondents" are necessarily diverse and unorganized. The issues of political economy
dominate for the most part though toward the end, when the "extra"
volume was appearing, there are some comments about prostitution.
The early numbers sketch out Mayhew's intentions for *London Labour
and the London Poor.* He also sets up a separate "loan office for the
poor" under the direction of his publisher John Howden to dispense
whatever donations came in to deserving cases. The size of this fund
was never large, probably because of the size and nature of the read-
ership. While the *Morning Chronicle* fund had contained £800, that
generated by *London Labour and the London Poor* seems not to have ex-
ceeded £30.

Many miscellaneous opinions crop up periodically. Mayhew believed indiscriminate almsgiving was bad; he thought money should
be given as loans and interest charged. "The Poor *are* poor generally
from a want of self-reliance," he said (21, 3 May 1851). "Any system
therefore (however well intentioned) which deprives them of all voice
in the management of their own affairs, can but tend to increase their
helplessness and poverty, and to keep them the same perpetual slaves
of circumstances." Though the specific results of this attitude seem
harsh at times—a five percent interest on loans, an attack on soup
kitchens and other charities—the understanding of the psychology of
poverty that lies behind it comes close to the modern notion that we
can only help people by giving them control over their own lives. It
is a blow against paternalism of every kind, and while that attitude
can be used to deny any welfare at all, Mayhew was never so simplis-
tic. Outside help was obviously needed; it was the mode that was
important to him.

Most topics in the "Answers to Correspondents" column are related
to his social surveys. For example, his experience taught him that
" 'those who have seen better days' constitute the worst class of the
poor" (29, 28 June 1851). Some topics, however, were quite different. He spends a number of pages speculating about the etymology
of various slang terms and entering into debate with readers over
other linguistic matters.

The discussion of different aspects of political economy provides the real value of the "Answers to Correspondents." When combined with the remarks in "Labour and the Poor," in volume 2 of *London Labour and the London Poor,* and in the four parts of *Low Wages* published in November and December of 1851, we can sort out the position Mayhew's experiences brought him to in the course of his investigations.

The most important aspect of his ideas is his angle of vision. The nature of his investigations had readjusted the point from which he looked not only at the matter of the causes of low wages but also at the whole issue of political economy. Just as he had decided essentially to limit himself to the working people's view of their situation, in formulating his own political economy he saw that received opinion was relevant mainly to capital or the employer: "Political Economy as it stands is super-eminently the science of trading. . . ." (40, 13 Sept. 1851) and "the fallacy of the whole appears to consist in ignoring the existence of the labourer, and not paying the same regard to his interests as to those of the capitalist class" (54, 20 Dec. 1851).

This failure Mayhew saw as the cause of all social unrest. Though at times he seems to suggest that the interests of the capitalist and the worker are inevitably opposed, as in his remarks on free trade being a blessing to the capitalist and a curse to the worker, like most Victorians he thought the interests reconcilable. He came to define his role as mediator between the two groups, as he said later in *German Life and Manners:* he writes, he says, to make mankind "kindlier and better towards each other . . . to induce them to believe that they are what they are, not from any merit of their own, but simply from the inscrutable decrees of the incomprehensible Providence above us" (1:163). The way he would do this would be dispassionately and objectively, and on the basis of the empirical evidence he had collected, to assert labor's case. His new political economy would take notice "of the claims of labour, doing justice to the workman as well as to the employer" (40, 13 Sept. 1851).

He began this work, which like everything he did in terms of this topic was to be unfinished, where he had begun, with the rate of wages. He provided a new definition of wages from labor's view, that is, "the *ratio* of the remuneration of the labourer to the quantity of work performed by him"[13] rather than the more orthodox definition of the ratio between population and capital expended. Thus wages were determined by the numbers of workers, the hours of work, the rate of working, the quantity of work, and the amount of the Wage Fund, a reference to the nineteenth-century idea, now discredited, that there is a fixed sum of money in the economy for the payment of wages.

With this explanation of wages, it became clear that the theory of supply and demand was simply not an adequate explanation of the ebb and flow of income. The supply of labor could be increased by altering the conditions of labor, as he demonstrated both in the *Morning Chronicle* series and in volume 2 of *London Labour and the London Poor*. The different ways Mayhew enumerated by which the alteration of working conditions could affect the rate of wages essentially boil down to requiring more work for the same or less pay; as he formulated first in "Labour and the Poor": "overwork makes underpay, and underpay makes overwork."

The accepted political economy told capitalists how to make more money by reducing costs, including the cost of labor. Thus current economic policy was inimical to the working classes since it made the reduction of wages and the elimination of jobs a desirable goal. Mayhew felt some other idea had to be substituted if the "two nations" were not to fall at each other's throats. He found that idea in the "tribute" system which was based on the assertion that production was a "partnership" between "the man of money and the man of skill" (*LW,* 35). A partnership being an association of equals, neither side should receive a disproportionate part of the profit generated by the two working together. The capitalist had to receive a fair price for the use of his money as well as for the risk he took in financing production. But the worker also deserved a fair price for his role in turning the raw materials provided by the capitalist's money into usable goods. The worker deserved "a certain proportion" of the *"increased value that the workman, by the exercise of his skill, gives to the materials on which he operates"* (42, 27 Sept. 1851).

This was and to some extent still is a revolutionary notion. Workers are not to receive whatever wage the market will support, but a fixed percentage of the value added by their labor. The crucial details of this system, however, Mayhew did not get around to describing. What percentage of the whole would be fair for the capitalist and what percentage for the worker? Would it be fifty-fifty? Or would the workers get 5 percent or .5 percent? It makes a big difference. The lack of these details limits the radical implications of Mayhew's position.

Mayhew also did not specify how the change in the method of accounting wages could come about. He was not against government regulation, though leery of it, nor was he negative about trade unions in general. In fact, there is very little evidence in his work that he was for or against any particular means of achieving social change, except his abhorrence of violent methods, in which category he, like most of his contemporaries, included strikes. He was naturally cautious, a Victorian who had both the strong desire to change things for the better and a natural caution against any specific method of doing so. Perhaps if he had been able to finish his work, he would have arrived at some more concrete proposals, even as he abandoned his initial belief in free trade being beneficial to the working classes. He was educated by his experiences. But such speculation belongs to the world of "might-have-been." For *Low Wages,* like "Labour and the Poor," like *London Labour and the London Poor,* and like "The Great World of London," was to remain forever incomplete.

The Criminal Prisons of London.   In 1856 when Mayhew and his brother were trying to complete *London Labour and the London Poor,* he had embarked on another related project. Unlike *London Labour and the London Poor,* this new endeavor was not intended to be a continuation of "Labour and the Poor." It was similar in the source of its material but different in form. Just as the title *London Labour and the London Poor* had indicated the scope and assumptions behind that survey, so too did the new title "The Great World of London."

This new work was conceived in the long tradition of the London sketch: light, journalistic accounts of the nooks and crannies of urban life. This genre of journalism descended ultimately from the eighteenth-century periodical essays of Addison and Steele in the *Tatler* and the *Spectator.* The characteristic form was a brief, amusing look at some unusual aspect of the city with, occasionally, a touch of social commentary. The greatest practitioner of this London sketch in the early nineteenth century was Charles Lamb. Leigh Hunt and others contributed to it also. Charles Dickens's journalism falls into the same category, and the journalism of "low life" discussed above in relation to the street folk was a part of this larger tradition.

Whether it was his publisher Bogue's idea or his, Mayhew seems to have abandoned his grand plan of a scientific survey of work and workers. He makes no claims here for his scientific approach nor for the goals of uncovering any "laws" about the economy. Instead, as he says in his prospectus, "the writer proposes being less minute and elaborate, so as to be able, within a reasonable compass, to deal with almost every type of Metropolitan Society." He planned general surveys of twenty-one kinds of society in London: the legal community, the criminal element, fashionable London, and so on.

As the form differed, so did the format. The book is printed in a more attractive way, with a large page unbroken by columns and with various typographical devices to indicate different divisions and subdivisions. It includes many illustrations, some taken from photographs, most of prisons. These latter were probably supplied by the prison authorities. A further difference is the introduction of footnotes which Mayhew uses for many of the references, sources, statistics, and quotations of authorities that had sometimes interrupted the narrative flow of his earlier work.

The use of these footnotes, which grow in length as he gets more involved in his investigations, demonstrates, however, how uncongenial the conventional journalistic London-life sketch was to Mayhew. When he was interested in a topic (and when he was not he usually dropped it quickly), he could not condense or simplify or omit. His mode was to be inclusive and to control his topic by classification. The two traits are responsible for the interest and value of his work, and they are also the reason the conventional concept underlying "The Great World of London" does not survive the first 100 pages.

After sixty-three pages of light, generalized pictures of London, he moved into what was intended as the first fulfillment of his planned general survey, but which turned out to be an extensive, detailed book of its own: *The Criminal Prisons of London,* as it was titled when published in book form in 1862. Mayhew later called it a "wretched fragment of a well-meant scheme."[14]

He came to the topic of the London prisons in these initial pages through a logical series of classifications. The general introduction "London as a Great World" approaches the subject from several broad angles. It begins with an effort to capture the variety of life in the city and then, via a balloon ride, to project a vision of the whole. (He liked to write descriptions of scenes from a high vantage point; in these early pages in addition to the view from the balloon he provides another sweeping survey from on top of St. Paul's Cathedral.) Unlike the general introduction, these views-from-on-high are relatively evocative because they are based on specific experiences. Mayhew also provides a statistical section on the size and population of London in which we recognize the "collector of facts" from the earlier surveys and general impressions of the city as one enters it by rail or through the ports.

After this comes a section on the "contrasts of London" (riches and poverty, charity and crime) which had been a cliché with London sketch writers for decades. Mayhew adds little to the familiar picture, although we recognize his hand by the number of statistics he used to evoke the familiar contrasts and by the passing references to people and scenes he had described in great detail when surveying the street folk. The introductory section closes with a discussion "Of the London Streets, Their Traffic, Names, and Character."

"Book the First" is a consideration of "Professional London" defined as "that portion of metropolitan society of which the members follow some intellectual calling . . . deriving their income from the exercise of *talent* rather than *skill*."[15] Mayhew tries to estimate their numbers and, using census figures, concludes they represent 2 percent of the metropolitan population. He argues for their economic and social worth to the country and closes with a list of the professions he will cover, beginning with "Legal London," entitled "division 1."

"Legal London" has its own general introduction, including a description of the various Inns of Court and the different law courts as well as the streets of lawyers' offices. (This is the area of Jaggers's office in Dickens's *Great Expectations*.) He touches on the legal mind, extols the honesty of English judges, and closes with the statistics of the various aspects of the trade. Since none of the courts were in session at the time he was writing this number (late March 1856), he decides to begin his "less minute and elaborate" survey with a description of the criminal prison system. He will spend, however, eight months doing so and produce 400 pages of text on the topic, and even then not be done with "subdivision 1."

To prepare for this work, Mayhew apparently did some preliminary reading, including Hepworth Dixon's *The London Prisons* (1850) and George Chesterton's *Revelations of Prison Life* (1856). (Chesterton had been governor of Tothill Fields prison and was an acquaintance of Mayhew's.) Mayhew had much of the official statistics that had come out of the prison system to hand. Furthermore, there had been in the past and continued to be considerable discussion in different media about prison discipline. He was not mining new fields, as in *London Labour and the London Poor*, nor providing data for confusing economic situations, as in "Labour and the Poor"; he was treading on somewhat familiar ground. Since he was not going to be allowed to exercise his greatest gift in this survey—that of interviewer—nor would he even be allowed to talk briefly to prisoners, his contribution in *The Criminal Prisons of London* is not of the same sort as in his earlier works.

Because of the familiarity of the material and because Mayhew had no chance to let his interviews distract him from his initial plan, *The Criminal Prisons of London* is a more organized work than *London Labour and the London Poor,* even though it too was published in parts (but monthly) and the parts printed unrevised when it was turned into a book. Mayhew visited the various prisons, sometimes more than once, but he did not seem to write up his piece until he had collected all the information he wanted. Thus, he could produce a "finished" picture. For the most part the topics that tempted him to digress were relegated either to footnotes or, in one case, to an appendix.

The introductory section described the different divisions of prisons, including those for offenders after conviction (which is all he was able to cover in his subsequent 400 pages) and those for offenders before conviction. He gives a numerical and descriptive analysis of the character of London criminals, making the same distinction between "habitual" and "accidental" criminals that he had detailed in the opening pages of the "extra" volume of *London Labour and the London Poor.* He also repeats from that earlier work (and to some extent from the initial pages of "The Great World of London") a description of the different types of professional thieves and cadgers. The introductory passage closes with some statistics and a description of the changes introduced by the 1853 act modifying the system of transportation of convicts to islands in the south seas. After this he attaches an appendix in which he describes in detail the different kinds of prison discipline currently in force.

There was no standardized prison system in England at this time. Not only could sentences for the same crime differ widely depending on judge and district, but the mode of convict life was frequently different at each prison. Not until 1865 was there any uniformity of treatment, and it was 1877 before a nationally administered penal system was in force. Mayhew's intention was to detail how each system worked and, he hoped, enlighten the public as to which was best.

All the regimes in nineteenth-century London prisons ultimately derived from the observations of the great eighteenth-century reformer, John Howard. In the process of exposing the horrifying conditions in eighteenth-century English prisons, Howard noted two main conditions that subsequent prison reform tried to address. The first was the unchecked intermingling of prisoners with the result that hardened criminals corrupted the inexperienced ones. Indeed, crimes were not infrequently planned in and directed from prison. The second condition he noted was the lack of any activity for the prisoners.

Nineteenth-century prison discipline addressed these two problems by introducing two systems, the "separate" system, in which prisoners lived and usually worked alone in their cells; and the "silent" system, in which they slept and worked in groups but were prohibited from speaking to one another. The two systems were sometimes combined, as at Millbank, where some inmates slept in solitary cells but worked together silently during the day. The common justification for the separate system was that it not only prevented the contamination of one prisoner by another but the isolation forced the convict to examine his past life and to look into his heart. Such self-examination, it was hoped, would lead to the reformation of the criminal.

The problem of idleness was more difficult. What work could prisoners be set to? In the convict prisons for offenders with long sentences there was some effort to make the work useful; the prisoners engaged in various kinds of clothing-making, laundering, or in industrial trades. But in short-term "correctional institutions," where sentences ranged from seven days to two years, the "labor" was generally useless: the treadmill, a revolving staircase which convicts had to walk up for a certain amount of time each day; the shot drill, moving a pile of cannon balls from one place to another, usually for seventy-five minutes at a time; and "picking oakum," separating and cleaning pieces of loosely twisted fiber impregnated with tar or creosote which was primarily used in caulking seams of ships. All of these types of "hard labor" were physically hard indeed, and their uselessness could be psychologically devastating.

In his appendix on prison discipline Mayhew gives a short history of the old prison system whose excesses and neglect had led to the nineteenth-century reforms. After this he takes up the various kinds of prison discipline, both those in force and those in theory. First is the "classification" mode, which was only an idea, for it was too impractical and expensive to implement. In it criminals were separated in cells and buildings according to their offenses. Next discussed is the "silent-associated system" and then the separate system introduced at the new "model" prison at Pentonville in 1840–1842.

The final discipline Mayhew discusses in this appendix is the "mark" system, not in operation in England but used in the transportation depot of Norfolk Island. Nearly all contemporary commentators on prison discipline—Mayhew himself, Dixon his source, and Dickens too—praised this system whereby a man was "sentenced to perform a certain quantity of labour [which] . . . the convict would be bound to perform before he could regain his freedom, whether he chose to occupy one year or twenty years about it" (105–6). Later in his survey, when Mayhew offered his suggestions for a better prison discipline, he would base it on the idea behind this "mark" system.

At this point, however, in his conclusion to the appendix, he observes that, based on statistics which show the crime rate has gone up, the present system is no better at deterring crime than the old system. The problem is twofold, he concluded: first, the silent and the separate systems were as extreme as the older one of no system at all. All that was necessary, Mayhew said, in order to "check the evils of unrestricted intercourse among criminals, is to prevent them talking upon *vicious* subjects to one another" (107). Enforcing total silence or total isolation tended to have a negative effect on the human mind, and the figures for insanity in the prisons were high.

Second, Mayhew concluded, the hard labor also had a negative effect. Criminals, as he had said earlier, were those who "will not work." The kind of "work" they are forced to do in prison simply reinforces their reluctance. If real rehabilitation is to take place, then the convict must change his attitude toward work. This must be a real change and not a "religious conversion" which was seen as the goal of most prison rehabilitation. No one is honest for purely religious motives, Mayhew said.

At this early point in his survey of the criminal prisons, Mayhew was not ready to go any further in his comments. Instead he turns to the description of the prisons themselves. He had to develop a new format for his presentation of this material, for that of "Labour and the Poor" and *London Labour and the London Poor,* relying on quotations from informants and the long biographical interview, was not applicable. His solution to the problem in *The Criminal Prisons of Lon-*

don is related to the mode he developed in his earlier works not for interviews but for description.

Many of the London sketch writers followed the example of their eighteenth-century forebears and, when describing a corner of the metropolis, tried to give a general picture of the place. They sought for representative and characteristic details which were then collected together and artistically shaped into an idealized picture every detail of which was true but which as a whole had never existed. Thus Dickens in "Meditations in Monmouth Street," passing an unnamed used clothes' display in London's East End, imagines the clothes lying on the pavement suddenly coming to life and forming a series of ghostly persons.

Mayhew, however, motivated not only by the genre of the London sketch but also by the requirements of scientific observation, deviated from this mode of general, idealized sketch in his descriptions, and with great effect. He tries to describe each place as he sees it at a specific moment in time so that the people waiting for the doors of the Asylum for the Houseless Poor in Cripplegate to open are seen on a cold winter evening and the scenes at the various markets in *London Labour and the London Poor* are determined by the time Mayhew was there. The result is a particularity of scene in which the specific details have been organized by the writer to make a powerful but also representative picture. Mayhew's descriptions were like photographs, part realism, part artifice.

In evolving a format for his descriptions of the prisons, Mayhew built on this characteristic mode. As in his earlier works, each individual survey falls into a pattern. He begins the section on each prison with a detailed description of the various London sights he takes in as he makes his way there. Thus he has a few paragraphs on the streets leading east from central London to Pentonville, and a sketch of the pleasant train ride south to Wandsworth. One of the longer of these introductory passages describes the London scenes on a boat ride up the Thames from Hungerford stairs to Millbank prison (now the area of the Tate Gallery). These descriptions have a liveliness of detail but are necessarily cursory and impressionistic.

Next he describes the history and architecture of the prison, both outside and inside. So much is similar to the format of his earlier works. The problem is what to do next. Instead of interviews with the prisoners, Mayhew presents a narrative of his day at whatever prison is under review. He reports the dialogue he overhears and the whispered asides his guides give him about various prisoners and scenes. He describes in detail what the prisoners are eating that particular day and the work that he observes in the workroom at that very moment. All of this creates a strong sense of participation on the part of the reader. Since he could not talk to the prisoners, we meet no individuals in our trips to the criminal prisons of London; as the title states, the emphasis is on the institutions not the inhabitants. Yet unlike most other works written about prisons during the period, because of his "day at" narrative structure, he gives us a sense of what it was like to be a prisoner in terms of the individual's experience if not in terms of his thoughts and feelings.

Yet Mayhew periodically tries to project himself inside the prisoners' minds: "we would cheerfully, had it been possible, have travelled with the prisoners to their destination at Portsmouth [where they were to labor on public works]; for, to the student of human nature, it would have been a high lesson to have seen the sudden delight beam in every face as the omnibus passed by some familiar scene . . ." (127). Despite the sentimentality of these projections—for Mayhew was no better than any other middle-class observer at second-guessing the lower classes when he could not talk to them—he manages to produce a frequently engrossing account of prison life as seen from the inside. Other than its synthesizing of information and opinion about mid-Victorian London prisons, this perspective on prison life is the value of *The Criminal Prisons of London* today.

Mayhew begins his survey with the various prisons for those who have been sentenced. He starts with the four "convict" prisons for those with sentences over two years: Pentonville (the "model prison"); Brixton (the Surrey House of Detention for short-term offenders which had been replaced by Wandsworth in 1851, but had been called back into use for women sentenced to long terms after the 1853 abolition of transportation for less than fourteen years); the "Hulks" (boats in the lower Thames which had originally transported felons, as in the opening of *Great Expectations,* but were now used as permanent prisons); and Millbank, built early in the century, a "depot" that held convicts of all sorts until places opened up for them at the other prisons. All these prisons were government institutions and run by a central authority.

At Pentonville Mayhew is impressed by the architecture but more uncertain about the separate system it enforced. A number of times in his narrative of the day at Pentonville he uses metaphors that equate the place with a tomb, albeit an impressively clean and spacious one. He also feels that the industrial training in tailoring and shoemaking given the inmates is not helpful in rehabilitation because it led to "no definite end" (153); the convicts did not receive enough instruction nor have a long enough time to become dextrous and hence they could not use the training outside the prison walls. Nonetheless, were it not that the solitary confinement seemed to increase the chance of insanity, Mayhew preferred it to the silent one because it made work desirable ("labour [becomes] so agreeable a relief to the monotony of solitude, that it positively becomes a punishment to withhold it"), and it also compelled the offender "to reflect on the wickedness of his past career with the view of his forming new resolves for the future" (169). Later he said "there is in *all* prisons a great deal too much care for the happiness of a being in the future world, and too little for the happiness in the present" (421).

The "day at" Pentonville is reported extensively. It includes the cleaning of the prison, breakfast, exercise, arrival of new convicts, work, and the closing of the prison, plus an account of a Sunday service at the chapel. The same categories turn up in the accounts of the other prisons, along with items unique to each one, such as the nursery at Brixton.

Brixton was the long-term prison for women, and here Mayhew was impressed by the gentleness of the female warders and strongly affected by the children, who, if born while the mother was in prison, were allowed to stay with her. Contemplation of these children returned Mayhew to the moral of *London Labour and the London Poor:* "the first great lesson of toleration [is] that even his [i.e., the observer and reader] own individual exemption from jail is due rather to the accident of his birth and parentage, than to any special merit on his part" (190).

If he was impressed by the appearance of Pentonville and Brixton, Mayhew was distressed by the Hulks at Woolwich, not only because the accommodations were cramped and unsatisfactory but because neither the silent nor the separate system operated in these floating prisons to which offenders were sent from Pentonville and Millbank to complete their sentences. As he says, the Hulks were "the receptacles of the worst class of prisoners from all the jails in the United Kingdom" (201) and because of the wanton association of criminals of various classes and the relatively free exchange among them, "whatever good is effected, therefore, by the systems of Millbank and Pentonville [by the separate and silent systems] is effectively destroyed at Woolwich" (202). He has a long day on one hulk, the *Defence,* including a visit to the library and to the military arsenal where the convicts worked during the day scraping sediment off cannon balls, followed by a somber few minutes spent in the marshy, gloomy convict burial ground. He also visited the *Unité* hospital ship and the *Sulphur* and *Warrior.*

The final convict prison Mayhew visits is Millbank, the largest, and built on the model of Jeremy Bentham's "Panoptikon." The constant surveillance, the desire for which motivated Bentham's pentagonal plan, had long been abandoned at Millbank and the pentagons were used for different purposes: one for reception, one for the workshop, one for women prisoners, and so on. The discipline was a combination: generally for six months the convicts were in isolation; after that they worked in silent association.

At this point Mayhew had been working four months on *The Criminal Prisons of London* and had published four parts. He now turned to the "correctional prisons of London" for short-term offenders: the Middlesex county prisons—Coldbath Fields for adult men and Tothill Fields for women and juveniles—plus the new Surrey House of Correction at Wandsworth for all classes. In the middle of this last survey the project collapsed, a final number appearing in December 1856. John Binny completed the survey of Wandsworth for the reissue in 1862, as well as that of the city of London correctional prison for all classes built at Holloway in 1849–1852.

Unlike the convict prisons, these correctional institutions were county-run and hence varied widely in their organization and discipline. Originally they had all been intended to *"correct* the indisposition to labour on the part of rogues and vagabonds" (274) but, with an irony that did not escape Mayhew, the useless, punishing labor enforced in them frequently had the opposite effect.

He spends close to seventy-five pages in his survey of Coldbath Fields, including two lively descriptions of the departure and arrival of prisoners and a number of reported conversations between prisoners and their visitors. There are also ancillary discussions on hard labor as a principle and on the weakness in the silent associated system practiced at this prison. He inserts all the opinions within the "day at" structure, however, and in this way maintains the immediacy of the narrative.

Mayhew uses this section on Coldbath Fields to detail various kinds of "prison labor," including the "hard labor" of the treadwheel, the shot-drill, and oakum picking, described above. Offenders with lesser sentences could be involved in tailoring, shoemaking, mat-making, or other trades. But Mayhew recognizes the futility in a short-term prison "where some of the men are confined for only a few days . . . to attempt to make labour profitable, owing to the impossibility of teaching the majority of the prisoners any handicraft in so short a space of time" (300).

He does not believe prisons should be schools or religious institutions where the only emphasis is on rehabilitation through education and industrial training. The criminal must do "penance" for his crime. Some punishment was necessary. Nonetheless, useless work simply hardened a felon in his abhorrence of it; as practiced, the punishment aspect of the sentence had become a positive barrier to any rehabilitation. Mayhew suggests a more sensible kind of prison discipline, one mentioned by Dixon and others, and a modification of the "mark" system in that it gave the prisoner some element of control. The problem is, Mayhew said, "the laws which regulate the world *outside* the prison walls are essentially altered, if not wholly reversed, *inside of them*." Outside men have to work to get food, shelter, clothing. *"But no sooner has a man set foot within a prison that all such anxieties cease"* (301). Mayhew's system would change that: "we would have every man placed, on his entering a jail, upon the punishment diet, i.e., his eleemosynary allowance of food should be only a pound of bread and water *per diem*. We would *begin* at this point, and make all creature comforts beyond it purchasable, as it were, by the amount of labour done . . ." (302–3).

Moreover, seeing the large group of men picking oakum in dead silence, Mayhew is moved to comment on the silent associated system in general, which he finds cruel and excessive: "to leave the tongue in a man's mouth, and yet to deny him the liberty of using it . . . is surely a piece of refined tyranny, [un]worthy of the enlightenment, if not the humanity, of the nineteenth century" (311). Not only does it lead to frustration and anger, but it is a waste of opportunity for the kind of instruction that would be the only way reformation could begin. He repeats his earlier statement: "surely all that is necessary in order to check unrestricted intercourse among criminals, is to stop all communion on *depraved* subjects" (335).

One other aspect of Coldbath Fields leads Mayhew into the realm of social comment. Nearly one-half of the prisoners in this short-term institution were sent there "owing to their not possessing sufficient money to pay the fine for which the police magistrate had commuted their particular breach of the law" (341); "they are incarcerated for their poverty, rather than their transgression" (342). Mayhew approves of fines in lieu of prison because, if prison is to be a deterrent, offenders must be kept unfamiliar with it as long as possible. He thinks fines should be the punishment for all "minor infractions of social rules" such as being drunk and disorderly, accidentally breaking windows, street-selling without a license, crying "sweep" in the street, etc. He also realizes that for a poor man even a small fine may be impossible to pay. Thus he advocates an installment plan for fines and, more radically, a sliding scale for the same offense since "the wealthier classes have not only less excuse for their offences, but also greater means of paying whatever penalty may be imposed upon them" (344).

He will pick up on this suggestion again in his next, last, and longest survey, that of the Middlesex House of Correction for women and juveniles at Tothill Fields. This prison, built early in the century on the site of one of the oldest prisons, Bridewell, was in the heart of Westminster. Practically on the doorstep of the royal palace, it was frequently used as an example of the contrasts of London. Its location leads Mayhew into an introductory discussion of the history of Westminster by which he tries to account for its various "rookeries" or vagabond colonies by their location near ancient sanctuaries. This in turn leads him to reassert the notion of crime as an inherited characteristic: "ethnic crime and pauperism would appear, not only to be consistent with the ordinary laws of human life, but to be as natural as hereditary insanity" (357). This opinion has consistently alternated with his equally frequent statement that nothing separated himself or his readers from these outcasts but the chance of birth. He was never able to make a final determination. If crime and vagabondage were hereditary, then no reform was possible, a state of affairs Mayhew as well as most Victorians could not consider. If reform could work, then crime and pauperism were not inherited. We can find several examples of this uncertainty of opinion. One such is his flat assertion "that crime is *not* referable to poverty" (382) followed by the observation on the next page that "it is mainly the poor and unlettered who belong to the criminal classes" (383).

He did try to tackle the problem presented by this opposition in his remarks on juvenile delinquency in this section of *The Criminal Prisons of London*. "The vagrant child [is] father to the felon man," he says, and thus society must discover the sources of juvenile crime in order to reduce the crime rate. After showing that none of the conventionally offered explanations for juvenile crime are supported by statistics, Mayhew offers his own theory: some people "are naturally of more erratic natures than others" (384) and will always be on the margins of social restraint; this, coupled with the fact that crime is frequently more lucrative than hard work, means that "we must do all we can to make theft less lucrative and more certain of detection, on the one hand, as well as to increase the rewards of industry, on the other, and to render it a more honourable vocation in the State" (386).

Still, since most criminals seem to come from the lower classes, other forces than just an inborn erratic nature must be operating. Not all uncontrollable persons turn to crime. What environmental element is at work? Mayhew thinks the answer lies at home. "Juvenile crime will be found to be due, like prostitution, mainly to a want of proper parental control," he says (386). But not all parents are willfully neglectful; situations outside their control may contribute— such as both parents needing to work, children idly associating with each other, and the state's failure to provide schools, and industrial and religious training. Bad housing contributes as well.

Nothing can be done to prevent the inborn tendency toward a life of crime, but the state can do something about the potential juvenile criminals who have improper "parental" control. Where parents fail, the state must "interfere" and become the "foster-father of the wretched little orphans" and see to it that they are well instructed and well trained (415). Years later, in *The Shops and Companies of London,* Mayhew would present a practical example of such foster-parenting. The state should fully train all first offenders, find them jobs, and insure them to their new employers. Second offenders after this treatment would be sentenced to life imprisonment.

England was far from such a system in 1856. In fact, Mayhew discovers to his horror that certain state institutions actually help turn juvenile offenders into adult "professional" criminals by eliminating their fear of prison. While in Tothill Fields, Mayhew sees that "children are sent to prison for the most trivial offences" (388). Initially he makes this observation mildly. But in his day at the prison he sees the list of "crimes" for which the boys are imprisoned. He cannot keep his anger out of his report: "we find little creatures of six years of age branded with a felon's badge—boys, not even in their teens, clad in the prison dress, for the heinous offense of throwing stones, or obstructing highways, or unlawfully knocking at doors—crimes which the very magistrates themselves, who committed the youths, must have assuredly perpetrated in their boyhood, and which, if equally visited, would consign almost every child in the kingdom to a jail" (406). As Mayhew tours the workrooms of the prison, this terrible injustice is forced on him with increasing power. He conducts a survey of the "crimes" the boys in the workrooms have been imprisoned for and concludes that "there is a considerable number who are confined for offences that not even the sternest-minded can rank as crime" (420). Not only is it unjust since every child in the world will throw a stone or spin a top when he should not, but also, for children of the poorer classes, prison can be a refuge once they know what it is like: "the place is almost a paradise in comparison to the hovels to which the poor little inmates have been generally accustomed, and the food positive luxury to their ordinary fare when at liberty" (409). So much for the deterrent effect of prison.

In *The Criminal Prisons of London* Mayhew had twice affirmed his faith in the magistrate's impartiality, but his experience in Tothill Fields strains his faith to the breaking point. Perhaps if he had continued his work he might have made a significant break with his class and with received opinion. But the end of his career as a social historian is only weeks away at this point.

He finishes his day at Tothill Fields, as far as juvenile offenders go, with a description of the arrival of new prisoners and the discharge of others. What he sees at the discharge confirms him in his explanation of the source of juvenile crime: *"Of all the young creatures discharged that morning, not a father, nor a mother, nor even a grown and decent friend, was there to receive them! . . .* We could not help speculating upon the impending fate of these discharged children, and of the shocking heartlessness of the State which can forget its duties as a father to them" (438).[16]

In the same way that the experience of Tothill Fields juvenile section led Mayhew to observations on the causes of crime, those in the female section led him to repeat and expand his ideas about female crime, mainly prostitution and petty larceny. His ideas about women are conventional and so are his responses to the nursery and the workroom where two hundred women are silently engaged in picking oakum.

Mayhew gives both the familiar biological explanation for women turning to crime as well as a popular psychological one. Like men, some women "find work inordinately irksome to their natures" and so, if they have to labor, these turn to prostitution "to secure the apparent luxury of an idle life" (454). (Women from other classes turn prostitute from "love of vanity.") In addition, women criminals have "the same insensibility to shame on the part of woman as dishonesty in man" (455) and hence lack the touchstone by which law and order are maintained—the fear of disapprobation. "The reason, therefore, why prostitution is the one chief delinquency of the female sex is because it is the one capital act of shamelessness, and that which consequently fits the creature for the performance of any other iniquity" (456). He insists on this point, remarking that "the most striking peculiarity of the women . . . in London prisons is that of utter and imperturbable shamelessness" (465). However, he does add that shame is a learned response and hence lack of it is not a sign of innate evil but rather of a failure of proper moral instruction.

These explanations of female crime were standard in mid-Victorian England. In the midst of repeating these conventional sentiments, however, Mayhew makes, almost as an aside, an interesting observation that is quite similar to notions of modern psychology. "It seems to us," he says, "that human beings like praise, simply because the admiration of others serves to increase their self-esteem." (We would now say "self-image" rather than "self-esteem.") Furthermore, "this self-esteem is essential not only to our happiness, but to our existence itself. It is of the highest importance for our welfare, for instance, that we should have faith in our own powers, since none can be of such use to us as we can be to ourselves" (455–56). This is an unusual observation, for in the Victorian period the instilling of humility and a sense of inadequacy were frequently seen as the proper exercise of parental authority. But this modern view contrasts sharply with some of his other observations about women, perhaps the weakest of which is his assertion that those who are "public women" and "shameless and affectionless" necessarily are rendered childless "so that the sight of these baby prisoners was at once a proof to us that the hearts of the women that bore them were not utterly withered and corrupt" (475).

The section closes with a visit to "The Female Prisoners' Own Clothes' Store" where prisoners' belongings are kept until their release. Mayhew and the matron project the lives of the women prisoners outside the prison from the clothes, particularly the bonnets, that were taken from them when they entered the prison. This whimsical exchange is the last he wrote for *The Criminal Prisons of London*. He begins the next section on Wandsworth Correctional Prison with an impression of the trip by rail from central London to Clapham Common, but the next ten pages on the history of the prison are all direct quotations from "the final report of the Committee of Justices appointed to superintend the erection of the House of Correction at Wandsworth" (489). John Binny apparently made the actual tour of the prison in 1862; at least he wrote it up then, as well as the surveys of Holloway Correctional Prison, and Newgate, Clerkenwell, and Horsemonger Lane jails.

At the same time that Mayhew was writing *The Criminal Prisons of London* he was conducting meetings to collect information. A number of these were with ticket-of-leave men, convicts on a system of parole that had recently been instituted. Mayhew calls them together to air their grievances, which include their difficulties in finding jobs, prejudice against them, and so on. At one, a felon tried to get his fellows to turn against Mayhew who, he said, was only interested in them in order to sell more books.

Mayhew was also in demand as a speaker at other kinds of meetings. Records of two of these, both groups agitating for the abolition of capital punishment, have survived. He was strongly opposed to capital punishment and had a number of thoughtful observations to make about it and about related issues of crime and punishment. He argued against capital punishment because it failed as a deterrent; it seemed to justify taking a life in retribution.[17] Beyond this, however, was personal experience. He had witnessed an execution where "he had seen that wretched man, a lunatic without question, killed in the most horrible manner; and he felt that, for the first time in his life, he had been present at the commission of a diabolical crime."[18]

In this latter address he also expanded his observations on the whole issue of crime. No criminal, he said, could ever be truly reformed in prison. Current systems fail because they do not follow "the criminal on his release from prison, and provide him with employment, and with the opportunity of leading a better life." He was not certain how prisons should be run "but he wished to give it as the result of his long acquaintance with the criminal classes, that he had never known one single instance where a criminal had been reclaimed by severity, though he had known very many who had been reclaimed by kindness." Mayhew was a man who learned from experience. These final words are a tribute to his humanity, and an appropriate capstone to his life's major work.

Chapter Four
Summing Up

Throughout the previous chapters, we have evaluated Mayhew's many different works individually. Now it is time to discuss his career more generally and to analyze the problems raised by the way in which he worked as well as the difficulties modern students and scholars have when using his social surveys.

Mayhew's life, despite its bright beginning and several high points, must strike a reader as a sad one. So much was possible back in the 1830s for the bright and talented young man, and in the event so much abandoned midstream, so little finished. It is hard not to be overcome by how many of his works are incomplete. Contemporaries writing about him many years later blamed his "indolent" nature for the failures of his life; undoubtedly there was something temperamental in his difficulties in following through. But Mayhew had considerable bad luck as well as bad judgment: his altercation with the publisher of *London Labour and the London Poor* owed something at least to the publisher's intransigence, and the sudden death of Bogue in 1856 was a dreadful piece of luck not only because it ended Mayhew's plans for continuing his investigative work but also because in retrospect it appears to have been the final break with his previous life. Furthermore, it was followed within two years by his father's death and the disappointment of the will. Surely Joshua's disinheriting of Henry was an excessive reaction to his bankruptcy.

The contrast between Mayhew's life before his social surveys and after is notable, and the long twenty-odd years after his last book was published are painful to think about. The change was not abrupt, but there was a gradual separation from the friends of his youth and a narrowing of associations. His circle in the late 1850s and 1860s seemed to shrink to his family. Then came those long last years when he apparently lived alone though on good terms with his daughter and her husband. (His son may have been living abroad.) This narrowing of his life is paralleled by a lessening significance of his work. He seemed to abandon the insights and attitudes achieved during the writing of his social surveys even as he drifted away from the connections he made during the height of his career. It is not a happy story taken altogether, yet Mayhew apparently remained sanguine and even-tempered through it all, a remarkable personal achievement.

His "indolent" nature, though at odds with the hard work involved in his social surveys, did make a difference in the nature of those works and as a result they present certain problems for the reader. His misquotation of Carlyle on the covers of *London Labour and the London Poor,* accusing him of sentiments which in reality Carlyle was bitterly attacking, are disturbing examples of his carelessness.[1] But this and all other problems in his work really result from their unfinished nature and their tangled publication history. Not knowing that the survey of the street folk does not represent Mayhew's intentions for *London Labour and the London Poor* had led a number of critics who either praise or criticize to mistaken judgments about the nature of his achievement. Not knowing that even the survey of the street folk is incomplete has led others, including Richard Altick,[2] to errors in reference and use of *London Labour and the London Poor.* Not knowing that the date of the four volumes of that work is a full decade after the investigations were conducted has led to a misuse and misapplication of Mayhew's findings. The general reader of *London Labour and the London Poor* does not necessarily need to know the "true history" of the volume but the scholar and critic must know it to use it correctly. The information is now all in print and has been for a number of years. In the absence of an authoritative edition of *London Labour and the London Poor* with full publication particulars attached to the text, students and scholars using his work must also consult the descriptions of the disparity between intention and final product and how they evolved.

There is a larger problem in Mayhew's social surveys, however, one that has clung to them from the very beginning, and which we must now meet head on. Exactly how accurate are his surveys? How reliable are his statistics? How much faith can we have that the reported interviews represent what was actually said by his informants? How can we be sure that individuals told Mayhew the truth? Did he lead his informants to tell him what he wanted to hear? Concern over these questions has been attached to his work since 1850 when the *Economist* attacked the contributions of the Metropolitan Correspondent because they were "almost exclusively the statements of the suffering artisans themselves" (16 Nov. 1850). The *Athenaeum* in 1851 also questioned the reliability of Mayhew's work after he published his negative remarks on the Ragged Schools. (Both these journals praised "The Great World of London.") Both modern historians E. P. Thompson and Gertrude Himmelfarb in their earliest pieces on Mayhew felt that H. Sutherland Edwards's comment that Mayhew's reports contained "an added colour of his own" suggests that his reported interviews might be suspect.[3] Finally, in a 1979 article F. B. Smith takes one interview with a convict who had been transported to Van Dieman Island and by using the records of the penal colony concludes that the convict spun a web of lies and omissions in the story of his life and the interviewer, Mayhew, swallowed it. Despite Mayhew's claims, he did not "verify even easily verifiable assertions." As a result, Smith feels that all of Mayhew's interviews are under a cloud.[4]

The question of Mayhew's accuracy will never be resolved to everyone's satisfaction. There is just not enough reliable information about how he worked: who helped work up the statistics and how, the means by which he found his informants, who accompanied him on his interviews, what questions he asked, how he took notes, how he checked on individual stories if and when he did, what principles he followed in turning the notes into the published reports, how the articles were checked and proofread. In the absence of this information, judgments about the reliability of his work will inevitably vary.

Before we try to sort out the different aspects of this problem, certain general observations are in order. First, although his reports are journalistic, they are similar, even identical, to much other social investigation of the period whether by individuals like the doctor Kay-Shuttleworth or the government itself in its blue books. Many of the same kind of questions, some clearly leading, appear in these reports and in Mayhew's. Further, whether we consider his social surveys journalism, embryonic sociology, or a unique combination of the two, we must recognize that they are not modern examples of these modes and hence they are not written to modern standards of scientific accuracy verifiable by independent means. To expect that of Mayhew's surveys is to ignore the nature of Victorian social science as well as the manner in which his reports were written and published.

Nevertheless, the problem of accuracy is a troubling one. Mayhew's social surveys are made up of three different kinds of observations and assertions. First, there are the *general* statistical surveys of various trades and groups of lower-class people and the descriptions of modes of work, aspects of the trade, and living and working conditions in the different branches of London working life. Second, there are the "biographies," the *particulars* on which the generalizations are presumably based, and third, there are his own personal *comments* on the significance of both the particulars and the generalizations. These three divisions of Mayhew's social surveys roughly follow the steps of an empirical procedure: a large collection of "facts" or particulars out of which emerge certain general patterns. The larger the number of facts and the more persistent the general patterns are, the more likely it is that the "laws" governing the situation—in "Labour and the Poor" the rate of wages—will emerge. Mayhew's insistence that he was a "mere collector of facts" accurately describes what he quickly realized he was doing, but his intention was always to have enough information to bring to light the general pattern.

Because his work is unfinished, however, it is the particulars that are his main contribution, and it is on the reliability of these particulars as expressed in the "biographical" interviews he published that the controversy over his accuracy is centered. No one questions that the general statistical surveys that precede each large series in the *Morning Chronicle* must be used with caution. They were hurriedly pulled together by unknown collaborators and equally hurriedly printed and proofread. Whatever errors, typographical as well as substantive, existed—and there were bound to be some—were never corrected. The same difficulty exists with the statistical charts Mayhew gave at the end of each major subsection of street folk in *London Labour and the London Poor,* though to a lesser degree. In the case of the street folk, Mayhew was collecting statistical information that had never been attempted before and because of the vagrant and transitory nature of street life would be very difficult to find in any circumstances. No individual figure can be used with impunity, but the overall picture created by the statistics in both individual street trades and in general are undoubtedly indicative of the "truth."

Although Mayhew's interpretation of the general statistics, as incorporated in his surveys or articulated in "Answers to Correspondents" and *Low Wages,* are important both in evaluating his work and in the study of economic theory in the nineteenth century, if we look for a fully articulated political economy such as John Stuart Mill's, we will be disappointed. But if we want a criticism that is based on specific investigation of some of the weaknesses of the accepted economic theory, then Mayhew has something to offer us. Unfortunately for the general reader, however, there is no single, coherent, available place where these ideas are expressed and developed. The reader who wishes to know or use Mayhew's economic theories must either comb through his works or use the summaries provided by others.[5]

That leaves the interviews reported as first-person statements. The mode of these interviews is discussed in the previous chapters: to repeat, Mayhew incorporates the questions asked into the answers and so, instead of presenting a dialogue between himself and his subject, he produced a long "biographical" statement uninterrupted by any other voice. In the preface he wrote for the 1851 publication of volume 1 of *London Labour and the London Poor,* he insisted on the accuracy of these reports: the work provided, he said, the "history of a people" for the first time ever, including a "literal" description of their lives "in their own 'unvarnished' language." He did not attempt to reproduce accent, the aspirated *h*'s and reversals of *v* and *w* of cockney speech being used exclusively in Victorian literature for comic effect. By his own admission, he also eliminated curse words and other "gross" language that would offend his readers. But beyond this standard and unexceptional editing, he affirmed that the published interviews represented the full and accurate accounts of what his informants had told him.

Except perhaps for some nervousness about the "added colour" asserted by Edwards, none of Mayhew's critics have claimed that he actually made up the reported interviews. Rather, the questions raised have been: did he select unrepresentative cases to report? did he ask leading questions? how thoroughly did he check the reliability of each witness before interviewing him or her, and how completely did he check the stories they gave him? did he omit information in the published interviews that would have contradicted or complicated the point he wanted to establish? did he "shape" the reported "biographical" interviews to make better copy?

Before taking up these questions, we ought to say a few words about the Edwards remark that has given some readers pause. H. Sutherland Edwards's *Personal Recollections* was published in 1900 when Edwards was 72. It is the source of much anecdotal information about the Mayhews, father and sons. Yet from his dates (he was sixteen years younger than Henry) and from Mayhew's own list of collaborators, it is probable that Edwards was closer to Augustus than to Henry; indeed Edwards and Augustus collaborated on a number of farces in the 1860s. In writing about Mayhew's days at the *Morning Chronicle* Edwards is perhaps relying on secondhand information. Further, what he says is vague: "London labourers of special interest, with picturesque specimens of the London poor, were brought to the *Chronicle* office, where they told their tales to Mayhew, who redictated them, with an added colour of his own, to the shorthand writer in waiting."[6] I have previously argued that this "added colour" might be the descriptions of the people he interviewed. Reading the reports, it is hard to know what else this "added colour" could be since the stories were relatively straightforward in their details and their figures.

Edwards's account is inaccurate in other respects. He does not mention, for example, that according to Mayhew himself he took extensive notes on the interviews, something the length of the published statements made absolutely necessary. In large meetings a shorthand reporter took down the individual statements with no intermediary. Edwards does not indicate that Mayhew conducted many interviews outside the *Chronicle* office, being anxious to get an impression of living and working conditions. Sometimes when he visited a workroom or apartment, he found workers who were not pre-selected and took their statements. Once he ran into a "slop" cabinetmaker on his way to sell some of his work; Mayhew stopped the man on the street and interviewed him on the spot. Nor does it seem that there are many "picturesque specimens of the London poor" among the skilled and unskilled workers whose stories make up the bulk of "Labour and the Poor." The occupants of the houses of refuge—vagrants, beggars, petty thieves, prostitutes, and F. B. Smith's returned convict—could be called "picturesque" as could many of the street folk in *London Labour and the London Poor,* and perhaps they are the people to whom Edwards is referring. In any case, his description is too incomplete and too unspecific to be the final word on Mayhew's accuracy.

It is important to understand also that Mayhew recognized many of the problems inherent in what he was doing. That is why he reassured his readers that he took extensive notes and why he gave periodic accounts of his difficulties in locating sources. Ultimately he relied on two elements to assure the accuracy of his overall report: first, some checking of sources' backgrounds and stories. This was not always possible to do, but failure to check thoroughly and completely was not necessarily due to carelessness or laziness. Mayhew was seeing a very large number of people daily and was under a deadline to produce copy three times a week in the beginning and once a week after that. Many of the people he interviewed had no written records to support their stories, and their possible references could be as obscure as themselves. Though it is not possible to know for sure, it seems likely that Mayhew took the word of various "gentlemen who knew the trade" or authorities such as Richard Knight of the City Mission, an evangelical organization that visited the poor of the East End in their homes, to establish his sources' reliability. He then checked elements of the individual stories that could be verified quickly and easily.

He was not content even with this. Although his intention was to arrive at the general "laws" governing the rate of wages, he knew that scientific "laws" emerge only from a very large number of particulars. Therefore, he really relies for the accuracy of the general picture on the *number* of interviews he conducted. He was concerned with the individual accuracy of the details in a single story, but he hoped that whatever inaccuracies existed in a particular interview would wash out when compared with other statements by individuals in similar situations. Thus, modern scholars who ignore the larger context of a single informant's story are misusing Mayhew's work.

One of Mayhew's methods of collecting as large a number of individual stories as he could was to hold large meetings. Thus he has meetings of East-End tailors, of West-End tailors, of needlewomen who had turned prostitute, of costermongers, of boy vagrants and thieves, and other groups, and in 1856 and 1857 of ticket-of-leave men and petty criminals. At one of these meetings the *Morning Chronicle* reported two thousand tailors in attendance. Mayhew instructed the men at the meetings to correct any statements they thought untrue and a shorthand reporter took down the proceedings. Sometimes the transcript of the meeting was given verbatim in Mayhew's subsequent report; more often he used the material he gleaned in this way as supporting evidence.

There are problems with using such a device to assure the accuracy and the randomness of the informants. Mayhew does not hold meetings for all groups he covers; in the series on toymakers for the poor, for example, he simply gives a few interviews with different individuals. But he normally strove for large numbers of informants. Even in those series where the large meeting was used to garner supporting evidence, he also reported individually collected statements from different parts of the trade.

For its time Mayhew's efforts at achieving accuracy through large numbers are impressive and unique for an individual investigator. Because of the pressure of the deadlines he did not publish "corrected" statements; he gave the reader what he got at the time. He never returned to these stories to weigh them against one another and point out the discrepancies. That is left for the reader to do, again not because of Mayhew's irresponsibility but because of the publication of the work on a daily or weekly basis and the fact that it is unfinished. Thus, any reader who wants to use an individual interview as evidence must do so with some circumspection. Mayhew would have expected that. Although in 1851 he insisted that "it is but right that the truthfulness of the poor generally should be made known" (1:iii), he undoubtedly knew that some informants had not told the truth or had suppressed part of it. Later, probably under the pressures of his fame and the "indolence" of his nature, he himself selected individual interviews to reprint without revision or comment. But when he was first conducting his interviews, he emphasized that each statement needed to be compared with others in order for the "truth" to be ascertained.

Still some questions about the interviews remain. First, how representative are the published statements? In the early numbers of "Labour and the Poor" Mayhew appears to have included almost everything he could lay his hands on, but as his sense of the labor situation in London clarified he became more selective about which interviews he included in his articles. When writing of the street folk in *London Labour and the London Poor,* he was also able to select because he knew enough about street life from his earlier investigations to be able to pick representative "street biographies" for the reader. Yet—and this is an important qualification—throughout all his investigations he tried to give statements from representative persons in every aspect of the trade. So he would include one or more interviews by a worker making a good regular wage, some by a worker in a middle-level job, and some by an exploited "slop" worker. Or when examining the question of lower-class drinking, he sought out teetotalers, reformed drunkards, and also workers who claimed they needed to drink on the job to keep up their strength. All their statements are full and presented without editorial comment. So Mayhew strove for both representative statements and inclusive coverage. Though any individual interview may not be representative, in general the number of different statements he reports in the various series assures reliable coverage.

There is still the question raised by Gertrude Himmelfarb and others as to whether Mayhew reported the more "colorful" or picturesque stories in order to make good copy. Reading the entire *Morning Chronicle* series straight through convinced me that in most cases Mayhew gave everything he could within the limits of space, his "Labour and the Poor" articles, for example, eventually taking up three full pages of closely printed newsprint. In the series on vagrants and houses of refuge, perhaps, he may have been drawn to the more "colorful" stories, but even here, as he interviewed all the residents of a low lodging house who came to a dinner at his expense, or as many others as he could during a one night's stay at a house of refuge, we sense an effort at balance. Some of the "street biographies" in *London Labour and the London Poor* are deliberately selected for their bizarre revelations, such as the early stories of a coster lad and girl. But mainly he was looking for informants who knew enough to give "the particulars of the trade" backed up by different types of street folk—intelligent, stupid, well-off, dirt poor, healthy, crippled, young, old, blind and so forth. Some of these stories are very "colorful," some are drab and impersonal. Here as elsewhere the total context is necessary to evaluate the individual story.

Another question raised by various critics is whether Mayhew asked questions that would lead his informants to give him the information he wanted. I have dealt with the issue of "leading questions" in Mayhew's social surveys at length.[7] By comparing his questions, deduced from the interviews, to those in the government blue books, I demonstrated that all Victorian social investigators asked similar leading questions. But Mayhew, unlike other investigators of his time, was interested in getting more than the "facts and figures" of work and wages from his informants. He wanted their thoughts and feelings about their situations and their lives as well. Because of this he includes a large number of "irrelevant" asides and seems to have given many of his informants opportunities for personal expression and revelation. Thus, though some "leading questions" undoubtedly resulted in predictable answers, the large number of personal details in the majority of the interviews create individual portraits which do not fill any preconceived plan.

Additional evidence for this is the number of times that Mayhew's editorial comment about a particularly colorful personality or group is at odds with our judgment after reading the statement. Mayhew is both sympathetic and disapproving of the "reverend" stenographic card seller; the reader only sees a complex and fascinating personality. Mayhew's remarks about prostitutes are mostly censorious, but the lower classes, particularly the street folk as revealed by their own comments, were generally more sympathetic, and after reading Mayhew's accounts, the reader's judgment is in line with theirs. Mayhew's remarks on patterers as a class are generally negative also, but the "biographies" frequently portray clever individuals who are not as far outside the norm as the interviewer's direct comments would lead us to believe. These revelations of personality in spite of his own stated feelings are evidence of the independence of most of the interviews from his judgments.

There remains one serious charge against Mayhew's reported interviews, one made both by the secretary of the Ragged School Union in 1850 and indirectly by Smith in his study of "Mayhew's Convict." Both essentially charge Mayhew with omitting information given him which was uncongenial to the particular point he was making, or at least not trying to check on a story he wanted to publish as it stood. In the case of the Ragged School controversy, the secretary charged that Mayhew said, when a policeman told him the children did not sell their Bibles but took them to church every Sunday and paid them off in installments, "Ah, well, never mind that; we don't want to put that down."[8] In his rebuttal Mayhew denied flatly that he had said such a thing and published statements by Henry Wood, who had been present at the interview, and Richard Knight, who had helped him locate some of his informants, both of whom vigorously supported his position. The published interview with the policeman does not support the secretary's charge, but it does not provide conclusive evidence of Mayhew's position either. However, as to the issue of the children selling the Bibles, which is the matter under dispute, Mayhew's evidence comes from the official reports of the Ragged School Union itself.

Smith's more thorough and thoughtful analysis also does not establish that Mayhew omitted unfavorable information about the convict. Rather, he suggests that the convict seemed to be editing his life's story in telling it to Mayhew in order to make himself look better than he was. Smith's charge against Mayhew is really not that he deliberately omitted material but that he was naive and failed to check the convict's statement. Smith may be right in this particular case, but I think he is wrong to extend the judgment beyond this case and also wrong to isolate an individual interview. It is also worth consid-

ering that, given the limited time Mayhew had to work up each article, had he chosen to devote more of it to the kind of rigorous
checking Smith seems to expect, he would have had far less time to
conduct interviews. The result might have been a few totally cross-
checked statements which might or might not be representative. Instead we have hundreds of statements,—some verified, some not—of
all different sorts of people. Given the format, we could not have
both thorough checking and large numbers. The reader must make
his own judgment as to whether Mayhew made the right choice in
concentrating on a large mass of statements to assure reliability rather
than personally checking out a few.

For what it is worth, I am convinced that though Mayhew may
have been fooled by some of his informants, though under the pressure of deadlines he may have been careless and erratic in his checking
of individual statements, though occasionally he may have been
drawn to the more picturesque specimens of the lower part of the
lower classes, he did not deliberately omit information he did not
want to hear, nor add other material to clarify or bend the interviews,
nor distort the stories in other ways. There is too much "extraneous"
information in individual interviews and too many statements ex-
pounding different points of view in nearly all his series. The inclusiveness plus the number reinforces my confidence in the general
reliability of particular cases.[9] But to repeat, this reliability depends
on the total picture that emerges from his different series, and to use
Mayhew's work accurately we must use it in toto.

Having considered the various reservations that have been expressed about his work, we can now turn to a discussion of its
strengths. There are many impressive ones.

Mayhew never got to the point of deriving all the laws of political
economy from the mass of particulars he had collected. He persis-
tently refused to explain or analyze facts until they were complete.
Though it keeps what he produced from having the general significance of Mill's *Principles of Political Economy* or Engels' *The Condition
of the Working Class in England in 1844,* Mayhew's refusal to theorize
without full empirical evidence is something for which we should respect him absolutely. Such "scientific" restraint in Victorian social
commentary is rare. Most investigators were all too ready with explanations for the Condition-of-England: not enough religion, too much
drink, innate inferiority, insufficient self-help, bad housing, lack of
proper sanitation, limited suffrage, and so on. The unworkable Poor

Law of 1832 was an example of what could happen when action was taken on the basis of such a priori judgments, although it is equally true that to do nothing to redress individual situations was also untenable.

From our vantage the conclusions to be drawn from Mayhew's facts in many cases seem only too obvious, but from his own point of view the general picture was far from clear. He was able to achieve what he did—and no other social historian of the period equaled his particular achievement—because he refused to draw conclusions on what he considered insufficient evidence. His sense of what would be sufficient was utopian perhaps, but by modern standards he erred on the right side by demanding more rather than less data.

This does not mean that he had no opinions either a priori or drawn from his experiences. He believed in self-help and admired the plucky street folk because they demonstrated the virtue so bravely. He tried to explain the character of the criminal element and street folk by both environment and heredity. He had his own impressive explanation of low wages. In *The Criminal Prisons of London* we see him in the process of learning from experience, coming closer and closer to a full recognition of the injustices of the legal system in terms of class. Other local judgments are delivered here and there. When convinced of an insight, Mayhew published it whether or not it was at odds with something he had said earlier. He had the frame of mind of a true scientist in his social surveys; he would follow truth wherever it led him. The indefinite nature of his subject—the human personality and the workings of the economic system—is mainly responsible for his inability to produce a tidy result. He was not a thorough social scientist because of the pressures of deadlines and the journalistic format as well as the lack of opportunity to revise. But he absorbed an astonishing amount of information and integrated into it an equally astonishing amount of personal observation. Perhaps it is not possible to sense the extent of his effort without reading his complete social surveys straight through, something I suspect few readers do. Without such a knowledge of the whole, however, it is all too easy to overrate individual statements, or, on the other hand, to underrate the entire achievement.

Out of the hundreds of "biographies" emerges the most extensive picture we have in mid-Victorian England of the poor and the dispossessed told, as Mayhew claimed, pretty much by themselves. Until we begin to look for other such "histories of a people," we cannot judge the nature of Mayhew's achievement. He was probably the founder of oral history and was the model for Studs Terkel's *Working*. [10] It is important to recognize the limitations and weaknesses of his work, but after all is said and done his social surveys remain as admirable works whose intentions we should respect as much as we delight in their expression.

To me, the single most impressive part of Mayhew's social surveys is the number of individual personalities he succeeds in revealing to us. In all ages the poor, the powerless, the people on the fringes of the social order are usually faceless and voiceless. In Mayhew's work this undifferentiated mass suddenly breaks into a series of intensely individualized portraits. As we turn the pages of the *Morning Chronicle* series, or *London Labour and the London Poor,* we feel we have been in direct contact with a part of Victorian society unknown before except from glimpses in novels by Dickens.

Mayhew achieves this through the combination of different forces. First and perhaps most crucial is his respect for his informants. As he said in volume 2 of *London Labour and the London Poor,* "There is but one way of benefiting the poor, viz., by developing their powers of self-reliance, and certainly not in treating them like children" (2:264). His assertion of their basic honesty in the preface to volume 1 reflects the same kind of respect. The result of his confidence in his subjects is that in his interviews a personal dynamic of mutual trust develops which enables Mayhew to break down the reserve normally caused by class barriers. He was curious without being condescending. His informants, sensing his genuine interest in the details of their stories, rewarded him with candid fluency. In addition, his talent as an interviewer—knowing when to give his informants free rein, when to follow up on questions, what to ask to evoke the feelings and attitudes of the people he spoke to—assured that the "biographies" were detailed and revealing. [11] Also his scientific propensities contributed to the success of his work. His conception of it on a "scientific-experimental" model assured an effort at his own neutrality and allowed the voice of his informants to emerge. In organizing his material, his determination to classify every category down to the finest point assured an ever more particularized set of data. The result was an extensive array of human beings with dignity, complexity, and personality. In any period Mayhew's contribution would be special. In his own time it was a marvel.

Notes and References

Chapter One

1. In my book *Travels into the Poor Man's Country: The Work of Henry Mayhew* (Athens, Ga., 1977), I collected what biographical material existed at the time in the first chapter, pp. 1–30. Other biographies of Mayhew include John L. Bradley, Introduction to *Selections from "London Labour and the London Poor"* (London, 1965), pp. vii–xl, and E. P. Thompson, "Mayhew and the *Morning Chronicle*" in *The Unknown Mayhew* (New York, 1971), pp. 11–50. Some family stories are found in an unpublished manuscript by Mrs. L. M. Coumbe, a descendent of Alfred Mayhew, which is the property of Patrick Mayhew of London.

2. *The Comic Almanac* (London: David Bogue, 1848), p. 47.

3. M. H. Spielmann, *The History of "Punch"* (New York, 1895), p. 268.

4. *Morning Chronicle,* 31 October 1850, p. 4.

5. Reported by Richard D. Altick, *The Shows of London* (Cambridge and London: Harvard University Press, 1978), p. 481n.

6. George Hodder, *Memories of My Time* (London, 1870), p. 213.

7. Bradley notes the first in his introduction. Mayhew suggested the boys' journal in 1872 to Frederick Locker. His letter is quoted by Patrick A. Dunae in "Penny Dreadfuls; Late Nineteenth-Century Boys' Literature and Crime" in *Victorian Studies* 22 (1979): 146. Miscellaneous items like this latter and Mayhew's connection with the georama project will continue to crop up as scholars mine the correspondence and journalism of the Victorian period.

Chapter Two

1. John L. Bradley, "Henry Mayhew and Father William," *English Language Notes* 1 (Sept. 1963):42.

2. Athol Mayhew, *A Jorum of "Punch"* (London, 1895), p. 51.

3. Raymond Williams, *The Long Revolution* (1961; reprint ed., Harmondsworth: Penguin, 1965), p. 292.

4. George Rowell, *The Victorian Theatre,* 2d ed. (Cambridge: Cambridge University Press, 1978), p. 1.

5. Michael R. Booth, *English Plays of the Nineteenth Century* (Oxford: Clarendon, 1973), vol. 4, p. 13.

6. John L. Bradley, "Henry Mayhew: Farce Writer of the 1830's" *Victorian Newsletter* 23 (1963): 21–23. Bradley repeats this point in his in-

troduction to his selections from *London Labour and the London Poor,* pp. x–xiii.

7. *The Wandering Minstrel* (New York, n.d.), p. 5; hereafter page references cited in parentheses in the text.

8. *"But however—"* (London, 1838), p. 20; hereafter page references cited in parentheses in the text.

9. In his introduction Bradley discusses briefly *The Barbers at Court, The Young Sculptor,* and *Mont Blanc,* p. xiii and pp. xxxi–xxxii. There were also various dramatizations of *London Labour and the London Poor,* but Mayhew does not seem to have been their author. Two such plays were *How We Live in the World of London* by J. B. Johnstone and *London Labour and the London Poor; or, Want and Vice* by J. Elphinstone. Both appeared in 1854. See Sally Vernon, "Trouble Up at T'Mill: The Rise and Decline of the Factory Play in the 1830s and 1840s," *Victorian Studies* 20 (1977):137.

10. F. David Roberts, "More Early Victorian Newspaper Editors," *Victorian Periodicals Newsletter* 16 (1972):17.

11. Edmund Yates, quoted by Roberts, ibid., pp. 15–16.

12. Richard Altick, *The English Common Reader* (Chicago: University of Chicago Press, 1957), p. 322.

13. Joel H. Wiener, quoted by Louis James, " 'Economic' Literature: The Emergence of Popular Journalism," *Victorian Periodicals Newsletter* 14 (1971): 13.

14. *The Waterloo Directory of Victorian Periodicals 1824-1900,* eds. Michael Wolff, John S. North, Dorothy Deering, phase 1 (Waterloo, Ont.: Wilfred Laurier University Press, 1976), p. ix.

15. Donald J. Gray, "A List of Comic Periodicals Published in Great Britain, 1800-1900," *Victorian Periodicals Newsletter* 15 (1972): 2–3.

16. Charles Mackay wrote the articles from Liverpool for "Labour and the Poor." As an outgrowth of those articles he published *History of the Mormons* in 1851. The book went through four editions between 1851 and 1856. Though initially published anonymously, the fourth edition stated the author was Charles Mackay. Nonetheless, the book is still frequently credited to Mayhew, undoubtedly because the first edition stated in the preface that the author had done his research in 1851 while engaged on "Labour and the Poor."

17. The information on the various journals in the following summary comes from the *Waterloo Directory* and Donald Gray, "List of Comic Periodicals" cited above.

18. Athol Mayhew, *A Jorum of "Punch,"* pp. 41–44.

19. A. M. Hookum, "The Literary Career of Henry Mayhew." M.A. thesis, Birmingham University, 1962, pp. 20, 22.

20. R. G. G. Price, *A History of Punch* (London, 1957), p. 353.

21. Quoted in Athol Mayhew, p. 121.

22. Ibid., pp. 45–46.

23. Spielmann, *History of "Punch,"* p. 17.

24. Price, *History of Punch,* p. 27.

25. Gray, *List of Comic Periodicals,* p. 7.

26. Price, *History of Punch,* p. 44.

27. John Bush Jones and Priscilla Shaw, "Artists and 'Suggestors': The *Punch* Cartoons, 1843–1848," *Victorian Periodicals Newsletter* 11, no. 1 (1978):3–15. Jones is currently preparing a complete index of authorship for *Punch.*

28. *Shops and Companies of London* (London, 1865), p. 174.

29. Charles Mitchell, *Newspaper Press Directory,* quoted in Gray, *List of Comic Periodicals,* p. 20.

30. Athol Mayhew, *A Jorum of "Punch,"* p. 45.

31. Henry Vizetelly, *Glances Back Through Seventy Years,* vol. 1 (London, 1893), p. 408.

32. *The Greatest Plague of Life* (London, 1847), p. 242.

33. *Men of the Time* (London, 1856), p. 542.

34. *Whom to Marry and How to Get Married!* (London, 1848), p. 271.

35. *The Fear of the World* (New York, 1850), pp. 53–55.

36. *Literary Gazette,* March 1851, p. 165.

37. *1851; or The Adventures of Mr. and Mrs Sandboys* . . . (London, 1851), p. 155.

38. *The Good Genius that Turned Everything into Gold* (London, 1847), pp. 200–201; hereafter page references cited in parentheses in the text.

39. Angela Hookum, "Literary Career of Henry Mayhew," p. 51.

40. The discussion of the state of nineteenth-century technical education is based on Gordon W. Roderick and Michael D. Stephens, *Scientific and Technical Education in Nineteenth-Century England* (New York: Barnes and Noble, 1973).

41. *The Upper Rhine; the Scenery of Its Banks and the Manners of Its People* (London, 1858), p. 319.

42. *What to Teach and How to Teach It* (London, 1842), p. 5; hereafter page references cited in parentheses in the text.

43. John L. Bradley discusses this adaptation in "Henry Mayhew and Father William," pp. 40–42.

44. The summary of the state of children's literature in this period comes from Brian Alderson, "Tracts, rewards, and fairies: The Victorian Contribution to Children's Literature" in *Essays in the History of Publishing,* ed. Asa Briggs (London: Longman, 1974), pp. 245–282, and Alec Ellis, *A History of Children's Reading and Literature* (London: Pergamon, 1968), pp. 5–75.

45. *The Wonders of Science; or, Young Humphry Davy* (London, 1855), p. xiv.

46. See Kenneth Fielden, "Samuel Smiles and Self-Help," *Victorian Studies* 12 (1968):155–76.

47. Price, *History of Punch*, p. 27.
48. *The Story of the Peasant-Boy Philosopher* (London, 1854), p. xii; hereafter page references cited in parentheses in the text.
49. *Young Benjamin Franklin* (London, 1861), p. vii; hereafter page references cited in parentheses in the text.
50. *The Boyhood of Martin Luther* (London, 1863), p. xi; hereafter page references cited in parentheses in the text.
51. John W. Dodds, *The Age of Paradox* (New York: Rinehart, 1952), pp. 373–74.
52. John Tallmadge, "From Chronicle to Quest: The Shaping of Darwin's 'Voyage of the Beagle,' " *Victorian Studies* 23 (1980):329.
53. *The Rhine and Its Picturesque Scenery* (London, 1856), p. 18.
54. *The Upper Rhine* (London, 1858), pp. vi–vii; hereafter page references cited in parentheses in the text.
55. Roderick and Stephens, *Scientific and Technical Education*, pp. 65–66.
56. *German Life and Manners as Seen in Saxony at the Present Day*, vol. 1 (London, 1864), p. vi; hereafter volume and page references cited in parentheses in the text.

Chapter Three

1. H. Sutherland Edwards, *Personal Recollections* (London, 1900), p. 60.
2. Quoted in *Report of the Speech of Henry Mayhew . . . at a Public Meeting . . . on . . . Oct. 28, 1850 . . .* (London: Bateman, Hardwicke, 1850), p. 6.
3. "Labour and the Poor," Letter 1, 19 October 1849. There is as yet no complete collection of Mayhew's contributions to the *Morning Chronicle* outside the newspaper itself. Two books of selections are *The Unknown Mayhew*, ed. E. P. Thompson and Eileen Yeo (New York, 1971), and *Voices of the Poor*, ed. Anne Humpherys (London: Frank Cass, 1971). Caliban Books of Firle, Sussex, issued volume 1 of a complete reprinting in 1980. It includes Letters 1–12. There are to be five more volumes. Further references to the series cited in the text by Letter number and date in parentheses.
4. The word *slop* to describe this sweated outwork derives from an old, obscure term for the ready-made clothing and other furnishings supplied to seamen from the ship's stores.
5. Duncan Bythell in *The Sweated Trades* (London: Batsford Academic, 1978), p. 253. Gareth Stedman Jones in *Outcast London* (Oxford: Clarendon Press, 1971) also discusses casual and sweated labor in Victorian England. He uses Mayhew's descriptions and analytical passages extensively and gives him high marks for recognizing the seasonal nature of much employment.

6. T. J. Edelstein, "They Sang 'The Song of the Shirt': The Visual Iconology of the Seamstress," *Victorian Studies* 23 (1980):183–210.

7. At what point Mayhew actually ceased to be the Metropolitan Correspondent is unclear. He said he was no longer employed by 4 October 1850, but ten letters from the Metropolitan Correspondent appear subsequent to that date, three of which are later reprinted in volume 3 of *London Labour and the London Poor*. In some passing remarks on the covers of *London Labour and the London Poor*, he suggests that he did the survey of the markets which ends the series in December. Perhaps he conducted the research that makes up these letters, and others wrote them up. There are also the three letters on dressmakers and hatters whose authorship is unclear.

8. Mayhew printed many comments on the covers to the weekly parts of *London Labour and the London Poor* under the title "Answers to Correspondents." The prospectus was on number 9, which is undated, but which appeared in early February 1851. Further references to material on the covers will be noted parenthetically (Part number, date) in the text.

9. Charles Mackay, *Forty Years' Recollections of Life, Literature, and Public Affairs*, vol. 2 (London, 1877), p. 152.

10. *London Labour and the London Poor*, vol. 1 (1861; reprint ed., London: Frank Cass, 1967), p. 43. This reprint as well as that by Dover in 1968 is identical to the 1861–1862 edition. Further references to this edition will be made parenthetically (volume, page) in the text.

11. Gertrude Himmelfarb made this point originally in "Mayhew's Poor: A Problem of Identity," *Victorian Studies* 14 (1971):307–20. She develops her argument in *The Idea of Poverty: England in the Early Industrial Age* (New York, 1984), pp. 307–70, a work published too late for me to use in this book. See also F. S. Schwarzbach, "*Terra Incognita*—An Image of the City in English Literature, 1820–1855," *Prose Studies*, May, 1982, pp. 61–84. He traces this notion through different sources, including Mayhew's *London Labour*.

12. See, for example, Peter Quennell, Introduction to *Mayhew's London* (London: William Kimber, 1951), p. 21.

13. *Low Wages, Their Causes, Consequences, and Remedies* (London, 1851), p. 15; hereafter cited in the text as *LW* followed by page number.

14. *Young Benjamin Franklin*, p. xiv.

15. *The Criminal Prisons of London and Scenes of Prison Life* (1862; reprint ed., London: Frank Cass, 1968), p. 64; hereafter page references to this edition cited in parentheses in the text.

16. James Bennett in *Oral History and Delinquency. The Rhetoric of Criminology* (Chicago and London, 1981) has two long sections on Mayhew's use of "oral history," particularly in relation to juvenile offenders. Our views of Mayhew in this context are similar. As Bennett says "my contribution to the study of Mayhew is a discussion of delinquency and oral history in more detail than has been done elsewhere" (p. 285, *n.* 4). He discusses Mayhew's

views on the causes of juvenile crime (pp. 50–55), and points out the limitations of Mayhew's analysis (pp. 55–58).

17. "On Capital Punishments," in *Three Papers on Capital Punishment* (London: 1856), p. 44.

18. Quoted in a report on his address to the Law Amendment Society in the *Illustrated Times*, 26 April 1856.

Chapter Four

1. In January 1852 Mayhew referred to Carlyle twice in "Answers to Correspondents." In one reference he ironically condemned Carlyle's hardline position on prison discipline in "Model Prisons." In the second reference he misapplied a passage from *Chartism*. In *Travels into the Poor Man's Country* I discuss these references, pp. 79–80.

2. In *The Shows of London* (p. 431) Altick puzzles over the reasons Mayhew did not include clockwork peepshows in his survey of street entertainers. Even James Bennett, who has read extensively in Mayhew's work, quotes passages from the sections in *London Labour and the London Poor*, vol. 2, which were written by Augustus, as though they were written by Henry. See *Oral History*, p. 38.

3. E. P. Thompson, "The Political Education of Henry Mayhew," *Victorian Studies* 11 (1967):58, and Himmelfarb, "Mayhew's Poor," p. 316. Edwards's remark is in *Personal Recollections*, p. 60.

4. F. B. Smith, "Mayhew's Convict," *Victorian Studies* 22 (1979): 439.

5. In *The Unknown Mayhew* Thompson and Yeo reprint some of two parts of *Low Wages*. Yeo's essay "Mayhew as a Social Investigator" in the same work discusses Mayhew's thought (pp. 51–95). In *Travels into the Poor Man's Country* I summarize Mayhew's thoughts on political economy, pp. 100–106.

6. Edwards, *Personal Recollections*, p. 60.

7. *Travels into the Poor Man's Country*, pp. 60–61.

8. *Morning Chronicle*, 22 April 1850.

9. James Bennett, *Oral History* (London and Chicago, 1981) has the same conclusion: "no evidence suggests that in his editing Mayhew falsified any factual point," p. 273.

10. Bennett, *Oral History*, p. 11.

11. See *Travels into the Poor Man's Country*, pp. 87–94, for an analysis of Mayhew's interviewing techniques. See also Bennett, *Oral History*, "Mayhew's Modus Operandi," pp. 265–71.

Selected Bibliography

The following bibliography includes significant editions of Mayhew's work as well as the more important books of selections. His collaborative works are listed at the end of each subsection. Only the plays published in acting copies are listed. In a few cases the introductions to books of selections are among the more important modern critical works on Mayhew, and hence these introductory essays are listed separately in the secondary source material under "Books and parts of books." Under secondary sources, I include full-length studies in article form, but only those books that contain extensive anecdotes or critical discussions and a highly selective list of reviews of *London Labour and the London Poor*.

PRIMARY SOURCES

1. Social surveys and related materials
"Answers to Correspondents." *London Labour and the London Poor*. Covers for the weekly numbers 5–63 (1851-1852). Never reprinted or collected.
"Labour and the Poor." Letters 1-82. *Morning Chronicle*, 19 October 1849 - 12 December 1850. Selections reprinted in *The Unknown Mayhew*, edited by E. P. Thompson and Eileen Yeo (New York: Pantheon, 1971), and *Voices of the Poor*, edited by Anne Humpherys (London: Frank Cass, 1971). Caliban Books of Firle, Sussex, issued volume 1 (Letters 1-12) of a complete reprinting of the Metropolitan Correspondent's articles in 1980. There are to be 5 more volumes.
"Labour and the Poor." *Report of the Speech of Henry Mayhew, Esq., and the Evidence adduced at a Public Meeting Held at St. Martin's Hall, Long Acre, on Monday evening, Oct. 28, 1850* . . . London: Bateman, Hardwicke, 1850.
London Labour and the London Poor. 4 vols. London: Griffin, Bohn, 1861-1862. Reprint, London: Frank Cass, 1967. Paperback edition: New York: Dover, 1968. Selections: John L. Bradley, *Selections from "London Labour and the London Poor."* London: Oxford University Press, 1965. Peter Quennell, *London's Underworld*. London: William Kimber, 1950 (vol. 4); *Mayhew's London*. London: William Kimber,

1951. *Mayhew's Characters*. London: William Kimber, 1951 (vols. 1–3).

Low Wages, Their Causes, Consequences and Remedies. Parts 1–4. London: At the office of *London Labour and the London Poor*, 1851. Selections in E. P. Thompson and Eileen Yeo, *The Unknown Mayhew*. New York: Pantheon, 1971.

"On Capital Punishments." In *Three Papers on Capital Punishments*. London: Cox & Wyman, 1856.

with John Binny. *The Criminal Prisons of London*. London: Griffin, Bohn, 1862. Reprint. London: Frank Cass, 1968. Initially appeared in parts as "The Great World of London," Parts 1–9. London: David Bogue, 1856. Mayhew wrote all up to page 498.

and others. *London Characters. Illustrations of the Humour, Pathos, and Peculiarities of London Life*. 2d ed. London: Chatto & Windus, 1874. The other authors are unknown; Mayhew contributed reprints of his earlier surveys. The first edition in 1870 has no material by Mayhew.

2. Plays and Novels

The Wandering Minstrel. 1834. New York: Samuel French, n.d.

and Henry Baylis. *"But however—"*. London: Chapman & Hall, 1838.

and George Cruikshank. *1851; or, The Adventures of Mr. and Mrs. Sandboys and Family, who came up to London to 'enjoy themselves,' and to see the Great Exhibition*. London: David Bogue, 1851.

and Athol Mayhew. *Mont Blanc*. London: privately printed, 1874.

and Augustus Mayhew (The Brothers Mayhew). *Acting Charades*. London: David Bogue, 1850.

——— . *The Fear of the World; or, Living for Appearances*. New York: Harper & Bros., 1850. The only English edition I located in the British Library was an 1855 reprint under the title *Living for Appearances*.

——— . *The Good Genius that Turned Everything into Gold; or, the Queen Bee and the Magic Dress*. London: David Bogue, 1847.

——— . *The Greatest Plague of Life; or, the Adventures of a Lady in Search of a Good Servant*. London: David Bogue, {1847}.

——— . *The Image of His Father; or, one boy is more trouble than a dozen girls, being a Tale of a Young Monkey*. London: H. Hurst, 1848.

——— . *The Magic of Kindness; or, the Wondrous Story of the Good Huan*. London: Darton & Co., 1849.

——— . *Whom to Marry and How to get Married! or, the Adventures of a Lady in Search of a Good Husband*. London: David Bogue, [1848].

3. Miscellaneous journalism

"The Great Exhibition." Nos. 1–9. *Edinburgh News and Literary Chronicle*. May–July 1851.

"Mr. Peter Punctilio, the Gentleman in Black." *Bentley Miscellany* (1838):609-26.

Report Concerning the Trade and Hours of Closing Usual Among the Unlicensed Victualing Establishments Now Open for the Unrestricted Sale of Beer, Wine, and Spirits at certain so-called "Working Men's Clubs," distributed throughout the metropolis. London: Judd, [1871].

"What is the cause of Surprise? and what connection has it with the Laws of Suggestion?" *Douglas Jerrold's Shilling Magazine* (1847), pp. 547–66.

Editor. *The Comic Almanac.* London: David Bogue, 1850–1851.

Editor. *Figaro in London.* Vols. 4–7. London: W. Strange, 1835–1838.

Editor. *The Morning News.* London: January 1859.

Editor. *Only Once a Year.* London: Stevens & Richardson, 1870.

Editor. *The Shops and Companies of London, and the Grades and Manfactories of Great Britain.* London: Strand, March–September 1865.

4. Educational and travel books

The Boyhood of Martin Luther. London: Sampson Low, 1863.

German Life and Manners as Seen in Saxony at the Present Day. 2 vols. London: William Allen, 1864.

The Prince of Wales's Library. No. 1. London: Office of the Illuminated Magazine, [1844].

The Rhine and Its Picturesque Scenery. London: David Bogue, 1856.

The Story of the Peasant-Boy Philosopher; or, "A Child Gathering Pebbles on the Sea Shore." London: David Bogue, 1854.

The Upper Rhine; the Scenery of Its Banks and the Manners of Its People. London: George Routledge, 1858.

What to Teach and How to Teach it: so that the Child may become a Wise and Good Man. Part 1. London: William Smith, 1842.

The Wonders of Science; or, Young Humphry Davy. London: David Bogue, 1855.

Young Benjamin Franklin. London: James Blackwood, 1861.

SECONDARY SOURCES

1. Books and Parts of Books

Beale, Thomas Willert. *The Light of Other Days.* 2 vols. London: Richard Bentley, 1890. Contains account of Mayhew's disastrous "Punch on the Platform" tour.

Bennett, James. *Oral History and Delinquency. The Rhetoric of Criminology.* Chicago and London: University of Chicago Press, 1981. Extensive discussion of Mayhew's contribution to oral history, especially as used with juvenile deliquents.

Bradley, John L. Introduction. *Selections from "London Labour and the London Poor."* London: Oxford University Press, 1965. The first biography of Henry Mayhew.

Edwards, [Henry] Sutherland. *Personal Recollections.* London: Cassell, 1900. Contains anecdotes of Mayhew family.

Forshall, Frederic H. *Westminster School, Past and Present.* London: Weyman, 1884. Contains account of Mayhew's running away from school.

Himmelfarb, Gertrude. "The Culture of Poverty." *The Idea of Poverty: England in the Early Industrial Age.* (New York: Knopf, 1984), pp. 307–70. Critical analysis of Mayhew's view of poverty and its influence on subsequent attitudes to the subject.

Hodder, George. *Memories of My Time.* London: Tinsley, 1870. Anecdotes of Mayhew family.

Humpherys, Anne. *Travels into the Poor Man's Country: The Work of Henry Mayhew.* Athens: University of Georgia Press, 1977. The first book-length study of Mayhew's social surveys.

Mackay, Charles. *Forty Years' Recollections of Life, Literature, and Public Affairs.* 2 vols. London: Chapman & Hall, 1877. Account of Mayhew at the *Morning Chronicle.*

Mayhew, Athol. *A Jorum of "Punch."* London: Downey, 1895. Mayhew's journalistic life through the founding of *Punch* told by his son.

Men of the Time. London: David Bogue, 1856. Early biography of Mayhew.

Price, R. G. G. *A History of Punch.* London: William Collins, 1957. Most modern evaluation of Mayhew's role in *Punch.*

Rosenberg, John D., ed. Introduction. *London Labour and the London Poor.* 4 vols. New York: Dover Press, 1968. Thoughtful and appreciative analysis.

Smith, Sheila M. *The Other Nation: The Poor in English Novels of the 1840s and 1850s.* Oxford: Clarendon, 1980. Discusses *Paved with Gold* with passing references to Henry Mayhew's work, but is wrong in some details of publication history and authorship.

Spielmann, M. H. *The History of "Punch."* New York: Cassell, 1895. Contains stories and comments about Mayhew by contemporaries.

Thompson, E. P. "Mayhew and the *Morning Chronicle.*" In *The Unknown Mayhew,* edited by E. P. Thompson and Eileen Yeo. New York: Pantheon, 1971. Thorough account of Mayhew and the publishers of "Labour and the Poor."

Vizetelly, Henry. *Glances Back Through Seventy Years.* 2 vols. London: Kegan Paul, Trench, Trübner, 1893. Contains anecdotes of Mayhew's life after 1852.

Yeo, Eileen. "Mayhew as a Social Investigator." In *The Unknown Mayhew,* edited by E. P. Thompson and Eileen Yeo. New York: Pantheon, 1971. An analysis of Mayhew's techniques and attitudes.

2. Articles

Account of Mayhew's bankruptcy. *London Times,* 12 February 1847, p. 8.

Auden, W. H. "An Inquisitive Old Party." *New Yorker,* 24 February 1968, pp. 121–33. Sympathetic review of *London Labour and the London Poor.*

Bradley, John L. "Henry Mayhew and Father William." *English Language Notes* 1 (September 1963):40-42. On Mayhew's *Prince of Wales's Primer.*

————. "Henry Mayhew: Farce Writer of the 1830's." *Victorian Newsletter* 23 (1963):21-23. On *The Wandering Minstrel.*

Briggs, Asa. "The culture of poverty in 19th-century London." *Scientific American,* July 1966, pp. 123–26. Analysis of *London Labour and the London Poor.*

Clayton, Herbert. "The Henry Mayhew Centenary." *Notes and Queries,* 11 ser., 5 (1912):145, 317–18, 433; 6 (1912):71–72. Contains some miscellaneous biographical information.

Dunn, Richard J. "Dickens and Mayhew Once More." *Nineteenth Century Fiction* 25 (December 1970):348–53. On possible influence of Mayhew's work on *Bleak House.*

Himmelfarb, Gertrude. "Mayhew's Poor: A Problem of Identity." *Victorian Studies* 14 (1971):307–20. First presentation of her views.

Humpherys, Anne. "Dickens and Mayhew on the London Poor." *Dickens Studies Annual* 4, edited by Robert Partlow. Carbondale and Edwardsville: Southern Illinois Press, 1975, pp. 78–90, 175–79.

"The Late Mr. Henry Mayhew." *Illustrated London News* 91 (6 August 1887):158. Obituary.

Metz, Nancy Aycock. "Mayhew's Book of Lists." *Hartford Studies in Literature* 14 (1982):41–49. Discusses the inclusiveness of *London Labour and the London Poor.*

Nelson, Harland S. "Dickens's *Our Mutual Friend* and Henry Mayhew's *London Labour and the London Poor.*" *Nineteenth Century Fiction* 20 (December 1965):207–22. On possible sources for some of Dickens's characters.

Obituary of Mayhew. *London Times,* 27 July 1887, p. 5.

Obituary of Mayhew. *Punch,* 6 August 1887, p. 53.

Pritchett, V. S. "True to Life." *New York Review of Books,* 17 March 1966, pp. 5–6. Review of *London Labour and the London Poor.*

Raban, Jonathan. "The Invisible Mayhew." *Encounter* 41 (August 1973):64–70. General survey of Mayhew's life and work.

Smith, F. B. "Mayhew's Convict." *Victorian Studies* 22 (1979):431–48. Analyzes a single interview and finds facts at variance with report.

Stevenson, David. "Mayhew and the London Poor: A Mediocre Genius and His Book." *University of Denver Quarterly,* Spring 1977, pp. 332–46. General survey of Mayhew's social surveys.

Sucksmith, Harvey Peter. "Dickens and Mayhew: A Further Note."

Nineteenth Century Fiction 24 (December 1969):345–49. Short discussion of Mayhew's possible influence on Dickens's novels, particularly *Little Dorrit*.

Thompson, E. P. "The Political Education of Henry Mayhew." *Victorian Studies* 11 (1967):41–62. One of first informative analyses.

3. Unpublished Materials

"Biography of Henry Mayhew for W. C. Griffin Handbook of Contemporary Biography." Manuscript of 1860 in the British Library.

Coumbe, Mrs. L. M. "The Mayhew Brothers." Manuscript in the possession of Patrick Mayhew, London. Contains some family stories.

Hookum, A. M. "The Literary Career of Henry Mayhew." M.A. thesis, Birmingham University, 1962. Surveys all of Mayhew's work.

Thomas, Alan Cedric. "Henry Mayhew's Rhetoric: A Study of His Presentation of Social 'Facts.' " Ph.D. thesis, University of Toronto, 1971. Analyzes the structure and mode of representation in Mayhew's social surveys.

Index